Emily Dickinson's Poetry

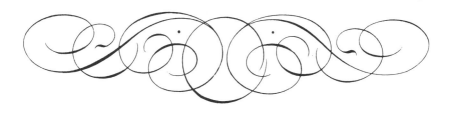

Robert Weisbuch

The University of Chicago Press   Chicago and London

ROBERT WEISBUCH received his Ph.D. from
Yale University in 1972. He is currently assis-
tant professor of English at the University of
Michigan. This is his first book.

The University of Chicago Press, Chicago 60637
The University of Chicago Press, Ltd., London

Library of Congress Cataloging in Publication Data

Weisbuch, Robert, 1946–
    Emily Dickinson's poetry.

    Includes bibliographical references and index.
    1. Dickinson, Emily, 1830–1886—Criticism and
interpretation. I. Title.
PS1541.Z5W38   811'.4   74-16678
ISBN   0-226-89146-1

Emily Dickinson's Poetry

To my wife, Susan Remington Weisbuch

'Tis Compound Vision—
Light—enabling Light—
The Finite—furnished
With the Infinite—
Convex—and Concave Witness—
Back—toward Time—
And forward—
Toward the God of Him—

—Emily Dickinson
poem 906

Contents

A Preface on Procedure

" 'Tis Compound Vision," Emily Dickinson exults in a poem about dying. She often willed these apparently ghastly, near ghostly projections of the mind to a moment when life ends and death begins—not to afford herself a gothic shudder or even to pry loose heaven's secrets. Everything Dickinson did is more sensible and important than it at first seems. She dramatizes that moment of dying, that "Hyphen of the Sea" as she once called it, to make palpable the imaginative balance she continually strove to maintain, between the "finished," the certain, and the adventure of the yet-to-be, the unknown and unknowable but beckoning "further heaven." To poise the mind at, but not implausibly beyond, this frontier is no aesthete's indulgence: "The Dying—as it were a Height / Reorganizes Estimate." The compound vision of the daily life and the infinite, "Back—toward Time—/And forward— / Toward the God of Him—," enables Dickinson to decide what matters and what does not. It teaches her to conform the present to the ultimates.

But this is only one form of a compound vision that is itself compounded of many kinds of attempts to make experience whole. Dickinson's is equally a compound vision in that her poetry contrasts and sometimes, remarkably, combines a self which is powerful, autonomous, and godlike with a self which is all-vulnerable, limited, and victimized. And it is more than a compound vision in that Dickinson's best poems simultaneously create a world and respond to that creation as if it were a given. The response itself may be double- or triple-minded: 'tis compound vision and compound witness at once.

Such mergings finally combine into Dickinson's poetic motive; and it is that Dickinson, not Emily of Amherst but the composite mind of the poems, that I hope to discover. To what uses does Dickinson put language? What is her mode of poetic construction? What expectations should the reader bring (and not bring) to her poems? These are the questions considered in the first part of this study, questions of style in the largest sense, of rhetorical strategies. Given the general answer that Dickinson develops her meanings by a peculiarly overt and furious process of analogy-making, by yet another form of compound vision in which usually discrete orders of discourse combine, the second part of the study asks what gets connected to what. It asks, further, where these connections originate as assumptions and where they lead as chosen beliefs. In short, what I'm after is a compound vision of the compounder herself.

This is merely a preface, and I do not wish to give the game away too early, to issue too many generalizations about Dickinson in lieu of a scrutiny of her poetry. My view of Dickinson will show itself in the first few chapters. But I would like to describe here the rules of the game as I have understood them.

Dickinson's unique interpretation of the English language must have been developed by long experiment, and we cannot know how many early experiments were flung away. But once she found her style, she kept it—kept it and mined its rich ore for the nearly eighteen hundred lyrics that have been found and published. Her best poems continually surprise us by exhibiting new possibilities of her language, but there are no distinct shifts either of style or of thought to be found in Dickinson's career. She thus robs the critic of one of his most valuable tools, the tracing of a chronological development. But the critic must somehow organize this large corpus, and the majority has opted for a categorization of themes. In *Emily Dickinson: Stairway of Surprise*, Charles Anderson posits four such categories—poetics, mind, nature, and death—to order his many acute readings of the individual poems; but such orderings are unfortunate in that any one Dickinson poem typically plays among several of these topics. Ruth Miller opens up an alternate possibility in her consistently powerful study, *The Poetry of Emily Dickinson*. She suggests that each of the bound fascicles, or packets, in which Dickinson left more than half of her known poems, can be reconstructed and read as narratives which typically move from the hope of an orthodox faith to doubt and finally to toughened faith. The reconstruction is clearly possible, as R. W. Franklin has shown in *The Editing of Emily Dickinson: A Reconsideration*, and Miller develops her theory most persuasively in considering one packet with great care. Her theory is interesting but speculative in that any combination of the individual poems may provide a sense of coherence, and even of progressive movement; thus I have not taken up her proposed organization, though others might well do so with profit.

Instead, I choose to view Dickinson's lyrics as one long poem, to the same extent that Whitman's lyrics constitute a *Leaves of Grass*. It is a key tenet of romanticism, put forth by Emerson in the past century and by Yeats in ours, that a writer's work, in its totality, should constitute a biography of his consciousness. To treat such a "life" critically, categories and subcategories may be necessary, but they had best be willing to destroy themselves by merging finally into a totality.

My search, then, has been for the underlying characteristics which unite the poems. But I isolate these characteristics only with the hope of finally achieving an integration which will not falsify the poems' variety. This method evolves from a strong belief that Dickinson's stylistic and thematic characteristics are nothing if not dynamic. It is misleading to consider this poet's attitudes as if they were little kernels of hardened belief. The problem with saying where Dickinson stands (say, on the question of a Protestant God) is that she can be found in two or five places at once. Her concerns manifest themselves as continuing self-debates, as varied and often conflicting dramatizations rather than as static position-papers. The individual moment, linguistically translated into the nuances of chosen words, will determine a particular resolution. Inevitably, that resolution will be challenged by another poem. Only by taking account of the full range of Dickinson's answers to her self-posed questions can we hope to discover the silent assumptions that shape the questions.

The reader should avail himself of Northrop Frye's brief essay on Dickinson in *Fables of Identity* and David Porter's fine book *The Art of Emily Dickinson's Early Poetry,* for Frye and Porter also consider Dickinson by investigating her recurring strategies and fictions. Despite this similarity of method—in fact, Porter and I both stress the terms "analogy" and "typology" though we apply them most differently—our emphases and conclusions vary greatly, and the reader might benefit by some comparison shopping.

A final rule which I have tried to follow is less peculiar to Dickinson.

The practical critic should be expected to offer an idea of his poet's general significance, but not to the neglect of individual poems. When confronted by a poem which seems to deserve and demand a detailed treatment, I have often risked clogging the flow of my argument to attempt to describe its individual complexities. A great deal of dialectical action occurs in Dickinson's poems, and there is no defense for passing over this action; for, without it, the poems would not be worthy of consideration at all.

I have incurred two kinds of debts in the writing of this study. The first is to those critics who have treated Dickinson with the seriousness she deserves. All too many pseudoscholars have attempted to picture this especially intelligent poet as a coy or incompetent chronicler of hypertrophied neuroses or as an imitator of greater poets original only in her freakishness. Far too much has been written on one or another secret life of Emily Dickinson and too little on Dickinson as poet. The critics to whom I am indebted—Aiken, Anderson, Bloom, Frye, Lynen, Miller, Porter, Sewall, Whicher, and Wilbur among many others—may disagree among themselves, but they have advanced the effort to understand both a poetry which transcends as it includes the merely personal and a life which is neither "tragic" nor "comic" but complex, proud, loving, and heroic even in its idiosyncrasies.

In the text, and even in this preface, I argue with some of the views put forth by Charles Anderson, Ruth Miller, and David Porter, and yet theirs are the studies which have most influenced my own. I hope they—and the reader—will remember that, if imitation is the most sincere form of flattery, debate runs a close second. In fact, while I have not included a bibliography—a remarkably full and reliable annotated bibliography by Willis J. Buckingham which includes scholarship and criticism to 1968 is now widely available (Bloomington and London: Indiana University Press, 1970) and I have managed to mention in my text and notes the studies which have seemed to me especially interesting—I would recommend the full-length studies by Anderson, Miller, and Porter as essential reading for anyone seriously grappling with Dickinson's poems.

I have relied almost exclusively on Thomas H. Johnson's editions of the poems and letters. The indebtedness of all readers and scholars of Dickinson to Johnson cannot be overstated. His editing has achieved nothing less than to restore Dickinson to the world; and his procedures in this awesome task seem to me a model of intelligent, even inspired scholarship. Richard Sewall's publication of *The Lyman Letters*, with a valuable commentary, has proved a most helpful supplement; and S. P.

A Preface on Procedure

Rosenbaum's *Concordance* (Ithaca, N.Y.: Cornell University Press, 1964) has served as a reliable map for image-hunting.

My other kind of debt, more personal, is to those who have provided guidance and encouragement in the development of this study: Richard Brodhead of Yale University; Richard Ohmann of Wesleyan University; Charles Summerlin of Lamar State College of Technology; James Wheatley of Trinity College, Hartford; and my senior colleagues at the University of Michigan, George Bornstein, John Knott, and Ira Konigsberg. Richard Sewall of Yale University, whose generosity is legend among Dickinson scholars, not only read the manuscript in its dissertation phase but also treated me to many of the important insights which will have become known with the publication of his epochal biography of Dickinson; and, at a later stage, Ruth Miller of the State University of New York at Stony Brook read the manuscript with painstaking care and afforded me much sound advice. My wife, Susan Remington Weisbuch, offered totally uncritical support throughout, often of heroic proportions. And finally, this project most owes whatever vitality it possesses to my two skeptical and magnificent preceptors at the Graduate School of Yale University, Marie Borroff and James McIntosh. Over a period of two years, neither once issued a censure without including a suggestion. Could I find the words to thank them adequately, I would be the subject, not the author, of a work on a great poet.

Introduction:
The House of Possibility

I dwell in Possibility—
A fairer House than Prose—
More numerous of Windows—
Superior—for Doors— . . .

(657)

1

Possibility is Emily Dickinson's synonym for poetry. Its house alone affords sufficient opportunities for observation and for voyages through the perceived vistas. Many windows, many doors; many visions, many quests. Because possibilities are endless, Dickinson's poetry posits no final truths. "Love to your World—or Worlds," she corrects herself in a letter to her friend Mrs. Holland (L 521).[1] This is a poet who will submit neither to borrowed dogma nor to any one world of her own hopeful making. She will not stop thinking.

Still, two major "worlds," two prevailing and apparently conflicting attitudes toward experience, run through the myriad visions. The first of Dickinson's worlds is a world of transcendence in which, to paraphrase Emerson's language in his essay "Circles," a deep is ever opening unto another deep. This first world is predictable: it is a natural outgrowth both of a literary time when visionary ideas were powerfully set abroad and of a personal, exuberant discovery of self in poetry. Dickinson discovered that the most ordinary word, tenderly nurtured in the mind's rich soil, could become a signifier of utmost mysteries, could grow like a vine into the upper air.[2] If the word, why not the flesh? In Dickinson's first world, commonplace objects and acts blaze into ultimate significance; the infinite is available for the right asking in every moment; transport is a matter of will, "Paradise is of the option" (L 319). Here, she is one with the independent party of New England optimism, one with Emerson and Thoreau.[3] In Dickinson's celebratory, Transcendentalist world, everyday events and objects are italicized into symbols, appearances rush toward essences, and possibilities never end.

But elsewhere Dickinson defines her power and freedom as consisting equally "in Vision—and in Veto!" (528), and that veto extends beyond socially sanctioned pieties to her own visions. The veto power of Dickinson's second pain-filled world stands ready to negate or qualify the self-legislated grandeur of the first. "It is difficult not to be fictitious in so fair a place," Dickinson writes of the natural world to Higginson, "but test's severe repairs are permitted all" (L 330). Dickinson would insist on testing her fictions, and they would often fail. The resultant despair is not simply a worldly pessimism; it is directed not against "so fair a place" as nature but against her own visions which have neglected a limit. Her second world is "second" because it is logically subsequent to her hopes. But why despair of what has never been? "To lose what we never owned might seem an eccentric Bereavement but Presumption has it's Affliction as actually as Claim —" (L 429). In this second world, the Transcendental possibilities of the first tantalize only to torture. The quester's very nature prevents realization of the intensely beheld goal; or, worse, the moment in which time is transcended crumbles back into *chronos*. His paradise in view but out of reach or reached only to be revoked, the quester achieves only a new dissatisfaction with the commonplace, which now becomes utterly barren:

> Had I not seen the Sun
> I could have borne the shade
> But Light a newer Wilderness
> My Wilderness has made—
> (1233)

Psychological limitations, fleshly fears, the failures of experience to fulfill hope, and, above all, the nullifying fact of mortality assert themselves in this second "mirror-world." These negations of vision create their own vision in turn: the symbolic intelligence which sees everlasting paradise in a commonplace pleasure must see death and hell in a commonplace pain. Thus, "Remorse" becomes "The Adequate of Hell—" (744); thus two terrible but unspecified separations from loved ones, perhaps by their deaths, are equated with the persona's own death in "My life closed twice before its close—" (1732). Dickinson does not proclaim and proselytize in this second world; she confesses. Natural enough to be a New England spinster and even more natural to desire to get from such a "here" to a Transcendental "There." But the intelligence that could cry "foul" against its most cherished visions is Dickinson's chief, glorious anomaly—glorious because its skepticism makes the visions which survive it real.

We should make our own confession here. The two worlds are not really independent except as we choose—or as Dickinson herself chose, in slighter poems and prose aphorisms—to abstract them momentarily. The two worlds constitute a spiral in which each grows out of the other. It is sometimes helpful for us and for Dickinson to consider these attitudes as polar opposites to clarify the terms of her self-dialogues. But Raymond Williams's defense of Dickens's shifting values applies fully to Dickinson's: "It is easy to show him, intellectually, as inconsistent, but my final point is that these deepest ideas and experiences tore at him, profoundly, in ways that make one see not inconsistency—the analytic abstraction—but disturbance—the creative source."[4] It is the nature of Dickinson's disturbances, in whose large terms we find our own, and the willingness of this supposedly secretive and willfully obscure creator to display her conflicts openly, without defense, that make her poetry matter.

2

This book is a critical study, not a biography; its story is the story of the poems, its main characters the two Emily Dickinsons, visionary celebrant and skeptical sufferer, who live together in the poems. Dickinson's actual circumstances are only a background for this story, but as background we should sketch them here. To do so, we can think of Dickinson's work as, in part, the offspring of three different families which interact but often quarrel: of the actual parents in actual Amherst; of the puritan ancestry behind them; and of the much looser group of powerful contemporary writers, primarily in Emersonian New England but in Victorian England as well.

The visionary thrust of Dickinson's first world constitutes a thoroughly rebellious response to the actual world into which she was born. This world is a New England in danger of losing its puritan soul, a New England in which, as Allen Tate has written, "The energy that had built the meeting-house ran the factory."[5] The limitations of Dickinson's particular parents—limitations frequently characterized in wildly unfair terms—are simply reflective of an age busy in denying its most important heritage, the life of the spirit. As Richard Sewall has argued, Dickinson's father in no way resembles his legendary reputation as another Mr. Barrett of Wimpole Street.[6] Still, it is a saddening experience to read some of the letters sent by Edward Dickinson to his fiancée Emily Norcross. The young lawyer writes doggedly of the life they will share in terms of duties and chastised pleasures and then, in a far more lively and natural voice, he recounts the events of his day and points to his future ambitions. It is not the absence of passion in Edward's view of marriage that is troubling but the hollow and mechanical expression he gives to the strictures he proposes, not the combination of abstract pieties and pragmatic goals but the variation in tone which suggests that each occupies a separate compartment of his mind and that the pieties are barely tolerated old guests. In his final letter to Miss Norcross before their marriage, Edward writes: "The time is short, My Dear, and we shall probably soon have occasion to enter upon the serious duties of life—Are we prepared? But I am too tired to 'moralise.' "[7] Edward's fatigue illustrates the distance of nineteenth-century New England from its puritan heritage, from the puritan sense of life as continually fraught with crises, and from the puritan habit of thought by which the most minute events are interpreted as ciphers of divine intention. The vestiges of puritan social dogma appear burdensome to Edward, and he makes no attempt to carry on the interpretive tradition which translates life into Life. Twenty-five years later, Edward's poetic daughter will write to her brother Austin, "we do not have much poetry, father having decided that its pretty much all *real life*" (L 65). Born into a representative family of the age, a family which retains the social rigidities of puritanism but lacks the passionate faith which once gave those rigidities justification, Emily Dickinson refuses to conform to her father's frightening definition of life. Her note to Austin continues, "Father's real life and *mine* sometimes come into collision, but as yet, escape unhurt!"

It is impossible to date the origin of an attitude, impossible to locate a moment when Dickinson first perceived that she would have to develop a separate reality for herself. But the outward manifestation of this sense may be dated from a negative act, a negative Calling, when, in her teens at the Mount Holyoke Seminary, Dickinson finds that she cannot stand up to commit herself to a perfunctory Christ.[8] By the age of twenty, in a letter to her conventionally religious friend Abiah Root, Dickinson is giving positive expression to her own commitment by creating an illegal, apostatic persona:

> You are growing wiser than I am, and nipping in the bud fancies which I let blossom—perchance to bear no fruit, or if plucked, I may find it bitter. The shore is safer, Abiah, but I love to buffet the sea—I can count the bitter wrecks here in these pleasant waters, and hear the murmuring winds, but oh, I love the danger! You are learning control and firmness. Christ Jesus will love you more. I'm afraid he doesn't love me *any*.
>
> (L 39)

In other words, in spite of all doubts, better the Ancient Mariner and his lived development of consciousness than the hermit who greets the Mariner on his return with conventional pieties. The letter portrays the cherished self-shock of a well-to-do Amherst girl at her own heretical development. Even at this early age, thoughts are deeds to Dickinson and so this business of letting fancies blossom, of constructing uncensored fictional worlds, is matter for fear and trembling. Yet the danger is delicious, for what has occurred is an escape:

> They shut me up in Prose—
> As when a little Girl
> They put me in the Closet—
> Because they liked me "still"—
>
> Still! Could they themselves have peeped—
> And seen my Brain—go round—
> They might as wise have lodged a Bird
> For Treason—in the Pound—
>
> Himself has but to will
> And easy as a Star
> Abolish his Captivity—
> And laugh—No more have I—
>
> (613)

The House of Prose, of conventional and prosaic conformity, here becomes a punitive closet; but the House of Possibility, of imaginative epistemological freedom, exists wherever the mind is. The poem recalls a moment late in another domestic drama, Shakespeare's *Lear,* when the King, now captured and about to be imprisoned with Cordelia, fully realizes that royalty is not robes but an internal state of being and that sovereignty exists not in rule but in love: "Come, let's away to prison. /

We two alone will sing like birds i' th' cage." But it is rebellious escape, not resignation, that Dickinson affirms. The little girl who is "shut up" by her family's cold and deadening respectability is equally the mature mental quester who is thwarted by the more general circumstances of daily, prosaic life. When both girl and poet are compared in turn to that *non sequitur* of a bird jailed in a dog pound, both girl and poet make a triumphant discovery: what has been chosen for me I need not accept; my thought can soar free of circumstance to reach the condition of a marvelously independent star.

From that vantage point, a scornful laugh is permissible, for in truth the would-be captors have put themselves in prosy captivity. In a likably arrogant poem sent to the father who had decided for "*real life,*" Dickinson reveals more precisely the nature of her poetic revolt:

> Sleep is supposed to be
> By souls of sanity
> The shutting of the eye.
>
> Sleep is the station grand
> Down which, on either hand
> The hosts of witness stand!
>
> Morn is supposed to be
> By people of degree
> The breaking of the Day.
>
> Morning has not occurred!
>
> That shall Aurora be—
> East of Eternity—
> One with the banner gay—
> One in the red array—
> *That* is the break of Day!
>
> (13)

The need to distinguish two antithetical modes of thought, to value the symbolic, possibility-building mind at the expense of mechanistic common sense, may lead to some symbolic excesses in the poem. The effort to distinguish gets in the way of a full development of imagery; the poem is trying to do too many things at once. But it is hardly what George Whicher claims it is, a poem of "resounding nonsense" sent "to tease her father for his insistence on the family's early rising."[9] Instead, it is a thoroughly serious attempt to show that even the advocates of father's *"real life"* use figurative language—"The shutting of the eye" is clearly synecdochic—and thus that their way of thinking is itself full of symbolic assumptions, though they are the sort of assumptions which deaden language and deny significance to life. The alternative voice, which does not "suppose" but confidently proclaims, makes of sleep a scene of self-reckoning, a type of Judgment. Similarly, the "sane" idea of morn as merely the breaking of the day is transformed into a scripturally capitalized Morn, *the* Breaking of *the* Day. The symbolizing mind allies itself with an alternative, literally apocalyptic sense of time: it looks forward to a dawn of eternity which will destroy the chronological time so reassuring to the "souls of sanity." This different dawn occupies the whole sky of myth. It combines the god-invoking classical term "Aurora" with carefully imprecise references to imagery from the Book of Revelation. [10] *That* is the dawn which the connective mind strives to imagine and with which it strives to identify. Its large desire makes the "sane" mind which settles for so little and neglects so much appear lost in folly; and it criticizes the sane mind by redeeming the language which sane and common usage so devitalizes. The poet's mission, as suggested here, is to revive in a more open-ended manner that puritan assurance that life is a meaningful quest, that the smallest acts are significant because life opens out.

Dickinson is not alone in this attempt. Her view from the House of Possibility is, after all, circumscribed: "I see New Englandly—," she quips at the end of an early poem (285). A poet who makes such an avowal around 1860 consciously places herself in the tradition of the transformed puritan sensibility which constitutes American romanticism. Like all of the American romantics—Hawthorne and Melville as well as Emerson, Thoreau, and Whitman—Dickinson chooses to see symbolically and to expand meanings to their furthest bounds. Like them, she dramatizes this methodology as a revolt against the life-draining elements of her culture; like them, she adopts an outsider's stance, a mood of continual desire, a mode of continual quest; like them, she longs for the spiritual nourishment but not for the dogmatic beliefs and tortured consciences of her great-grandparents.

Dickinson's identity with the American romantics is somewhat obscured by her own lack of historical concerns. She is far less concerned than her fellows with the idea of America and far less involved in the particular political issues of the day. Whitman's scorn of effete "foo-foos" is powered by his vision of America as a potential New Eden, a prelapsarian garden of bodily and spiritual health; Dickinson's scorn of "soft, cherubic ladies" is powered instead by a vision of the potential of existence in general, in which personal Edens are always possible. She nowhere speaks, as Melville does in the sunnier early years of his career, of a new American literature, totally different from and greater than the literature of the European past. She never feels compelled, as Thoreau does, to spend a night in the Concord jailhouse to protest unfair taxes, and she never writes tracts against slavery—she never writes tracts.

From one point of view, this detachment is deplorable. The extent to which Dickinson's concern for the universal self in universal experience negates a concern for urgent social questions may be seen as the most extreme proof of the unhinged nature of New England Transcendental thought. More empathetically, we can see this detachment as Dickinson's own brand of fatigue. She is tired of bromides from the pulpit, of moldy, prescribed laws of life. "I do not respect 'doctrines,' " she tells Mrs. Joseph Haven to explain her non-attendance at a church service (L 200). It may well have been the presentational form of New England politics, tied as it was to sermon-like rhetoric, which caused Dickinson's disinterest. To her mind a disengagement from the passing social scene would allow for a more complete engagement with a permanent cause: the advocacy of a method of thought which translates into a method of life. Because this method has center stage to itself in Dickinson's poetry, she becomes, in this sense, the epitome of the American romantic.

But if Dickinson prized any contemporary writer above all others, it was not Emerson or any other American but George Eliot: " 'What do I think of *Middlemarch?*' What do I think of glory—except that in a few instances this 'mortal has already put on immortality' " (L 389). No wonder Eliot could strike such a response: the Eliot who writes, "If we had a keen vision and feeling of all ordinary human life, it would be like hearing the grass grow and the squirrel's heart beat, and we should die of that roar which lies on the other side of silence,"[11] finds a secret American sister in the Transcendental Dickinson who writes, "Had we the first intimation of the Definition of Life, the calmest of us would be Lunatics!" (L 492). Of course there was much more to George Eliot than the romantic quotation suggests: a probing intelligence, an acknowledgment of the real and limiting, a perception of mixed human fates. She could credit the dreamy hopes of a Dorothea Brooke at the same time that she stresses their impossibility.[12] In her second world, the world of limit and negation, Dickinson resembles the critical author, not the dreamy heroine, of the early chapters of *Middlemarch*.

There is no single explanation for Dickinson's recognition of what she called "the Thief ingredient," the ingredient by which romantic afflatus would be nullified or inverted into pain. We cannot expect a complex mind to be influenced singly or simply. Dickinson's reaction against easy, untaxed transcendences is in part simply a quality of visionary integrity. It might be seen, too, as her father's *"real life,"* transformed into an acknowledged but resented brake. In cultural terms, when Dickinson's second world is presented in its quieter, more resigned aspect, when, for instance, a persona admits to helplessness and calls on a higher power for aid, we find a puritan strain of humility and dependence; while in its angrier, more resentful aspect, when Dickinson posits no god or a cruel one, we find the anguish of modern spirit, Henry James's "imagination of disaster."

Actually, we need not look backward or forward to discover attitudes similar to Dickinson's, but simply sideways. It is helpful to remember that romantic New England is also Victorian New England; ideas can cross oceans. Not only in George Eliot, but in the attitudes of all the great Victorians, we find a fear like Dickinson's of oracular cheating. The English romantics have died, some in despair and others in awful complacence; they had not awakened to find their dreams true, not on this earth. To a Victorian like Arnold, as Dwight Culler writes, "The Joy of the Romantic poets, and of childhood ... had some element of illusion about it, of a divine illusion, which is unsatisfactory to modern man." Arnold's solution, Culler continues, is to create a poetry of "imaginative reason."[13] Leaving out Arnold's explicitly social concerns, Arnold's relation to the romantics is like Dickinson's relation to herself.

But we need not stray from Dickinson's New England home to locate similar self-questionings. Dickinson's first, bardic world is the world of the early Emerson, the Emerson who would teach men that they could see God face to face and not die—and who would add, echoing Blake, that every man is his own Christ; Dickinson's second, confessional world is the skeptical (and especially skeptical-through-longing) world of such contemporaries as Melville, whose Ishmael warns man not to stare too long into the fire. If puritan faith is a source of optimistic romanticism, puritan hell-fire can work its transformed fears; and Yankee skepticism can be extended by a Melville or a Dickinson into metaphysical doubt. Further, such "optimists" as Emerson and Whitman had begun to doubt their initial exuberance, had begun to qualify their skyey visions and tie them to the death-bound earth by the time Dickinson might be influenced by them. But, more important, from the first all of the American romantics had opted for a certain fragmentation of thought, a willingness to give each attitude its head, to organize

the world around one image one day and its opposite the next—
Emerson calls his works "a sort of Farmer's Almanac of Mental
Moods."[14] Thus, even the abstract dualism of Dickinson's two worlds
seems representative.

To a degree it is; and, in particular, when the images which organize
the world become dire, when the grass of Whitman's "Song of Myself"
is replaced by the "Chaff, straw, splinters of wood, weeds, and the
sea-gluten," the "few sands and dead leaves" of his "As I Ebbed with
the Ocean of Life," we are fully prepared for Dickinson's second world.
Still, I would argue that Dickinson's House of Possibility exists in its
own particular neighborhood. What in Emerson or Whitman seems
subsequent retreat and even failure is part of Dickinson's constant
method from the beginning. Not only do we find her two worlds
growing sequentially out of each other in many poems; but in the
finest poems and even in individual phrases, the oracular and skeptical
voices and visions become one: "The Risks of Immortality are perhaps
its' charm—A secure Delight suffers in enchantment—" (L 353);
"Ecstasy is peril" (L 989). The story I tell in this book concerns
self-conflict only in the service of a final wholeness. Dickinson's world
of joy prevails, but only by taking into full account all the fears and
negations of the second world and transforming them into her one fixed
value, a vitalizing dread. Emerson, for one, complained that he could
forge no such reconciliation: "The worst feature of this double
consciousness is, that the two lives, of the understanding and the soul"
(very much like Dickinson's two worlds, in reverse order) "... really
show very little relation to each other: never meet and measure each
other; one prevails now, all buzz and din; and the other prevails then,
all infinitude and paradise; and, with the progress of life, the two
discover no greater disposition to reconcile themselves."[15] Dickinson's
major achievement may consist in her demand that romantic hope
must admit pain and disappointment, that freedom must not ignore
but include necessity, that paradise must be achieved by quest through
the "buzz and din." Still, the tension between the two worlds is every-
where evidenced and it is this tension—apparent in the smallest
minutiae of style as in the largest narrative patterns—that most clearly
identifies Emily Dickinson. This tension will serve as the bounding line
for our considerations of Dickinson's rhetorical strategies, metaphysical questionings, and fictive patterns alike; for only by acknowledging
continually the multiform conflict can we perceive the energy of its won
resolutions.

Analogical Poetics

> *For Pattern is the Mind Bestowed*
> *That imitating her*
> *Our most ignoble Services*
> *Exhibit worthier.*
>
> (1223)

1

We can speak, at a high level of abstraction, of Dickinson's "two worlds"; but each of the individual poems shadows forth a world of its own. Perhaps the essential quality of Dickinson's verse is its compressed inclusiveness. All her near-1,800 poems are extremely brief lyrics—I doubt that any other poet in the non-haiku world has written so many poems of less than forty lines—and yet even her briefest poems seem unbounded in scope, seem to be taking in, from a particular angle, everything at once. If we are finally to put together Dickinson's compound meaning, we must begin with the method by which she achieves such scope—especially because her method has been misunderstood and her very soul attacked on the basis of this misunderstanding.

Even admiring critical studies are rife with expressions of bewilderment and anger. Yvor Winters indicts Dickinson for "irresponsible obscurity"; Jay Leyda suggests more carefully that many of the poems neglect to mention their "omitted centers," real-life circumstances that lead to the poems but go unnamed; Ruth Miller theorizes that Dickinson "refines a style to disguise what has happened in her internal world";[1] and less sympathetic attacks on Dickinson's "private

11

symbolism" are legion.[2] The confusion set in early. When her awed but baffled mentor, the man of letters Thomas Higginson, asked for a clarification of some poems she had sent him, Dickinson replied, "All men say 'What' to me, but I thought it a fashion—" (L 271). No fashion: after more than a century, normally sensitive readers still ask that vulgar, accusatory "what" of a poet who upsets their normal expectations.

Dickinson is a difficult poet but she becomes incomprehensible only when we neglect to raise the questions necessary for an understanding of any poet. In what ways does this poetry create meaning from language? For what kinds of meaning should we look?

We can begin to answer these questions by considering the kind of obscurity which worried Dickinson herself. "While my thought is undressed—I can make the distinction, but when I put them in the Gown—they look alike, and numb," she complains in another letter to Higginson (L 261). She fears that the demands of poetic composition—rhyme, meter, all the elements of decorum, and especially, perhaps, the popular idea of poetry as a comment on a particular aspect of life, a footnote to existence—will limit the scope and obscure the outline of an individual thought. But the apparently humble note to Higginson, which takes up the clothing imagery he himself had employed in an advisory article to young writers,[3] may have been written more as a hint toward proper appreciation than as self-criticism. For by the time she wrote the letter in 1862, Dickinson had discovered a poetic method which does not dress but illustrates, thus *is*, the pattern of her thought.

The essence of the method is analogy, and analogy becomes a way of poetic life. As "I dwell in Possibility" develops, Dickinson reveals, with characteristic wit, that her House of Possibility is a non-house: it is all of phenomenal nature, with "The Gambrels of the Sky" affording "an Everlasting Roof." She concludes by defining more precisely her activity within that "house":

> For Occupation—This—
> The spreading wide my narrow Hands
> To gather Paradise—
>
> (657)

Translated into the language of logic, this hand-spreading becomes a method for expanding analogical relations into inclusive visions. Dickinson's typical poem enacts a hypothesis about the world by patterning a parallel, analogical world. This is the linguistic basis for

Dickinson's revolt against a mentality unwilling to look deeply into things: to make words mean as much as they can, to take them out of the dull round of cliché, to renew them by realizing their connotative and etymological potential, and to reorbit them in analogical combination. At each stage of this process in Dickinson's best poems, the persona serves to make the word flesh, to register the human consequences of the transformed meanings. Thus the very creator of a poetic world will respond to it, often with Frankenstein-like shock and always with surprise. Dickinson's visionary and confessional strains merge perfectly in the rhetorical grain of such poems.

This claim that Dickinson insists on the consequential nature of word choices echoes T. S. Eliot's famous praise of an earlier poet: "A thought to Donne was an experience; it modified his sensibility."[4] In fact, many admirers of metaphysical verse have found in Dickinson their one romantic friend and have attempted to define her as a late child of the metaphysical tradition. The similarities are more concrete than a vague claim for reassociation of sensibility would suggest. I call Dickinson an analogical poet because analogy suggests an extended equation (*a* is to *b* as *c* is to *d*) carried out by a rigorous logic whose comparisons are always functional and never merely decorative. Further, we may think of metaphor as a completed analogy, in which the progressive logic of the associations is buried; conversely, we may think of analogy as a metaphor-in-the-making, in which the associative process calls attention to itself. This description jibes with Eliot's definition, in the essay just cited, of the metaphysical conceit: "the elaboration (contrasted with the condensation) of a figure of speech to the farthest stage to which ingenuity can carry it."[5] Eliot goes on to note that Donne's poetry abounds in compacted metaphors and this is equally true of Dickinson's. But the distinction which places Donne and Dickinson in the analogical camp holds: if we grant that no metaphor ever completely closes the distance between its two terms, both Donne and Dickinson distinguish themselves by maintaining an extraordinary tension between tenor and vehicle, a tension which emphasizes the fact that a comparison is being made and that its logic reveals the nature of the poet's (or his persona's) mind. Dickinson's willful confusion of categories, her merging of terms from ordinarily discrete realms of experience, call attention to themselves. Time frequently becomes space:

> Between the March and April line—
> That magical frontier

> Beyond which summer hesitates
> Almost too heavenly near . . .
> (1764)

Similarly, an emotional condition is described in terms of geographical travel:

> The lonesome for they know not What—
> The Eastern Exiles—be—
> Who strayed beyond the Amber line
> Some madder Holiday—. . .
> (262)

In turn, place is internalized: "Gethsemane— / Is but a Province—in the Being's Centre—" (553). And conversely, human parts become material objects, as in the line "The Eyes around—had wrung them dry—" (465), where eyes confoundingly become cloths as well as the hands that wring cloths dry. In the same famous poem, "I heard a Fly buzz when I died—," we find an example of sensory synaesthesia, as the fly is described "With Blue—uncertain stumbling Buzz—." But Dickinson also creates a more unusual synaesthesia of nature, a reordering of natural causality, as in the things-as-perceived phrase, "The Dust did scoop itself like Hands— / And throw away the Road—" (824). Such "confusions," typical in strategy if not in vocabulary to the metaphysicals as well, do not announce an identity but a perceived resemblance. The analogical poet displays his connective process and thus makes less of a claim for how the world is put together than for how his mind puts it together.

But Dickinson's analogical strategy differs from the metaphysicals' in a quality so crucial that any comparison must be severely limited. We can get at this special quality by examining the most simple of Dickinson's characteristic analogical structures. This first kind of analogical progression, the analogical collection, develops by a series of perceptions or stories. Each is at least partially analogous to the others and each reveals a new aspect or consequence of putting the world together in the particular, often unstated way which links the otherwise disparate examples. In other words, each scene is illustratory, and our attention is finally drawn away from its specific content to the general principle which relates it to the other scenes. Concept subordinates examples, but the examples afford the concept its suggestive scope and almost literally bring it to life. Consider this simple poem:

14

How many schemes may die
In one short Afternoon
Entirely unknown
To those they most concern—
The man that was not lost
Because by accident
He varied by a Ribbon's width
From his accustomed route—
The Love that would not try
Because beside the Door
It must be competitions
Some unsuspecting Horse was tied
Surveying his Despair
(1150)

After she simply states the linking idea, Dickinson elliptically tells two illustratory tales. The first story reads like a murder mystery with a happy ending. A man is saved, without ever realizing it, from a "scheme" concocted either by nature or by his enemies, say a falling rock meant to harm him, because by mere chance on this particular day he "varied by a Ribbon's width" from his habitual path. The woeful second story balances the unrecognized good fortune of the first. It introduces a far more complex situation, a set of relationships worthy of a Victorian novel. A young man, on his way to offer a proposal of marriage to his lady, is dissuaded by the appearance of a horse. He interprets, perhaps misinterprets, the horse as a sign that "It must be competitions," that another suitor is present, that his lady is unfaithful. The young lady "most concerned" with the scheme, the aborted proposal, is only a door's width away, but she is so far away from recognizing and righting her lover's misgiving that Dickinson never mentions her directly. Ironically, it is only the dumb horse which surveys her lover's despair. The poem shows that Dickinson can tell a tale with evocative compactness, but it leaves us with more than two stories. Their totally different genres and consequences notwithstanding, both illustrate the same dictum and thus create a sense of the great range of chance. The poem frightens us by suggesting that we are ignorant of the frequency and power of chance, because chance often pertains to what does not happen; our lives are not in our keeping. Most effectively, chance is made neither solely benevolent nor malevolent. That, too, is a matter of chance.

And by the time we finish the poem, we recognize that its two apparently mimetic scenes are themselves "chance" choices from an infinity of possible exemplifications of the poem's unifying proposition. The scenes are not mimetic but illustratory, chosen, temporary, analogous. The poem is finally sceneless, and this scenelessness is the fully unique quality which identifies Dickinson's lyric technique. There is nothing quite like this scenelessness in any other poet. We are more accustomed to poetry which does posit a referential situation, complete with a scenic component: anything from a bourgeois living room to a pastoral garden, from a particular historical setting to the universe.[6] (We could say that *Paradise Lost* contains all of these scenic components, for instance.) Most poetry is at least internally occasional, in the sense that a certain state of affairs serves as a goad to reflective speech. We may value the expression of the meditated situation far more than the motivating situation itself ("Lycidas" is a good example); but a poem usually contains a referential reality, even if that reality is totally fictional, invented. Even in metaphysical poetry, the primary scene is fixed. The language characteristically keeps one arm of its compass on the situation of a lovers' parting while the other arm circles in search of a definitive simile. Most often, the boundary of a Dickinson poem is not a particular scene or situation but the figure of the analogy as it moves from scene to scene. Dickinson gives us a pattern in several carpets and then makes the carpets vanish.

This final scenelessness makes itself felt even more strongly in analogical collections which leave their unifying principles entirely implicit. Such is the case in this much celebrated poem:

> Did the Harebell loose her girdle
> To the lover Bee
> Would the Bee the Harebell *hallow*
> Much as formerly?
>
> Did the "Paradise"—persuaded—
> Yield her moat of pearl—
> Would the Eden *be* an Eden,
> Or the Earl—an *Earl?*
>
> (213)

The first stanza questions whether the sexual consummation of love might not be the end of love. Harebell is to bee as the maiden is to her lover and, with a nice pun on "girdle," sexual consummation is compared to the bee's invasion of the flower. In the second stanza, the lover-bee becomes an earl, the maiden-harebell a paradise, and her submission the yielding of a "moat of pearl." While its analogies still relate directly to the sexual problem of the first stanza (entrance into paradise by a moat of pearl is a beautiful figure for the sexual act), the more abstract, vaguely biblical language of the second stanza intimates an analogous, more universal and metaphysical fear. The poem raises its bet. If that which is most desired is by definition something we do not possess, then will not whatever becomes known lose its sublime status without elevating the knower? Will not any Eden, not just the sexual paradise, cease to be an Eden? The poem takes us from the bee's domestic garden to The Garden, Eden. The apparently trivial act of a harebell and a bee becomes an illustration of personal, sexual doubts; that fear then becomes a cosmological doubt, an illustration of the despairing thought that only by a failure to achieve the thing sought can the thing itself remain worthy of achievement.

The poem's raising of the bet is particularly effective because the philosophical question does not replace the more immediate personal one but grows naturally out of it. The voices of Dickinson's two worlds, oracular and confessional, combine to spread a personal grief into a law of all experience. We end up here, as in all of Dickinson's analogical collections, with a kidding of empiricisms: what is presented as deduction finally reveals itself as a drama of designed examples. We are not concerned finally with the habits of bees and flowers or knights and moats; less ridiculously, we are not even concerned primarily with sexual ethics or theological justifications. The analogical examples go toward a general denial of that fond hope that one can have his cake and eat it. But this is not to say that the imagery is merely explicatory. If empiricism is kidded, pure reason is dragged from its tower to do the joshing. Sexual fears, part of our constant experience, vitalize the abstract fear they example. In the second stanza, God's ways, which may or may not engage us immediately, depending on who "we" are, gain immediacy by their almost anatomical conjunction (in the words "yield her moat") with the earlier sexual metaphor. And, whatever our degree of theological concern, the second stanza forces us to recognize the scope of the negative law it illustrates. That law includes God, includes essence itself. By the time we derive the law, its imaging has hit upon so many areas of our consciousness—social, libidinal, natural, mythic, cosmological—that whatever areas have not been hit feel the shot nonetheless. And the divisions of consciousness are acknowledged only to be obliterated.

17

Dickinson's raising of the bet may occur as a progression from the personal and practical to the universal and metaphysical, as in the preceding poem; or the progression may be reversed, so that apparently impersonal questionings of the world are transformed into emotional urgencies. But here again, though the emphasis may alter in the course of a poem, psychological fears and philosophical thoughts do not compete, but blend:

> So has a Daisy vanished
> From the fields today—
> So tiptoed many a slipper
> To Paradise away—
>
> Oozed so in crimson bubbles
> Day's departing tide—
> Blooming—tripping—flowing—
> Are ye then with God?
>
> (28)

The observations of endings seem calmly philosophical until the final line shows that they are motivated by a question crucial to the speaker. Again in this poem, minor and contrasted analogies abound. The Daisy "vanishes" like a missing person; the sunset-tide bleeds away; the daisy vanishes from one garden, the slippers arrive at another. The seventh line climaxes the analogical process and prepares for the surprisingly direct question which links the analogies. It takes one gerund related to each of the three diversified images and organizes them into a temporal progression: all things first bloom like daisies, then trip off like children in slippers, and finally fade away like sunsets which seem to flow away like tides. Are ye then with God? Will I be? The bland equation of three kinds of nature—vegetative, human, and cosmic—creates a total question of entropy which spurns categorization.

We can see now that Dickinson's local confusions of categories have an even more crucial function than Donne's similarly "made" metaphors. Donne's metaphors typically establish a basic "outer" situation which they simultaneously transform according to the persona's "inner" state of mind. Dickinson's sceneless analogical collections, by their very lack of "outer" situations, forgo that playful competition between experience and its interpretation. Instead, those local confusions of category are extended to become the structural principle of the analogical collection, with its free and ingenious mergings of disparate thoughts. Dickinson's analogical aesthetic tries to eliminate such traditional dichotomies as inner and outer. Her poems do not dramatize the projection of mind onto matter but the organization of a mind-world continuum in a pattern of chosen language. Thus, Dickinson's use of analogy is more romantic than metaphysical, as befits her actual moment in history.[7] Charles Rosen's brilliant remark on romantic cognition and language applies particularly to Dickinson:

> The uncontrolled expansion of concepts until they referred potentially to everything and therefore to nothing so that the processes of association were completely liberated and magnified was a process repeated until it could seem like a vulgar and maddening trick.... But it is a trick based upon a profound comprehension of speech, a realization that there is no possibility of authentic and direct communication without some looseness, some play in the mechanism of language.[8]

But even here we must take care not to nullify Dickinson's individuality by placing it. It is not a Wordsworthian spontaneity, an overflow of powerful emotions rendered in an imitation of natural diction, that informs the analogical collection. No poet has written more elliptically than Dickinson; no poet better illustrates what John Lynen calls "the odd self-consciousness which makes the American abnormally aware of his symbolizing."[9] Dickinson does not quite present us with what Robert Langbaum has described as a romantic "poetry of experience." The poems do not develop a view of an experience in complete conjunction with the narrative unfolding of that experience, as Wordsworth does in the *Prelude* and as Coleridge does in his conversation poems; instead they define the essence of a whole range of experiences by the development of a versatile analogue, just as Coleridge does with the sea voyage in "The Ancient Mariner." When Dickinson's poems pose as reportorial, the speaker does not proclaim, "I was there—this happened to me"; instead, he implies, "I was somewhere—the exact place doesn't matter—and this analogy will constitute the meaning of that experience, minus the experiential trimmings. As such, the analogical development will be a new experience of its own." The poems do not lack a situational matrix—that would be impossible—but mimetic situations are transformed, transported to a world of analogical language which exists in parallel to a world of experience, as its definition. Thus Lynen is only partially right in saying that "Emily Dickinson is always turning event into circumstance *as her poems develop*" (italics mine).[10] That transformation takes place in the formulation of the opening analogy. Already, "event" has become design, though in its development the poem may exchange a simple analogy for a more complex and inclusive one. Dickinson's poems present us with a second spontaneity, with an over-the-shoulder view of the "later" process by which a poet's mind attempts to make sense of experience by acts of concentrated language.

This is to say that we get into terrible trouble if we read Dickinson's poems too literally, and especially if we read them as displacements or obscurations of particular experiences in her life. It is also to say that we cannot stress too much the freeing of language from its usual associations that occurs in the analogical collection. The most grisly images may go toward establishing a sane and even spiritual context of both personal and philosophical importance. The genius of one poem consists in its retention of savage, appetitive illustration right through the final analogy, which nonetheless purifies the conception:

> As the Starved Maelstrom laps the Navies
> As the Vulture teased
> Forces the Broods in lonely Valleys
> As the Tiger eased
>
> By but a Crumb of Blood, fasts Scarlet
> Till he meet a Man
> Dainty adorned with Veins and Tissues
> And partakes—his Tongue
>
> Cooled by the Morsel for a moment
> Grows a fiercer thing
> Till he esteem his Dates and Cocoa
> A Nutrition mean
>
> I, of a finer Famine
> Deem my Supper dry
> For but a Berry of Domingo
> And a Torrid Eye.
>
> (872)

The memorably ghoulish images of the first three stanzas work by the ironic reduction of man to a dainty dinner, served up to the hungry and savage forces of nature, which are anthropomorphized into social gentlemen. This is not so much a confusion of categories as a full reversal. But puns on sustenance can go in an opposite direction. (Think of a phrase like "food for the soul" and of the church

20

Communion services.) The speaker's "famine" is "finer" than the tiger's because it is less literal, because it describes not a destructive need but a creative spiritual desire. The "Torrid Eye" and "Berry of Domingo" make the speaker long for an epistemological completion, for a closer, more passionate relationship with a hidden omnipotence. In this sense, the earlier, savage reversals are themselves reversed. But they establish the ferocity ("sincerity" certainly would be too mild a word) of the speaker's frustrated desire. And, more surprisingly, they give the speaker's desire a past history. Each of the preliminary analogies presents a more complete appetitive history than the preceding one: the maelstrom is simply starved before it, catlike, "laps the Navies"; but the vulture has been teased by the sight of the slow-dying "Broods" he wishes to "force," to devour rapaciously; and the tiger already has partaken of a leftover, a "Crumb of Blood," before he dines on his main course of man and finds himself henceforth dissatisfied with any less luxurious repast. A law is progressively established. The greater one's past satisfaction, the greater his longing for the sustenance that is no longer available. As the final term in the series, the speaker most exemplifies this law, though of course its application has been altered completely. Once, the speaker did achieve the sublime moment of spiritual fulfillment, and it is that, as it is with the tiger and his human food, which makes the present offering, his own "Dates and Cocoa," so cruelly insufficient. The poem may be thought of as a wild and disconsolate rewriting of Wordsworth's Immortality Ode, a dirge to lost powers, a dirge in which mere intimations of the thing itself torture rather than console.

A much slighter poem goes even further to remind us that the analogical collection need not present a steady progression, a gradual raising of the bet. At times, the progression demands a sudden leap of the mind:

> By such and such an offering
> To Mr. So and So
> The web of life woven—
> So martyrs albums show!
> (38)

At first, the poem seems to concern the most ordinary social gift-giving. The final line fills in the blanks ("such and such" and "so and so") by a startling application: the offering of a life to a principle worth dying for. Yet even as social gift-giving is transformed into a supreme

21

sacrifice, the last line manages to retain the lesser domestic illustration by including the image of a homely album.

It is in this ability to surprise without falsification that we see most clearly the positive value of Dickinson's status as a private poet. Very few of her poems were published in her lifetime, infrequently in the local Springfield *Daily Republican* and once, anonymously, in a *Masque of Poets* edited by her idolator and fellow-poetess, Helen Hunt Jackson. If, as Ruth Miller suggests, Dickinson very much desired a public reputation in the early years of her writing, she very quickly came to disparage publication: "Publication—is the Auction / Of the Mind of Man," begins a poem now frequently reprinted (709). Freed from the pressures of a public career, Dickinson was freed from ordering her imagination in terms of subjects. This is one of the strengths of a poet who does not say to himself, "I'll write Endymion this year and Hyperion the next." When a word, a phrase, a motto, or a formulated idea came to her attention, Dickinson was free to chase it through all sorts of referential categories and to note the reciprocal effects.

The phrases and prefabricated ideas that floated through Dickinson's mind most often were Calvinist, and Dickinson's relation to her cultural heritage is exactly coequal with her attitude toward language in general: appreciative and rebellious, appreciative of vital meanings by rebellion against hackneyed ones. In our final example of the analogical collection, for instance, we would hardly know the puritan ethic of work and sacrifice for the surgery Dickinson performs on it:

Who never lost, are unprepared
A Coronet to find!
Who never thirsted
Flagons, and Cooling Tamarind!

Who never climbed the weary league—
Can such a foot explore
The purple territories
On Pizarro's shore?

How many Legions overcome—
The Emperor will say?
How many *Colors* taken
On Revolution Day?

How many *Bullets* bearest?
Hast Thou the Royal scar?

Angel! Write "Promoted"
On this Soldier's brow!

(73)

The analogy moves from deserts to South American mountains and then to what first appears a European battleground but soon becomes heaven.

The emperor's questions of the third stanza seem to be irrelevant to the pattern, even to contradict it by asking simply for what the soldier has accomplished, until they are shown to be only preliminaries for the real question of what he has suffered. As the poem ends, the tamarind is transformed into spiritual drink, Pizarro's purple territories become heaven, and the emperor becomes St. Peter. The war is transformed into an internal battle, the soldier into a soldier of life. In a roundabout way, the poem revitalizes another theological cliché, for the soldier has "lost" his life to find another, crowned life. The illustratory scenes of the poem finally find a home within a Christian tradition. But by the time they arrive there, the poem has formulated such a sweeping field for its initial paradox that a Christian "new Life" becomes only part of its pattern, an ultimate example. In poems like this one and "As the Starved Maelstrom laps the Navies," Dickinson defeats the theological ennui of her culture by a policy of "surround and conquer." This is how the poems of analogical collection support and illustrate Richard Wilbur's idea that "At some point Emily Dickinson sent her whole Calvinist vocabulary into exile, telling it not to come back until it would subserve her own sense of things."[11]

But Dickinson's analogical collection, with its scenelessness, explains a more important and inclusive characteristic of her poems. Readers invariably comment on the extraordinary degree to which Dickinson rivets their attention so completely on her use of language. For many years, critics attributed the attraction of Dickinson's language to her exotic vocabulary. William Howard exploded that myth by his statistical proof that "Dickinson uses no more unusual words than do Emerson, Keats and Lanier."[12] Unfortunately, both Howard and David Porter[13] replace the old red herring with a new one. They claim that we naturally focus on Dickinson's language because of the brevity of each poem. Yet great epics constantly achieve a concentration of meaning which any number of mediocre lyrics lack.

The special attention we pay Dickinson's language is partly attributable to its surprising confusions of category. But we must return to the scenelessness which constitutes the basis of Dickinson's strategy for a full explanation. Even the narrative poems of analogical collection

23

refuse to compose a mimetic situation. That is, they posit no specific situation which occurs apart from the language and which the language only serves to interpret. In fact, Dickinson teases us mercilessly to accentuate this quality of her poetry. In "So has the Daisy vanished," we expect the comparative "so" to be the metaphorical vehicle for a retarded basic situation, yet it is compared only to other images on the same level of abstraction. The "so" plunges us into an analogical *in medias res*. In "As the Starved Maelstrom laps the Navies," we begin by thinking that the opening "as" indicates a temporal coincidence, for example, "as the starved maelstrom laps the navies, the sailors cry out." Instead, we discover that the "as" is a "just as," pointing to analogical comparisons.

In both poems, Dickinson is parading the extraordinary self-containment of her language. Insofar as Dickinson's transportations of meaning do not revolve around a situation, they form the situation. An understanding of what the poet is doing with her language constitutes our only recourse for an understanding of the poem's drama. It is this anti-occasional scenelessness which explains one of Dickinson's strangest and boldest remarks (L 397): "Subjects hinder talk."

2

This extreme interpretation of the lyric, this extreme subordination of subjects to structures, is not limited to the analogical collection. The principle of a sceneless poetry holds true equally in poems outside our first analogical category, in poems where we are given only one scene, because the scene is transparently an imagined one. Consider this poem which operates by the structure that we will examine next, the single, extended analogy:

> Come slowly—Eden!
> Lips unused to Thee—
> Bashful—sip thy Jessamines—
> As the fainting Bee—
>
> Reaching late his flower,
> Round her chamber hums—
> Counts his nectars—
> Enters—and is lost in Balms.
> (211)

This bee hardly pretends to the same status as the bee which is buzzing around my study right now. Dickinson's bee serves to analogize a thought. The poem transforms "Eden" from a place in the mythic past to an ever present quality which can take many forms, many chambers: "Eden" is whatever the individual seeker considers his greatest desire, his fulfillment. The poem's bee then acts as proof-by-imagery of the validity of the speaker's wish: to delay her Eden, whatever form it may take, until she is almost sadly sacrificed, faint from a lack of it; to delay it so that by its late coming she can value fully her desire's consummation and sacrifice herself happily, "lost in Balms." As in the "harebell" poem, a paradise becomes a paradise because it is what we do not easily possess. The bee-flower analogy also vividly describes a characteristic series of reactions to *any* fulfilled desire: first an awe of the long-awaited, by now unexpected offering; then that odd intellectual interlude (here, the tallying of nectars), the rational comprehension that "yes, it's really happening and so this is the quality of its overwhelming value"; and finally, a joyful renunciation of critical distance, a submissive immersion in the atmosphere the joy creates. We could imagine several more stanzas to the poem, each picturing the "same" relation by different analogies (though admittedly each analogy would add a new flavoring to the relation, just as the lip-bee analogy balances the theological reference of the first line with a more sensual possibility and thus suggests all sorts of joys "in between"). In Dickinson's second distinguishable analogical progression—the extended analogy, whose full import is progressively revealed as different aspects of the analogy are developed—scenelessness remains the chief characteristic.

And the chief difficulty: Adrift in a subjectless sea of thought, we seek for solid earth. But we are not really adrift—the clearly identifiable patterns of thought serve as our keel—and our impatience only creates mirages. Because Dickinson's poems of extended analogy frequently appear incomprehensible and equally often call forth the most exotic of responses, I want to forgo a survey of them to focus instead on what seems to me the single most difficult poem Dickinson wrote.[14] It is high time to test the notion of analogical scenelessness as an interpretive method. This is the poem that I have chosen:

> My Life had stood—a Loaded Gun—
> In Corners—till a Day
> The Owner passed—identified—
> And carried Me away—

And now We roam in Sovereign Woods—
And now We hunt the Doe—
And every time I speak for Him—
The Mountains straight reply—

And do I smile, such cordial light
Upon the Valley glow—
It is as a Vesuvian face
Had let its pleasure through—

And when at Night—Our good Day done—
I guard My Master's Head—
'Tis better than the Eider-Duck's
Deep Pillow—to have shared—

To foe of His—I'm deadly foe—
None stir the second time—
On whom I lay a Yellow Eye—
Or an emphatic Thumb—

Though I than he—may longer live
He longer must—than I—
For I have but the power to kill,
Without—the power to die—

(754)

Published interpretations of the poem invariably rest on a particular identification of the speaker and the "owner." The poem is a woman's celebration of being loved, a frontier romance. The poem concerns the poetic capacity as it is brought to life by poetic inspiration, a mastering muse.[15] In either case, the poem is a riddle to be solved. It wittily suggests a specific idea which it does not mention directly. If this is true, then we must judge the poem a failure of underdetermination, for it suggests totally different ideas to reasonably acute readers.

I think we can raise the poem above the level of a Rorschach test if we cease to think of it as a simple allegory in which one image "stands for" one idea. I will read the poem twice: first by the development within the poem of its opening analogy, which refers to the general idea of someone's "life"; then by the suggestive images which seem to relate the poem's general meaning to certain specific topics. First the analogy within the poem; then the range of possible "outer" analogies to the inner analogy. We must begin with the inner analogy because an understanding of the poem depends on a recognition of its attitude, its structure of intent. Dickinson aids us in this procedure. If we think of the poem as a critique of a certain view of relatedness which applies to all sorts of relations, we find ample reason for leaving the persona and its owner unnamed. We are being led to consider the design of the analogy, freed from the connotations which invariably arise out of a single subject. That design is powered by the suggestive analogy of the first line. The verb "had stood" skillfully negotiates between the condition of animation (My Life) and the inanimate object to which it is compared (a Loaded Gun) by referring both to a description of physical position and to a condition of psychological stasis. The "I" of the poem is not so much a personality as a personification of the speaker's general life, in itself an abstraction. The construction of the analogy establishes the poem's mode of narration and imagery: the scenes of the poem are not real, natural places, but symbols of My Life, of an attitude toward the self and its relation to the owner; by extension, temporal states and acts in the poem ("Our good Day" and "Night," and even "live" and "die") are not merely sequential but, like the poem's descriptions of motion, are characterizations of the relationship.

The analogy's most important function—so obvious that we take it in at first but do not easily focus on it—is to merge the categories of animate and inanimate and thus to mold the poem's attitude toward its speaker. If we resist the temptation to attach specific significances to the life-gun and its owner until we have watched the poem develop the bare relationship, we discover that it is not a poem which celebrates power and loyalty but a poem which warns against the delusion of achieving self-realization through subservience. The speaker unwittingly creates a demonic world, a world where the only choices are purposelessness or self-negating subservience, and where the "I" becomes an "it." Possibilities of self-fulfillment and equal, loving relationship are never considered. However sympathetic we are to the psychological state of the poor life-gun speaker, the poem criticizes her assumptions by dramatizing both the dangerous delusions of borrowed power and the resultant despoiling of potentially harmonious and loving connections to the world outside the speaker-owner relationship. At first this reading may seem even more quixotic than those I have rejected; but remember that the persona herself seems surprised by her final utterance.

The opening stanza establishes the irony of borrowed power very quietly:

> My Life had stood—a Loaded Gun—
> In Corners—till a Day

Chapter Two

The Owner passed—identified—
And carried Me away—

The owner activates the life-gun in that he brings time, "ᵗ Day," and motion to a condition of total stasis. But the maiden has not been freed from her tower, the Life from its comparison to a gun. Like a passive instrument, the Life is identified and carried away. It achieves neither its own vitality or its own purpose. In terms of dramatic progression, the impasse has been broken too quickly for us to accept the speaker's relief. The hero of a comedy does not solve his problems in the first act. And this premature *deus ex machina* is suspicious: it puts us on guard for unseen difficulties and for the possibility of an eventual counter-resolution.

As the speaker's tone turns from an appeal for understanding to a joyful celebration of power, our suspicions of the speaker's truth increases:

And now We roam in Sovereign Woods—
And now We hunt the Doe—
And every time I speak for Him—
The Mountains straight reply—

The life-gun's thoughtless joy in the relation is overtly undercut by its real status as a passive instrument activated only by an external control. The pronoun "We" in the first line claims an equality which then is canceled by the ventriloquism of the third line. The life-gun speaks only for its owner, only to achieve his ends. Here, the poem introduces its second kind of irony, the plundering of nature. Not only is the life-gun's purpose controlled by the owner, but that circumscription creates an evil purpose. The pastoral scene is made ambiguous, as pastoral always is, by the activity of hunting.[16] The loveliness of the pastoral scene is never developed. Instead, the scene is used for a boast of power. The woods are "Sovereign," supremely powerful, not in themselves but because "We" can roam through them and exert a power over them. The mountains are made to "straight reply" to the life-gun's speech; the ability to create an echo serves as a boast of domination over natural grandeur. The life-gun fails to see that the mountains speak just as it does, without will.

This distance between the speaker's sense of his situation and the poem's, between statement and meaning, further increases in the third stanza:

And do I smile, such cordial light
Upon the Valley glow—
It is as a Vesuvian face
Had let its pleasure through—

The sense of the persona's activated potential as violent and violating becomes plainer in the description of the life-gun's "smile" and the resultant "cordial light" that glows upon the valley. The initial analogy has not been dropped, the life-gun has not been personified. Rather, the real horror of the analogy is brought out. The smile and the cordial light are the gun-shot and its destructive explosion. The smile is malevolent just as the gun's speech is injurious. The poem introduces humanizing social actions only to transform them into the distorted meaning lent by the life-gun analogy. The life-gun has been activated only to show forth its "Vesuvian" face, the mindless and cruel pleasure of volcanic power.

A strange alteration is occurring in that third stanza. Unless we see that volcanic face as the owner's (and this would disrupt the physical exactness of the poem, for the face which "shows through" the gun must be the flash of firing, not the gun's owner and shooter), the life-gun is beginning to speak in relation to itself, as though it can pull its own trigger. Yet from the analogy we know that no such independence is possible. Instead, the life-gun has equated its purpose so thoroughly with the owner's that it is beginning to perpetuate him; another illusion of selfhood and self-expression.

And when at Night—Our good Day done—
I guard My Master's Head—
'Tis better than the Eider-Duck's
Deep Pillow—to have shared—

To foe of His—I'm deadly foe—
None stir the second time—
On Whom I lay a Yellow Eye—
Or an emphatic Thumb—

Though I than he—may longer live
He longer must—than I—
For I have but the power to kill,
Without—the power to die—

These final stanzas so openly expose the speaker's error of uncritical servitude that, at last, she must acknowledge the disastrous consequences. At night, "Our good Day done," the life-gun is content to guard its owner, and in fact glories in the slave-like function which prevents a sharing of the "Eider-Duck's / Deep Pillow."[17] (This is the point at which literal-minded readings of the poem as a frontier romance begin to get nervous and resort to abnormal psychology.) The gun continues to separate itself from the owner, now accurately renamed a master, only to show the circumscription of its life by its abiding loyalty. The life-gun relates to its master in no libidinal, equal manner but only in destroying his foes. Though now it actually does pull its own trigger with "emphatic Thumb," the gun is in essentially the same position as when it spoke in stanza two—spoke not with the owner but against the doe.

The foes are unspecified, like the life-gun and the master. We can consider them as night thoughts, repressed fears and memories, if we wish to think of the fifth stanza as a continuation of the night scene. Whether we give the foes this psychological interpretation or not, the life-gun acts protectively and, as before, violently to prevent any challenge to its master. Its "emphatic Thumb" is turned against the world, against whatever lies outside the master.

The poem's concluding sonnet-like turn, which has been attacked almost universally as hopelessly obscure, simply extends the initial analogy to its final, tragic consequences. The life-gun's kickback occurs as it is forced to project its situation into what is at once the future and the larger consequences of the present. The hidden hopelessness of its situation become all too obvious when the power which had seemed so fine, and which has revealed its destructive intent less and less euphemistically, is finally described as "but the power to kill, / Without—the power to die—." This paradox is but the frighteningly literal consequence of the opening analogy. The life has become the gun to which it compared itself; its only capability is destructive. As for the paradox of the first two lines of the stanza, the status of the gun again controls the status of the life. Dickinson employs a yin-yang of life and death, whereby the capacity for dying measures the real power of the life.[18] In the sense of life as mere existence, the life-gun may outlive its master; but the master *must* outlive the gun in the sense of life as animate self-actualization, for in that sense the life-gun has not lived at all. Or, if we say that to live here means to gain the immortal life achieved through death and that this life cannot be attained by the servile gun, then "My Life had stood—a Loaded Gun—" dramatizes the dictum of another poem:

Analogical Poetics

> Who has not found the Heaven—below—
> Will fail of it above—
> For Angels rent the House next ours,
> Wherever we remove—
>   (1544)

A life that is a loaded gun cannot find, it can only hunt and kill. Just as in the opening stanza, the life-gun once again voices a fear of stasis. Its tone once again becomes confessional, pleading. Even the exact rhyme-endings of lines two and four, abandoned after the first stanza, return. Poetic technique mirrors the horrific meaning. In one sense, despite all its furious activity, the life-gun has altered its condition not at all.

We do not solve Dickinson's poems by guessing at "what she's really talking about" but by contemplating the self-sufficient design of action. Once we have done that, we can consider its implications. First, the voice of the analogy teaches us to think of the speaker primarily as an animate being, one of us. This speaker voices a pattern of joy eroded by self-betrayal, mental states appropriate only to the human realm. Our study of the imagery may turn up more particular and even contradictory identifications of the life-gun; but it is important to recognize that these other identifications are subordinate. The owner-master is more of a stick figure and can be considered anyone or any personified principle afforded dominion over human action.

The poem presents one resolution of a debate which Dickinson's poetry continually carries on with itself. Is it better to maintain an independence, however limited in power, or to gain power by ceding oneself to a greater? Various poems narrow the debate to questions of marriage, or of absolute belief in a particular conception of the deity, or of the submission of poetic creation to any single, controlling doctrine; other poems, like "My Life had stood," will keep terms like "Master" (or "Wife," in other such poems) sufficiently ambiguous to include all these possibilities and any others to which one could apply the design. The debate often expresses itself in the imagery of "My Life had stood," yet the resolution is often opposite. In another poem,

> 'Twas my one Glory—
> Let it be
> Remembered
> I was owned of Thee—
>   (1028)

31

And in a letter which appears to have been written about the time "My Life had stood" was composed,[19] Dickinson complains to Higginson, "I had no Monarch in my life, and cannot rule myself, and when I try to organize—my little Force explodes—and leaves me bare and charred—"(L 271). Yet in the same period, Dickinson responds to Higginson's specific criticisms with a spirited defense of her independence: "You think my gait 'spasmodic'—I am in danger—Sir—You think me 'uncontrolled'—I have no Tribunal" (L 265). And in many poems, she renounces the attraction of being owned. In "I should have been too glad, I see" (313), a "new Circumference" is rejected because

I should have been too saved—I see—
Too rescued—Fear too dim to me. . . .

Dickinson's "Master" poems vacillate between two opposite fears which beset all the American romantics. In *City of Words,* Tony Tanner notes the "abiding American dread that someone else is patterning your life, that there are all sorts of invisible plots afoot to rob you of your autonomy of thought and action, that conditioning is ubiquitous." Dickinson's "Master," whether an actual person or a personified system, thus prevents the realization of an American dream, the dream "that while other, older countries are ridden by conventions, rules, all sorts of arbitrary formalities which trap and mould the individual, in America one may still enjoy a genuine freedom from all cultural patterning so that life is a series of unmediated spontaneities." But in rejecting the master, one only returns to the state of the immobilized life-gun. You dispose of one fear only to find another, "the dread of utter formlessness, of being a soft, vulnerable, endlessly manipulable blob, of not being a distinct self."[20] It is out of this fear that Thoreau complains in a letter to Harrison Blake of his amorphous real self, "a mere arena for thoughts and feelings; definite enough outwardly, indefinite more than enough inwardly." The final irony is contained in Tanner's description of this formless state as "endlessly manipulable"; escape from the master only primes one to desire a return to him.

Puppet or blob? Transcendence at the cost of freedom or freedom at the cost of meaning? Dickinson elsewhere imagines other, happier possibilities; but as long as she works this dialectic no one poem settles the issue, no development in the direction of one position can be discerned in the chronological arrangement of the poems. Poetically, Dickinson's concern is more with the possibilities and limitations of each choice than with finally advocating either. Here, as elsewhere, we must resist the temptation to take one poem as definitive of any permanent state of our poet's psyche.

As I said earlier, the alternative of independence is not actively present in "My Life had stood—a Loaded Gun—" except as the speaker's chosen analogy negates it, and thus we focus on the speaker's psyche. What we get is not so much a defense of independence as a condemnation of subservience. The poem is remarkable in that it includes many of Dickinson's pro-master arguments and transforms them into fatal errors. An attitude which is portrayed elsewhere as an ennobling and self-fulfilling fidelity to an inspiriting ideal here appears as a debasing servility, a retreat from the integrity of struggle and doubt. The life-gun here has attempted to transport herself from Dickinson's world of limitation to Dickinson's world of unbounded realization, and she has caught herself cheating.

This understanding of the "inner" analogy provides us with an understanding of the poem that is sufficient. But we need not stop here. Those critics who consider "My Life had stood" a poem about love or about the creative process limit the poem unduly but they are not simply projecting their own preconditioned responses on the poem. The analogy develops by images which do point toward those "subjects." I have argued that we must give the poem the broad scope it demands, that we have to see these particularizations as subordinate to a general design which could apply to almost any topic we could imagine. Specific images allow the poem to suggest specific applications without subjugating its design to any one of them. In other words, we have a poem that takes shape around an analogy and talks about "everything" in terms of that analogy; yet its illustratory imagery allows it to talk more about some things than others.

For example, it would be ridiculous to deny that the eider-duck pillow and the general attitude of the persona in "My Life had stood" suggest a love relation. We are meant to be put off by the renunciation of a sexual consummation in stanza four—its possibility, like the "We" pronoun and the humanizing social gestures of speech and smile, is raised only to be negated by adherence to the life-gun analogy. We are put off in such a way to indicate that the poem's critique is not directed so much against the wedded state as against the attitude of helplessness which creates the initial analogy, the analogy which in turn determines the bedroom status of gun and master. The sexual abnegation is simply part and parcel of the larger abnegation of life in the poem, an abnegation caused by an active refusal of all possible relations other than this one in which the "partners" are so absolutely unequal as to spoil any marriage and debase the human condition.

33

The application of the poem to a love relation simply repeats in a smaller circle the poem's general meaning. The ways in which the poem's imagery points toward the theme of poetic practice (suggested most obviously by the possible pun on speech in the second stanza, and by imagistic similarities between this poem and other poems which openly concern poetry) are more challenging. In fact, the pistol imagery of a late letter suggests a way in which we can read the poem as a description of the power of language, with no ethical meaning whatsoever. Dickinson begins a letter to her cousin Louise Norcross by contemplating the activity of letter-writing in itself:

> What is it that instructs a hand lightly created, to impel shapes to eyes at a distance, which for them have the whole area of life or of death? Yet not a pencil in the street but has this awful power, though nobody arrests it. An earnest letter is or should be life-warrant or death-warrant, for what is each instant but a gun, harmless because "unloaded," but that touched "goes off"?

(L 656)

Throughout this ingenious and fast-moving string of analogies runs the idea of a static potential ever ready to be ignited into explosive action. We might say that the gun here is an instant loaded by language, its effect determined by the intent of its utilizer. We can find further support for such a reading in another poem whose imagery of destruction is not a moral argument but a claim for the hidden power of language and, by synecdoche, of life:

> Could mortal lip divine
> The undeveloped Freight
> Of a delivered syllable
> 'Twould crumble with the weight.
>
> (1409)

In the context of these potential sources, "My Life had stood" may be read as a longer version of the same claim. Read thusly, the poem suddenly loses its ironic implications. The speaker becomes a personification of an instant, or of dormant mentality or language, which then is "identified" and loaded with meaning, by a mastering muse. The apparently cruel hunting of the doe becomes an image for the process by which the poet captures nature in language. As for the Vesuvian face of stanza three, a passage from one of the mysterious "Master" letters[21] provides a possible gloss:

Vesuvius dont talk—Etna dont—one of them—said a syllable—a thousand
years ago, and Pompeii heard it, and hid forever—

(L 233)

Again, we are outside a moral realm in a description of power; when the
speaker of our poem claims dominion over nature, we can interpret this
as a simple, Whorfian claim for the way in which language determines
our view of things. In stanza four, the life-gun's defeated "foes" are
whatever elements oppose vitality. Finally, the idea of a word as
everlasting transforms the life-and-death paradox of the last stanza. It
can be read in parallel to this analogical figure:

> The Poets light but Lamps—
> Themselves—go out—
> The Wicks they stimulate—
> If vital Light—
>
> Inhere as do the Suns—. . .
>
> (883)

The master-poet may die, but he will live in his artifacts forever. And the
wick he stimulates, the language, will thus live on, though in a literal
sense language, as an abstract, is neither alive nor dead. A poem which
begins, "A Word made Flesh is seldom / And tremblingly partook"
provides an even closer parallel to our last stanza:

> A Word that breathes distinctly
> Has not the power to die
> Cohesive as the Spirit
> It may expire if He—
> "Made Flesh and dwelt among us"
> Could condescension be
> Like this consent of Language
> This loved Philology.
>
> (1651)

The repetition of the phrase "power to die" seems to clinch the matter.
The master of "My Life" is "This loved Philology" which brings to life
the personified instant-made-word. Our previous reading of the "inner"
analogy is wholly negated.

Not true, of course. But I am not arguing with myself as a rhetorical

35

exercise. This alternate reading prompts a crucial issue. The poem in itself does not suggest this interpretation; the reader would need special knowledge to derive it. If the reading is valid, then the oft-heard complaints against Dickinson's coyness, or, more specifically, against her supposed "private symbolism" become valid. The poem is reduced to the status of an overingenious and underdetermined guessing game.

Happily, this alternative reading fails to account for many details of "My Life had stood"; it contradicts the pleading tone of the poem's voice; and it posits a speaker (language personified) for whom the life-gun's emotional utterances are absurd. (No other poem in Dickinson's canon presents an unnamed first-person speaker who is a personified abstraction.) Furthermore, if we compare "A Word made Flesh" to our poem, we discover crucial differences. In "My Life had stood," the speaker does not gain but loses humanity by his analogy to an inanimate object. The life-gun is not "partaken" as a kind of Eucharist wafer, but used, shot at game, at that which will be partaken. The analogy's spatial implications negate any notion of loving infusion. The point of the analogy is that the infusion is an illusion;[22] and this becomes most clear in the use of the phrase "power to die" in "My Life had stood" as opposed to its use in "A Word made Flesh." It is impossible to read the syntax of the lines "For I have *but* the power to kill / Without—the power to die—" as a boast; it is a complaint and a confession.

We can specify that confession by reference to another poem which more truly does reflect on the meaning of "My Life had stood." It is a poem on the everlasting persistence of the word, this time not the abstract "Word" but a word produced by a particular individual. Here, the spirit which informs the word is malarial and the effect is no cause for celebration:

> A Word dropped careless on a Page
> May stimulate an eye
> When folded in perpetual seam
> The Wrinkled Maker lie
>
> Infection in the sentence breeds
> We may inhale Despair
> At distances of Centuries
> From the Malaria—
>
>   (1261)

In "My Life had stood," the words are shot carelessly since the "loaded gun" poet allows himself to be controlled by an external cause and thus denies his own responsibility. The result is a despairing malaria of the spirit, complete with "Yellow Eye," which indeed does harm others.[23] In fact, Dickinson's poetry as a whole argues for our original reading of "My Life had stood." The potency of language is celebrated amorally for its vitalizing power in inverse proportion to the stress placed on a human, intentional producer of language. If words "kill" unintentionally, that is a tragic but unavoidable result of the hidden power of language and of life; it is precisely that which also affords the vitality, the only meaningful life. But when it comes to intentional woundings, Dickinson characteristically sympathizes with the victim and, as in "My Life had stood," implies that the killing agent is not herself truly alive:

> She dealt her pretty words like Blades—
> How glittering they shone—
> And every One unbared a Nerve
> Or wantoned with a Bone—
>
> She never deemed—she hurt—
> That—is not Steel's Affair—
> A vulgar grimace in the Flesh—
> How ill the Creatures bear—
>
> To Ache is human—not polite—
> The Film upon the eye
> Mortality's old Custom—
> Just locking up—to Die.
>
> (479)

The persona of "My Life had stood" is not satirized as harshly as is this woman. As a first-person speaker the life-gun appeals to our sympathy, though less so as the ironies of which it is unaware become apparent; and however fundamental the persona's error, at least it is passionate, and at least the persona finally recognizes—as this lady of steel cannot—that she has "but the power to kill / Without—the power to die—."

Yet it is essential to see that the loaded gun's emergence into power is a false emergence, precisely because authentic power is so important to Dickinson. We are free to consider the "Owner" in "My Life had stood" as personifying poetic inspiration; but we must recognize that he represents a particular kind of poetic inspiration, particularly external to the self and therefore, by the basic pattern of the poem, a negation of authentic inspiration, illusory just as the life-gun's inspiriting by the owner is shown to be illusory in the overt development of the analogy. We see, at last, that Dickinson is playing a "private" game of a serious kind in "My Life had stood," a game which does not contradict but enriches the meaning of the poem's inner analogy. Throughout "My Life had stood" Dickinson transforms imagistic patterns which celebrate life's power in many other poems into a hellish vision of self-deception. She allows a range of possible applications which move from nature to the human, from a peripheral description of the power of things in the abstract to a central condemnation of making a thing of one's human self in order to gain power. The amoral or even benevolent power of nature, of things in the abstract, cannot justify a careless and conscious use of such power in the human realm. This is a false analogy, an analogy which the poem raises to oppose. As our interpretation of the poem as a poem about poetry moves into the human realm, its images become smaller concentrics within the analogy's more general circumference. As a poem about life, "My Life had stood" deplores an idea of the self as a passive vessel which can be fulfilled only by the surrender of individual purpose. As a poem about poetry or, more accurately, as a poem which contains a poem about poetry, "My Life had stood" deplores an idea of poetry as a mere instrument for any nonpoetic cause. It implicitly criticizes received dogma as a false muse.

No reader will agree with every detail of this lengthy interpretation, but I hope that it has swept away the widely held assumption that Dickinson is impossibly obscure. If we do not assume that Dickinson creates ambiguities in order to be coy or to protect undignified emotions, we discover that the ambiguities exist in order to redirect attention. This poet does not want us to pin her symbolic language onto a particular experience but to consider that language as the expression of a pattern which encompasses many diverse experiences. She does not withhold facts of her private experience but censors irrelevant particularizations to create archetypal autobiographies.[24] These are autobiographies of the best sort, in which the persona seems to discover his life's essence only in the process of writing its description. Dickinson's best poems, exemplified by "My Life had stood," surprise themselves by the connotations of their chosen analogies and readjust themselves phrase by phrase. The poem is a voyage which determines the consequences of a thought, of a relational hypothesis; when the poem's voice is embodied in a first-person speaker, as it is in "My Life had stood," then the fate of the persona is coequal with the destiny of the analogy. "My Life had stood—a Loaded Gun—" provides a transparent gown for dynamic speculation. Thus it very nearly achieves Dickinson's ultimate and unattainable goal, the goal which the master inside the poem prevents:

> Costumeless Consciousness—
> That is he—
>
> (1454)

3

Anti-Allegory

Good art, including the good illustration, must probe.
—Arnold Kettle, *Introduction to the English Novel*

1

If scenelessness is one of Dickinson's weapons in her battle against "hindering" subjects, symbolism is the other. Dickinson's symbolism is not an exception to her intensely analogical poetic but a part of it; for a symbol, broadly defined, is simply an incompleted analogy in which the analogue is the only term and its subject(s) is left unstated. In fact, we began to consider Dickinson's symbology at the moment we began to consider her analogical technique. The analogical collection contains explicit local analogies in abundance, but finally all of the explicit analogies become a compound symbol for the unstated law which relates them; and the single, extended analogy is simultaneously a symbolic narrative—what we termed the "outer analogies" of "My Life had stood" constitute its symbolism, a hinted but unspecified group of subjects to which the entire analogy can be applied.

Where does inner analogy end and symbol begin? Dickinson integrates the two techniques so completely that it is difficult to be definite. Still, we can clarify the distinction by scrutinizing a poem which is less difficult than "My Life had stood" but which similarly develops a single analogy to point outside of itself. The analogy here is not stated directly, but it is established clearly in the first few lines:

Anti-Allegory

> You've seen Balloons set—Haven't You?
> So stately they ascend—
> It is as Swans—discarded You,
> For Duties Diamond—

We can construct the analogy for ourselves without much trouble: the stately ascension of a balloon is as surprising and spectacular as a hypothetical transfer of swans from their horizontal, aquatic paddling to equally graceful vertical, aerial flight. As in "My Life had stood," the vehicle overtakes the tenor in the second stanza:

> Their Liquid Feet go softly out
> Upon a Sea of Blonde—
> They spurn the Air, as 'twere too mean
> For Creatures so renowned—

The imagery plays on the sea-to-sky transfer of the swans, though a balloon is still the nominal tenor. I say "nominal" because phrases like "Duties Diamond" and "spurn the Air" produce a symbolic impact which suggests that the real subject extends beyond either balloons or swans. This outer analogy, which constitutes the poem's symbolic meaning, clarifies itself in the third stanza:

> Their Ribbons just beyond the eye—
> They struggle—some—for Breath—
> And yet the Crowd applaud, below—
> They would not encore—Death—

The imagery has become appropriate to both anthropomorphized balloons and airborne swans, and it makes clear that together they constitute a strangely literal emblem for anything or any creature, especially the human sort, which attempts to rise above its limitations, to reach toward any upper heaven.

The consequences of the analogy also are strangely literal and naturalistic.

> The Gilded Creature strains—and spins—
> Trips frantic in a Tree—
> Tears open her imperial Veins—
> And tumbles in the Sea—

41

The balloon-swan rips and falls into the sea. What we have here is an emblem of tragic action, of heroic desire thwarted by natural limitations. The language has been managed so carefully that the balloon can support the burden of this meaning without bursting, for it has become more than a balloon.

Yet the poem, aware that it has stretched its own limitations to the breaking point, ends with a different interpretation. The language and syntax thus far have imitated the action they describe. The language became lyrical in the second stanza, which most invoked the swan half of the analogy; it became "frantic," metrically "struggling for breath," in the broken phrases of the third and fourth stanzas as the balloon-swan gashed itself; and now the poem ends by deflating its outer analogy as the language drops down with its subject to the colloquial earth:

> The Crowd—retire with an Oath—
> The Dust in Streets—go down—
> And Clerks in Counting Rooms
> Observe—"'Twas only a balloon"—
>
> (700)

The clerks are wrong in their heartlessness, of course; they share Father Dickinson's exclusive belief in a nonsymbolic *"real life."* But their invocation suggests an outer analogy far less glorious than an analogy to tragic action. It calls to mind an analogy to economic enterprise, to that unsubstantial stock-market phenomenon of the nineteenth century commonly called a "bubble" or "balloon." The greater analogy has not been deflated in any final way; this last stanza simply displays the poem's potential range of reference. It suggests that what is an emblem of tragedy to the empathetic, symbolizing mind is "only a balloon" to the crowd of small-time materialists. We see as we are, and the poem's own attitude here is not unthinking unconcern but the tortured admission of limitation so characteristic of Dickinson's confessional mode.

Poems like "My Life had stood" and "You've seen Balloons set—Haven't You?" do double duty. They ask the reader to connect implied outer correlatives as well as to follow the development of the inner analogy. But at other times, Dickinson will grant her symbols center stage by eschewing internal analogies altogether. The result is a third kind of analogical structure, which at first glance appears to be a simple, story-like narrative; but the images which tell the story are managed so that they become symbols of a greater pattern of ideas, a pattern whose nature is such that it can be exemplified but not directly stated. Our third analogical category differs in kind from the other two, first, because it only implies analogies and, second, because its implications, its "outer" analogies, are invariably plural and occasionally conflicting, as in the balloon poem.

The chief quality of Dickinson's symbols is their homeliness—she even plays on this quality in the crowd's response at the end of the balloon poem. It is as if Dickinson is challenging herself by continually choosing the most resistantly mundane images as symbols for matters of the spirit. And strangely, in actual fact, these most far-flung poems of an extremely anti-occasional poet often came into being out of very unremarkable personal experiences. This process is most clearly evidenced by those letters to personal friends which include poems, poems which always relate tangentially to the subject at hand and which always transcend that subject. But perhaps the most startling example of this transformation of personal experience into archetypal autobiography can be reconstructed from a few letters and a poem not included in them, but almost surely developed out of the same commonplace thoughts that went into them.

At age twenty, several years before she begins to write the poems by which we know her, Dickinson whimsically tells her brother Austin of a daring excursion:

> ... after tea I went to see Sue—had a nice little visit with her—then went to see Emily Fowler, and arrived home at 9—found Father in great agitation at my protracted stay—and mother and Vinnie in tears, for fear that he would kill me.
>
> (L 42)

The next year, it is Dickinson who is surprised by a family member's late return home. In playfully metaphysical language, she writes to her future sister-in-law, Susan Gilbert,

> We were much afflicted yesterday, by the supposed removal of *our Cat* from time to Eternity.
> She returned, however, last evening, having been detained by the storm, beyond her expectations.
>
> (L 97)

Several years later, time and eternity become the earnest underpinnings of a "late arrival" poem:

> Tho' I get home how late—how late—
> So I get home—'twill compensate—

43

Better will be the Ecstasy
That they have done expecting me—
When Night—descending—dumb—and dark—
They hear my unexpected knock—
Transporting must the moment be—
Brewed from decades of Agony!

To think just how the fire will burn—
Just how long-cheated eyes will turn—
To wonder what myself will say,
And what itself, will say to me—
Beguiles the Centuries of way!

(207)

Dickinson's persona takes the place of the wandering cat, and the wandering becomes a symbol for independent speculation. No longer are we placed in a scene of comic domestic drama, though a sequence of fear and relief at a tardy return home repeats itself here. The "Night" of the first letter has been lent symbolic status by its placement as the culmination of "decades of Agony" and "Centuries of way." It is now an almost gothic condition more than a time, a condition of being ultimately lost in unpierceable mysteries. This same stretching-out of time transforms those who wait from a protective New England family to an unnamed group in Eternity who did not wander, who apparently played it safe and were saved. No longer is father's reaction in question, but "what itself, will say to me"; the inanimate pronoun depersonifies Edward Dickinson, and in his place stands a speaking principle, an unnamed deity figure, possibly but not necessarily the other Father, the one in the Trinity. Only possibly, for one function of Dickinson's symbology is to free her not only from the domestic world but also from the specifications of any particular theological or metaphysical myth. Thus we must define the "home" of the poem negatively, by saying that it is no longer the Amherst homestead nor has it become a Christian heaven. In the poem's bare symbolic pattern, "home" has become the place of origin and return, the place which must be left to be achieved again.

So, too, the persona is no longer the cat or Emily Dickinson but any seeker who has to strike his own path. Like Coleridge's mariner, this epistemological persona may end up at the same place as the more conventional hermit-like elders, but he first will leave home, confront mysteries, and earn his way back. In fact, the persona may become a representative of all striving humanity by the concluding line's inclusive

"Centuries of way." In a different way, the poem gains simple dramatic force over the letters by the persona's yet-incomplete act: the persona speaks by faith alone, while still away from home. The poem has a present-tense, lived-experience impact even in its symbolic, analogical form which the letters lack. There is just enough doubt to define the confident attitude of the projection as an achievement of faith. The hardships of quest will be compensated only "so I get home," only if, to borrow imagery from "Come Slowly—Eden," the bee has not fainted forever before the Eden-Flower offers itself. In this poem, that Eden must be sought out actively; but as in "Come Slowly—Eden," the frustrations will increase the joy of the seeker and elevate the status of what is sought after. "Better will be the Ecstasy" for both the wanderer and those who have stopped waiting; more glory to the quester, more love shown to the "itself," by the hair-breadth entry just before the "Night" descends.

All this from a cat's delinquency! But however personal the origins of the poem, and however much Dickinson alters archetypes in it and designs her own charged images out of commonplace materials, it is unfortunate that her symbolism is usually described as "private." The term is unfairly pejorative, for it suggests a solipsistic motivation and an incommunicable effect. In this spirit, Eleanor Wilnor faults Dickinson for "the extreme privacy with which her canon was created; never being exposed to any real criticism, she was never forced to face the critical agony of realizing that a word for her might be something far different to another mind, and the slipperiness of her language was therefore never brought home to her."[1] If certain words have hidden and quirky meanings for a poet, and if the poet cannot make the meaning plain within a single poem, that would be a real fault. And it is true that Dickinson often establishes a full range of connotations for an image in one poem and then repeats the image in other poems without explicit explanation. But I have tried to show that Dickinson constructs surrounding contexts which implicitly explain the meaning of images most exhaustively. Granted, a knowledge of all 1,775 poems makes comprehension readier, and a dictionary of Dickinson's images, in imitation of Foster Damion's dictionary of Blake's symbology, would be a worthy project for any scholar; but the reader who does not wish to recapitulate the critic's task is at no impossible disadvantage. As William Howard concludes upon the completion of his statistical studies of Dickinson's poetry, "what we are dealing with is the use of a word, almost any word, in an extended metaphorical sense as a stylistic habit and not with the use of a word primarily because of some private appeal it has for the poet."[2]

Howard's conclusion holds true even in especially "bare" symbolic narratives where symbols define each other with little or no help from a surrounding context of ordinary usage. For instance, from an examination of several poems we would discover that Dickinson uses the word "east" as a synonym for dawn and thus ties the idea of oriental splendor to the moment of reawakening life. Similarly, we would find that the word "west" is a metonym for an impending sunset, and that sunset in turn is a possible type for a brilliant end to life, a sort of defeat of death by dying beautifully. But denied that prior knowledge of Dickinson's meanings, we would learn them in the course of this single poem:

Said Death to Passion
"Give of thine an Acre unto me."
Said Passion, through contracting Breaths,
"A Thousand Times Thee Nay."

Bore Death from Passion
All His East
He—sovereign as the Sun
Resituated in the West
And the Debate was done.

(1033)

The passion which no longer can ally itself with youthful life simply finds a new subject to glorify, the ending of a life cycle. As sunset partly imitates and partly completes the sunrise, an elderly passion redirects its attention and in so doing recapitulates its early triumph by relighting the day-life from a different position, its western goal. The redirection bears plural interpretations: from a temporal love to a spiritual one; from a hold on Eden in the East to a hold on apocalypse and immortality in the West. But no special knowledge is needed for the comprehension of the poem's simple "mind over matter" dictum, for the analogy of "passion" to the "Sun" makes plain in more condensed and effective language everything we have said about "East" and "West."

Another extremely brief poem defines itself even more exclusively through its symbols:

To Whom the Mornings stand for Nights,
What must the Midnights—be!

(1095)

These synecdochic symbols are sufficiently suggestive in a regular manner to need no internal, analogical assistance. A thorough examination of her poems would disclose that Dickinson's mornings are times of natural gaiety, rational clarity, and friendly community; that her nights, in their bad aspect, are times of fear and alienation, of subterranean thoughts, epistemological blindness, and experiential blankness; and that midnight, as night's apex, is the moment of supreme unbelief and the death of the grave. (Just so, Noon, as the morn's apex and midnight's opposite, is the transitory moment at which the sun reaches to God, earth becomes heaven-like, experience fulfills itself in baroque splendor, and the mind reposes in faith.) A thorough examination of these two lines lets us in on all these "private" meanings and adds a harrowing conjecture to jell them into a specific horror. This is to say, Dickinson's "private" symbolic narratives, like all her poems, are available to public comprehension.

2

Methought that of these visionary flowers
I made a nosegay, bound in such a way
That the same hues, which in their natural bowers
Were mingled or opposed, the like array
Kept these imprisoned children of the Hours
Within my hand,—and then, elate and gay,
I hastened to the spot whence I had come,
That I might there present it!—oh! to whom?
                    (Shelley, "The Question")

The poet-persona belongs to Shelley, not to Dickinson, but he states the problem of symbolic narratives perfectly. The poet gathers his flowers, his visionary thoughts, into a composite nosegay. He arranges these flower-thoughts in the order of their natural occurrence; he retains their wild variety within a form, his hand. He returns to the spot where he began, circles back to his first vision, and finds himself alone with his nosegay and no one to receive it. No sweet moral, no maiden of abstraction, seems suitable to his deepest thoughts. The flower-vision cannot be transferred, cannot be translated; it simply states itself.

What Shelley expresses as a problem is also a veiled boast. It is the cherished discovery of the romantic poet that his poetry needs no justification as an aid to a less imagistic, more doctrinal truth, that poetry's prior reason runs too deep and too strong to be dammed by notional understanding. Like allegorists, the major romantics want to explain "everything": Wordsworth names as his goal "truth, not individual and local, but general, and operative" and Coleridge wants his poems "to convert a *series* into a *Whole.*" But the poet's definition of truth has changed. No longer is it to be found in explicit religious and philosophical systems, but in a radically undoctrinaire spirit which infuses the soul and the world, "the one life within us and abroad." Thus the poem no longer points and teaches; it *is* and reveals. I quote Geoffrey Hartman at length on Wordsworth, for he states the case with great precision:

> All truth, said Coleridge, is a species of revelation. Revelation of what? The question cannot be answered without a certain kind of pointing, as if truth were here or there, as if life could be localized, as if revelation were a property.... Pointing is to encapsulate something: strength, mind, life. It is to overobjectify, to overformalize.... Yet pointing in this larger sense cannot be avoided; it seems inextricably tied to the referential nature of signs or the intentional character of thought. All Wordsworth can do is emancipate the direction of the reference.[3]

That is all Dickinson can do in her symbolic narratives. Her words must mean more than they say, but they need not mean what somebody else has said. Her words need not illustrate that "war of authorities"[4] common to traditional allegory, but self-proposed possibilities of life. The particularly illustrative structure of Dickinson's symbolic narratives places her, more definitely even than her characteristic themes, in the romantic tradition. Her poems participate in a major romantic form which I call anti-allegory.

Anti-allegories often pose as heuristic allegories, as a series of events, scenes, and attitudes in search of an abstract, referential explanation. Because their situations are clearly illustrative and appear potentially encyclopedic, anti-allegories are, in a broad sense, allegorical. They force the reader to seek out causal implications. In search of them, the reader looks to see where the language points, to which authoritative orders. In fact, he may find in the poem many gestures toward such orders, but finally he is forced back by this very plethora of suggestion from a monistic, referential interpretation, forced back to a holistic description of the poem's pattern in terms of nothing but itself.

Dickinson's "surround and conquer" policy is simply a more direct version of an allegory-frustrating technique which abounds in English romantic poetry. The English, proper and embarrassed to the last, often explain away their most ambitious anti-allegories as "dream poems." Two such dream poems, Coleridge's "Kubla Khan" and

Browning's "Childe Roland to the Dark Tower Came," can serve as models. Both construct natural landscapes which are subverted by supranatural imagery to mean far more than themselves as realistic descriptions. But what exactly do they mean? Xanadu, with its beautiful compound of wildest nature and utmost art threatened by the "tidings of war" which are somehow contained in itself, may enact the life cycle or the Fall. It may imply a principle of poetic imagination, that the imagination which "builds in air" can never be satisfied by the most splendid real creations; it may imply an idea of self-destuctive depravity in even the purest mind; or it may imply even in its preface the moral concept of accepting the failure of permanence in a world of time. Likewise, the two gothic, even surreal plains through which Childe Roland passes may represent the pre-Christian and post-Christian, the prehistoric and the modern, nature and civilization, the unconscious and the rational—even the poet's individual talent and his participation in a tradition. The images of each plain suggest a disparity between them but refuse to limit their definitions to any one allegorical possibility. We know only the general nature of their disparity. When Roland crosses the river which separates the two plains, he means to stab a vermin but fears he has murdered a struggling child. He fears that in his terror to escape the instinctual, natural plain he may be killing off the best, not the worst, of himself; he may be destroying innocence rather than darkness and infection. Even here, the poem's images do not point a referential meaning but engulf several. In both poems, we are left with patterns made bare by their very abundance of suggestion and with patterns which, by their very nakedness, seem to dramatize "everything."

Not only do both poems return finally to themselves, they personify that return. The last image in "Kubla Khan" is of the poet who has "drunk the milk of Paradise," the poet who wishes he could do what, in fact, he has just done. Roland becomes "one more picture" in a "living frame" formed by his precursor poet-knights, and his last words exclaim himself and the title of the poem which he has become, *"Childe Roland to the Dark Tower Came."* In both poems, the speaker becomes the final, defining emblem, the only emblem sufficiently large and dynamic to take account of the poem's range of meaning.

Anti-allegory always concerns itself. Other shadowed "subjects" are seen through the poem's filter, and the poem finally makes the nature of its filter its chief subject. In other words, it contains a critique of the narrative pattern it employs. Coleridge's Xanadu is his version of a *locus amoenus*, the traditional setting of grass, shade, and water which corresponds to a mental set of rest, relaxation, and retirement. But there are dangers in the *locus amoenus* itself, dangers more integral to the setting than the threat of hedonistic irresponsibility to the poet who relaxes there:

> The *locus* is distinctly conceived as a refuge from the processes of time and mortality (indeed, in its generative aspects, as an antidote to them.) But the conception is illusory, not only because one must eventually return to ordinary life, but also because the brook may freeze, the grass wither, the tree fall into the sere and yellow leaf.[5]

But Coleridge's Xanadu is remarkable in that it takes these dangers into account within its setting: "A sunny pleasure-dome with caves of ice," "The mingled measure / From the fountains and the caves." The landscape contains all time, all changes, within its dynamic realm. But still it cannot avoid the "lifeless ocean" and "Ancestral voices prophesying war!" The *locus amoenus* will never do, not even in its most comprehensive form. The dome's shadow "midway on the waves" must be replaced by the poet's "dome in the air" to gain a timelessness through time.

As "Kubla Khan" is a *locus amoenus* and yet criticizes the whole idea of its chosen genre, so "Childe Roland" is a quest which criticizes and redefines the quest motif. Roland's journey is chivalric and poetic, a portrait of the artist as a voyaging and doomed knight. His apparent goal turns out to be disastrously dreary and inconsequential, a "round squat turret," not a meaningless symbol but a symbol of the end of meaning. Roland conquers the symbol by replacing it as his final goal with himself and his journey, with the poem itself. The striving replaces the striven for, the poem-in-unfolding replaces the sought-after climax in significance. As in Shelley's "Question," the poet is left with himself and his experience as his quest's only explanation. The inspired poet-knight becomes his own inspiration.

A Dickinson poem, so central that I will discuss it again in another context, bears a startling resemblance to Browning's quest-critique; but Dickinson's anti-allegory criticizes more peculiarly, in silence:

> Our journey had advanced—
> Our feet were almost come
> To that odd Ford in Being's Road—
> Eternity—by Term—
>
> Our pace took sudden awe—
> Our feet—reluctant—led—

> Before—were Cities—but Between—
> The Forest of the Dead—
>
> Retreat—was out of Hope—
> Behind—a Sealed Route—
> Eternity's White Flag—Before—
> And God—at every Gate—
>   (615)

The most remarkable quality of this remarkable poem is that it ends—ends in absolute incompletion, ends at the point where Roland's journey had just begun:

> Then pausing to throw backwards a last view
> To the safe road, 'twas gone! Grey plain all round!
> Nothing but plain to the horizon's bound.
> I might go on; nought else remained to do.
>   ("Childe Roland," stanza 9)

Dickinson does not go on, not in this poem. She has scrapped the quest's gradual development through time to give us a set picture smack in the absolutely alienated middle of things, a picture even more abstract and nonvisual than Browning's grotesque scenes. Yet the poem is not an allegory of death. As Geoffrey Hartman suggests, "In this little quest-romance, Eternity is always *before* you."[6] That is, the quest through life is defined as a single moment, the moment of dying, for that is as far as the mind can go in its terrestrial life. The poem's apparent incompletion redefines the sense of an ending. The poem ends where the mind's certainty ends, on a middlemost point of perplexity. The mind's eye foggily sees beyond the "Forest of the Dead" to the "Cities" of reward, but by definition the mind of this life, even at its outermost limits, cannot will itself to pass through to gain intimate knowledge. It can only hypothesize imaginatively, fictionalize plural gates and plural gods. Dickinson will settle for no intermediary quest of lesser scope than life and death, and in this poem she refuses her imagination a fictionalized finale for the only quest sufficiently inclusive to deserve the name. Either the quest motif is guilty of trifling in lesser concerns or, if it expands to Dickinson's requirements, it is guilty of pride in positing a goal, a defined end, at all.

Dickinson's "Journey" is more extreme than Browning's, not only in its redefinition of the quest-romance, but also in its quasi-allegorical stance. Its equation of the "odd Fork in Being's Road" with "Eternity" predicates a fully allegorized, Bunyanesque landscape. But it is "Eternity—by Term—," as if to say "Well, that's what they glibly call it." And in the stanzas that follow, as the symbols become increasingly complex ("Eternity's White Flag," for instance, suggests both a final, dazzling purity and Eternity's willingness to make a truce with, to admit the successful quester), the persona's relation to those symbols becomes unique, her own unsanctioned and ambivalent response to a traditional hope she cannot make her own without qualification. Dickinson dares a fully allegorical stance and then actively transforms it. We are left not with a "translation" of traditional dogma but with a fully individual sense of things which, by respatialization, employs traditional terminology only to alter it radically.

Dickinson's anti-allegories, and their extremity, are characteristic of American romanticism. The extremity concerns not only a willingness to employ allegory against itself but also an impatience with literal, evolving narrative time, an impatience which Emerson and Whitman share.[7] Though puritan thought is close-ended, though experience is strictly interpreted by a preformed theological abstract, the habit of scrutinizing the mundane for universal meanings lays the foundation for an American version of anti-allegory. Once freed from the dogma of a particular referential subject, analogy-making becomes possibility; development no longer derives from the predetermined cosmology but from the symbol whose evolution forms the poem's cosmology. In fact, it is in America that anti-allegory receives its most extreme formulation. Coleridge often spatializes his idea of a poem's development as a circle, but only in relation to the poem's return upon itself or its conversion of a series to a whole. It takes Emerson, in his early essay "Circles," to invent a spiritually imitative epistemology for the genre:

> The eye is the first circle, the horizon which it forms is the second, and throughout nature this primary figure is repeated without end. It is the highest emblem in the cipher of the world. St. Augustine describes the nature of God as a circle whose center was everywhere and its circumference nowhere.... Another analogy we shall now trace, that every action admits of being outdone. Our life is an apprenticeship to the truth that around every circle another can be drawn; that there is no end in nature, but that every end is a beginning; that there is always another dawn risen of mid-noon, and under every deep a lower one opens.... Permanence is but a word of degrees.[8]

Dickinson's relation to Emerson is uneasy—as uneasy, in fact, as Emerson's to Augustine and to Milton, whose phrases from *Paradise Lost,* here unacknowledged and deliberately twisted, contribute to the last few sentences of the quotation—and her frequent insistence on

"Circumference" often goes to stress the limitations of the human mind-eye. But whatever the temperamental and philosophical differences between the two, Emerson's statement expresses the implicit credo not only of Dickinson's symbolic narratives but of her general poetic techniques. Dickinson's scenelessness creates an expandable circumference of meaning. Her "raising of the bet" actuates the dictum "that there is always another dawn risen of mid-noon, and under every deep a lower one opens." Her symbols radiate outward through concentric scenes and what they signify comes dangerously close to a boundless reference: "there is no end in nature," "Permanence is but a word of degrees."

A poetry of this nature creates special interpretive problems. We are used to dealing with levels of meaning; as Northrop Frye says, criticism is allegory to begin with. But how are we to deal with a poetry which flies after what Emerson calls "The Flying Perfect" without ourselves escaping into the gas?

We can escape such an interpretive fate only by acknowledging the precise imprecision of Dickinson's symbolic language. As Dickinson's confusions of category merge terms from ordinarily discrete realms of discourse, so her individual symbols radiate their meanings through ordinarily discrete realms of discourse. For instance, the word "home" appears in nearly a hundred poems. It is almost always a place of safety and rest, but it may connote only a familial domicile or it may connote an envisioned heaven, an ultimate home; it may be the place from which a quest begins or the place of epistemological completion earned at the end of a quest; or, as in "Tho I get home how late—how late—," it may include all these meanings, though in that poem of a projected future the ultimate home and the epistemological completion are stressed. By the same token, Ruth Miller's definition of Dickinson's symbol of the sea, as "the place of transition between life and afterlife,"[9] errs only by limiting the symbol to a chronological and theological reference. If we wish to take account of all the meanings of "sea," the symbol's definition must become less precise. It is simply the opposite of "home," the place of risk, or query, of changes of all kinds. It entices the wildness of the spirit to quest.[10] Miller's definition of the symbol has an allegorical rigidity while Dickinson's allows for concentrically expanding and contracting connotations, for analogical meanings within the single word.

This distinction is central to an understanding of Dickinson's anti-allegories, and the failure to allow for the precise imprecision of her symbols has caused serious misreadings. Consider a typical symbolic narrative which utilizes the "sea" image. "I started early—Took my Dog—" immediately announces itself as mythic:

> I started early—Took my Dog—
> And visited the Sea—
> The Mermaids in the Basement
> Came out to look at me—
>
> And Frigates—in the Upper Floor
> Extended Hempen Hands—
> Presuming Me to be a Mouse—
> Aground—upon the Sands—
>
> But no Man moved Me—till the Tide
> Went past my simple Shoe—
> And past my Apron—and my Belt
> And past my Bodice—too—
>
> And made as He would eat me up—
> As wholly as a Dew
> Upon a Dandelion's Sleeve—
> And then—I started—too—
>
> And He—He followed—close behind—
> I felt His Silver Heel
> Upon my Ankle—Then my Shoes
> Would overflow with Pearl—
>
> Until We met the Solid Town—
> No One He seemed to know—
> And bowing—with a Mighty look—
> At me—The Sea withdrew—
>
> (520)

Every critic who has contemplated this poem in writing considers the sea merely an objectification of death. That meaning is surely there, but not in so simple a form. Dickinson's "Dog," in its extreme personal loyalty, is often a symbol of self-identity, and it is selfhood which the sea threatens. The sea is not merely death, and it is not merely evil. It is an agent of pearly disintegration, it wishes to effect on the persona "a sea change / Into something rich and strange." The sea's "Mermaids" and gesturing "Frigates" are themselves "rich and strange"; they suggest that the poem is at least partially about a confrontation with one's own mythic, even irrational imagination. In addition, the sea's masculine personification and his implicitly sexual assault upon the persona in stanza three suggests an identity with the mastering principle, that male owner we met as a different analogical figure in "My Life had stood—a Loaded Gun—." In fact, we might gloss the persona's analogy of herself to a "Dew" which the sea-master will "eat up" with a statement from an early letter written by the poet to her future sister-in-law, Susan Gilbert:

> How dull our lives must seem to the bride, and the plighted maiden, whose days are fed with gold, and who gather pearls every evening; but to the *wife*, Susie, sometimes the *wife forgotten*, our lives perhaps seem dearer than all others in the world; you have seen flowers at morning, *satisfied* with the dew, and those same sweet flowers at noon with their heads bowed in anguish before the mighty sun; think you these thirsty blossoms will *now* need naught but—*dew?* No, they will cry for sunlight, and pine for the burning noon, tho' it scorches them, scathes them; . . . Oh, Susie, it is dangerous, and it is all too dear, these simple trusting spirits, and the spirits mightier, which we cannot resist!
>
> (L 93)

We cannot take this gloss too literally. I am not suggesting that this is a poem about the fearful aspects of marriage, but I am trying to establish that the poem also is not about "the transition between life and afterlife." The sea is a symbol of all the experiential unknowns and of all the denied irrational urges. If we wish to think of the poem's landscape and action as primarily internal and psychological, we should note that the persona initiates the action by visiting the sea and that the sea finally withdraws "with a Mighty look" which suggests that his defeat is only temporary. That is, in that this is a poem about death, it is about confronting the thought of death, and then of refusing to entertain it. For good reason: the thought of death gets out of control, just as the tide seems to break the limits of the moon's regulatory spell on it, and threatens to become the actuality of death. But we must say more than this. If the sea is a symbol of death, then death itself is an emblem of many fears, mysteries, and desires. Likewise, the retreat to the "Solid Town" is not simply a return to life, but a return to conventional society, to common sense, to a self-assurance bought at the price of passion, to father's *"real life"* defined as the exclusion of imaginative realization. The poem develops the sea symbol to construct a paradox reminiscent of the chief Melvillian paradox, stated by Charles Feidelson, Jr.: "The phantom is ungraspable as long as we stand on the bank; and the ocean is annihilative once we dive into it."[11]

Like Melville's whale, Dickinson's sea combines the desired phantom and the feared annihilation in a single symbol.

To interpret Dickinson's symbols, we must imitate their precise imprecision. We must resist the temptation to pin down a poetry which depends on expansible meaning. For instance, can we really say that the subject of the following poem is "the difference between light verse and the higher use of wit" or "the writer" as she "looks back upon the work she produced four or five years ago and finds it trifling" or even "poetic accomplishment"? Or, in a radically different vein, can we say that "this poem renders the relationship between life on this earth and afterlife"?[12]

> We play at Paste—
> Till qualified, for Pearl—
> Then, drop the Paste—
> And deem ourself a fool—
>
> The Shapes—though—were similar—
> And our new Hands
> Learned *Gem*-Tactics—
> Practicing *Sands*—
>
> (320)

To qualify all the forgoing interpretations as overhasty statements of single-minded intention, as allegorical readings of an anti-allegory, does not leave us in a position of know-nothingism. The poem asserts a world of continuum, of continually inclusive evolution, where no activity, however trivial, is wasted. (The poem would thrill Huizinga and other play theorists.) Poetic construction is only one possible analogy-completer and the correlative of life and afterlife another. The only arts mentioned bear an obviously analogical intent: from an effort which produces only artificial gems, paste, we learn the techniques of true gemology. Certainly the images of playful construction pull toward an artistic reference, but the opening plural pronoun lets everyone in on the act; the poem may refer equally to the art of constructing one's life in general. The poem is not a "reflection on" a particular subject: it calls to mind the most specific and most general references at once. Its own "gem-tactic" consists in the incredible versatility of its symbolic pattern, a cutting edge which can be applied to all sorts of philosophic stones.

It is a recognition of the specific nature of any symbolic narrative's cutting edge which keeps us from an uncritical eclecticism. The reader's responsibility is to ask the right question: to formulate a theme broad enough to support the poem's burden and to refuse to transform analogical illustration into factual statement, biography, or arbitrarily dreamed-up allegory. Imagine how either a flat-footed Marxist or an overreaching biographical critic could butcher this symbolic narrative:

> The Malay—took the Pearl—
> Not—I—the Earl—
> I—feared the Sea—too much
> Unsanctified—to touch—
>
> Praying that I might be
> Worthy—the Destiny—
> The Swarthy fellow swam—
> And bore my Jewel—Home—
>
> Home to the Hut! What lot
> Had I—the Jewel—got—
> Borne on a Dusky Breast—
> I had not deemed a Vest
> Of Amber—fit—
>
> The Negro never knew
> I—wooed it—too
> To gain, or be undone—
> Alike to Him—One—
>
> (452)

The victory of the moral proletariat! The poet's confession of racial supremacy! Well, not quite, although the social standings of Earl and Malay are appropriate to the attitudes they represent. The poem devalues a pious passivity, an unengaged intellect, in comparison to a passionate activity, an involvement with experiential risk. The earl's proud humility toward the pearl (a typical anti-allegorical symbol of general meaning, definable only as supreme beauty and significance) is shown up as a superstitious fastidiousness, and fastidiousness in turn becomes a serious failure of the spirit. For all his piety, the earl will not "gain or be undone"; to attain the pearl in life or to become pearly in death are not "alike" to him. He will not activate the life within him to gain the life abroad. Even the syntax contributes to the passive-active contrast: in the second stanza, the "I" of the gerundive subordinate clause is replaced in the main clause by the "Swarthy fellow." (Obviously, the phrase does not mean that "the swarthy fellow prayed for me as he dove" but that "I prayed, while he performed.") The poem is a psychological study in part—even as he is learning his lesson, the earl continues to assert the "swarthy," "dusky" inferiority of the deep diver who is unconsciously instructing him—but the psychological study is clearly subordinate to the poem's instructive purpose. This is perhaps the most daring aspect of Dickinson's anti-allegories. They carry on the moral recommendation of certain attitudes, the "teaching" function of traditional allegories, without referring to extrapoetic codes of conduct. The poem gracefully transforms material to spiritual gain to illustrate a forceful moral: that nothing will come to the man who waits in selfish fear—not wealth in any real sense of the word, not paradise, not beauty, not a realization of the meaning of things, not any of the potential values contained in Dickinson's pearl. Yet this recommendation of risk does not derive from any particular moral system and it does not apply to any particular sphere of action.

The effect of Dickinson's symbols depends finally on a merger of her two worlds. The bardic and confessional attitudes come together in Dickinson's symbology. Her anti-allegories combine a quality of parable with a sense of lived experience. Thus individual actions become universally essential while detached ethics become existentially real. From a greater distance, we can see another, less technical reconciliation. Many of the symbolic narratives enact a disappointment or a failure, and as such they contribute to Dickinson's world of veto, of negation. Yet they enact these negations with an exuberance of language that calls to mind Yeats's phrase of respect for vital suffering in "Lapis Lazuli": "Gaiety transforming all that dread."

4

Persona as Voice, Persona as Style

I'm Nobody! Who are you?
Are you—Nobody—Too?
Then there's a pair of us?
Don't tell! They'd advertise / banish us—you know

How dreary—to be—Somebody!
How public—like a Frog—
To tell one's name—the livelong June—
To an admiring Bog!

—Dickinson, poem 288

Do I contradict myself?
Very well then. . . I contradict myself;
I am large. . . . I contain multitudes

—Whitman

1

The "I" of the poems is not Emily Dickinson of Amherst, Massachusetts. Dickinson is emphatic in a letter to Higginson: "When I state myself, as the Representative of the Verse—it does not mean—me—but a supposed person"(L 268). We may choose to qualify this warning against biographical inference by characterizing it as the kind of statement a poet makes to protect his inner life from his own desire to investigate it; and personae are deliberately chosen and thus, however fictional, somehow indicative. Still, Dickinson's multitude of personae—constantly contradicting one another in tone as well as "opinion"—discourages any hope of finding the real, final self in any one poem. If we are to draw a composite picture of the Dickinson who matters most, the Dickinson whose sensibility informs the poems, we must survey her variety of poses. A methodology is suggested by the language of Dickinson's disclaimer, in which even the fictional persona is relegated to the subordinate, resultant status of "Representative of the Verse." "Verse" can be taken as the analogical rhetoric that we have studied or as those syntactical features of style that we have yet to consider; and we will question the relation of Dickinson's poses to each in turn.

Throughout, I have equated a bardic, oracular voice with Dickinson's Transcendentalist faith and a confessional voice with Dickinson's alternating skeptical sense of limitation and grief. These equations need qualification and complication, but they can serve as the poles of Dickinson's spectrum of poses. At the negative extreme, an analogy develops to reveal the psychological state of a tragic persona. We already know something about this kind of progression, for "My Life had stood—a Loaded Gun—" is an especially clear illustration of it. The analogy—my life: a loaded gun—is completed by the more buried equation—the master (or mastering passion or belief) of my life: the owner of the gun. From that point on, the vehicles (gun and owner) swallow the tenors (my life and its guiding principle) in the persona's overt narrative statement; but irony is created because we, at least, remember the nature of those tenors and recognize the gulf between the proper function of a gun and the proper function of a life. The consequences of the analogy develop silently in the middle stanzas and then explode as the tenors reassert themselves and the speaker finally recognizes the terrible problems involved in the analogy. In the final stanza the narrative is revealed as the projection of a state of mind for, as John Lynen has written of another poem, "What started out as an action turns out to be a state of affairs."[1] Or more precisely here, what started out as an action turns out to be the state of the persona.

At the opposite end of our spectrum, the single, extended analogy may be employed for a completely different purpose. It may develop without an individuated speaker to reveal the poet's own thoughts. A relatively direct expression develops its own kind of complexities, as in this poem which celebrates a process of literary creation:

> This is a Blossom of the Brain—
> A small—italic Seed
> Lodged by Design or Happening
> The Spirit fructified—
>
> Shy as the Wind of his Chambers
> Swift as a Freshet's Tongue
> So of the Flower of the Soul
> Its process is unknown.
>
> When it is found, a few rejoice
> The Wise convey it Home
> Carefully cherishing the spot
> If other Flower become.

When it is lost, that Day shall be
The Funeral of God,
Upon his Breast, a closing Soul
The Flower of our Lord.

(945)

As a poem whose subject is itself, the poem actively enacts the process it describes. Its own "italic Seed" is the analogy—this (poem): Blossom of the Brain. The blossom's flowering, the developing growth of the analogy into an encompassing vision, is illustrated as it is stated by the analogical association of otherwise unrelated natural images (the wind, the freshet's tongue). Then the poem considers the poet's responsibility to his idea. The "Wise" who find this blossom—and the reference here is primarily to the poet who finds this fructification of spirit in himself, not to the reader—"convey it Home"; that is, they take it to heart, find its deepest meaning. And that is exactly what the poem does in its final stanza. It interprets the flower analogy sacramentally; it makes the creative process a sign of Godhead, for the loss of the seed is "The Funeral of God," the death of meaning. The poet is another Mary, "for that which is conceived in her is of the Holy Spirit" (Matt. 1:20). A loss of the seed must close the soul of "our Lord," Jesus, for the seed, like Jesus, is God's experiential representative. This new extension of the analogy may appear wildly heretical—every man his own Christ—but it is supported by puritan theology. Ernest Benson Lowrie's paraphrase of a passage from Samuel Willard's *Complete Body of Puritan Divinity,* an inspired guidebook to puritan orthodoxy, could serve as an accurate gloss of this poem's procedure:

> In the essential order the prime analogate is in God and is applied analogously to the creature. But in the order of knowing the process is reversed. The mind begins with the derived perfection as it is known within the creaturely sphere, and then elevates it through the dialectic of the incommunicable qualities so that it becomes worthy of God "in a more sublime and supereminent manner."[2]

The derived perfection of the seed has been elevated in Dickinson's poem to become worthy of God's significance. Poetically, this final, theological fructification of the analogical seed is startling but earned, for the "Blossom of the Brain" has been renamed "The Flower of the Soul" before it becomes "The Flower of our Lord" and throughout the poem Dickinson has emphasized the godlike omnipotence and mystery of the poetic process. This particular blossom, this very poem, is not lost. The "spot" where its seed, its single analogy, sprang up *has* been "cherished," and with its sacramental conclusion the blossom in fact has become an "other Flower."

Of course, the two poems we have cited as opposites are not as far apart as they seem. The involved sufferer of "My Life had stood—a Loaded Gun—" does not voice simply a spontaneous overflow of emotions; we spent a long chapter examining the art and logic of her utterance. Likewise, the impersonal sage of "This is a Blossom of the Brain—" does not set forth a dry theory of analogical poetics; the poem is as full of passion as an awe-filled prayer. Our hypothetical polarities are justified in that the one poem is basically confessional while the other is basically revelatory. We can state the polarity in terms of the ways the poems employ the verb of being. The "is" of "My Life had stood" is a temporal indicator, while the "is" of "This is a Blossom" states a definition. But again our polarities are not absolute. "My Life had stood" finally transforms narrative, chronological time into "a state of affairs," and "This is a Blossom" defines itself by an analogy to temporal growth. In all, whatever stance Dickinson takes, her best sufferers are intelligent and her best sages are impassioned. The two figures are linked by a belief that is implicit in the development of "My Life had stood" and that gains explicit statement in "This is a Blossom": the way your analogical language develops suggests what kind of world you have chosen, what kind of person you are.

In fact, whenever the bardic or confessional tendency is totally negated by the other, Dickinson produces distinctly inferior poetry. The confessional persona will use the maddened logic of analogy to express gushing sentiment:

> Distance—is not the Realm of Fox
> Nor by Relay of Bird
> Abated—Distance is
> Until thyself, Beloved.
>
> (1155)

More frequently (and less disastrously) the rebellious transcendental seer takes over to voice advisory aphorisms from on high:

> Count not that far that can be had,
> Though sunset lie between—
> Nor that adjacent, that beside,
> Is further than the sun.
>
> (1074)

Both these "distance" poems seem incomplete. We expect the first to spread out and the second to zero in, but they just end. Only that concentration of meaning and those daring hyperboles which persist even in Dickinson's slightest poems keep the first example from being embarrassing and the second from being pompous. Luckily, such instances are rare. Ingenious compounds of bard and sufferer abound. A third group of single, developing analogies ranges between our two hypothetical poles. In these poems, Dickinson attempts that most ancient social function of poets, naming. These poems deserve more attention than they have received, for they offer a way out of the puppet-blob alternatives that we considered in relation to "My Life had stood" and the other master poems. As Tony Tanner notes, language affords a third alternative, in which the writer can "find a freedom which is not a jelly and . . . establish an identity which is not a prison."[3] Since Dickinson is not, after so much history, in the founding position of an Adam toward her culture, we might describe this group more accurately as poems of renaming. Language is an inherited system, an imposed Master, but Dickinson can jostle it to master the Master. In the activity of naming, more particularly, Dickinson can acknowledge the otherness of nature and avoid egotistic subjectivity; but simultaneously, by drawing attention to this naming activity, Dickinson can assert her individuality of perception and thus become, in Tanner's phrase, the artist of oneself.

The more obvious purpose of these poems is to revitalize language and the world upon which language acts, and they operate by a humanization of the process of definition. Two extraordinary procedures regularly occur in these poems. First, the single, extended analogy comes to be associated with a rage for order, with pompous logic and deadening system; thus it is often challenged and occasionally overthrown in the course of the poem. Second, our two opposite personae, the sage and the sufferer, sometimes combine and sometimes compete within a single speaker's voice.

We can view an example of both processes in a renaming poem which dramatizes the idea that links "My Life had stood" to "This is a Blossom," the idea that symbolic language expresses the self:

"Morning"—means "Milking"—to the Farmer—
Dawn—to the Teneriffe—
Dice—to the Maid—
Morning means just Risk—to the Lover—
Just revelation—to the Beloved—

Epicures—date a Breakfast—by it—
Brides—an Apocalypse—
Worlds—a Flood—
Faint-going Lives—Their Lapse from Sighing
Faith—The Experiment of Our Lord—

(300)

Because "morning" means according to who you are, the single analogy is overthrown by the analogical collection. But Dickinson is willing to accept such relativity only as a psychological fact of life, not as an abnegation of absolute meanings. She sets up a hierarchy of values. Each stanza progresses from the most utilitarian meanings of "morning" to the most symbolic, from associations engendered by ordinary self-concern to associations engendered by sublime ideals of risk and self-sacrifice. In the final three lines plainly named character types are replaced first by an idea of nature, then by a metaphor of those about to die, and finally by a full-fledged abstraction. Dickinson thus builds to the quality of faith, the only "subject who" is able to get outside its self completely to view an overall pattern to "morning." That pattern, "The Experiment of Our Lord," may be seen in retrospect to include all the more limited meanings, and thus the structure of the single, developing analogy is reestablished. Thus too, the voice which has identified momentarily with sufferers finally separates itself to establish a sage-like overview.

Sage and sufferer combine in one figure in a poem where the extended analogy is more finally and violently overthrown:

"Heaven"—is what I cannot reach!
The Apple on the Tree—
Provided it do hopeless—hang—
That—"Heaven" is—to Me!

The Color, on the Cruising Cloud—
The interdicted Land—
Behind the Hill—the House behind—
There—Paradise—is found!

Her teasing Purples—Afternoons—
The credulous—decoy—
Enamored—of the Conjuror—
That spurned us—Yesterday!

(239)

The single analogy here gives way permanently to the analogical collection, for "what I cannot reach" turns out to be all sorts of things: apples, distant houses, sunsets. Dickinson makes "Heaven" relative, literally surrounds it with quotation marks, to give it a psychological and epistemological impact and to show that by its ungraspable essence it is ever present as an idea, a desire, in the most commonplace phenomena of everyday life. This expansion of meaning subtly transforms itself into an illustratory narrative in the third stanza which presents a Sisyphus-like vision of unending quest, of noble if credulous and always frustrated aspiration. "Heaven" is seen as the outward bounds of nature and then personified as a magnetic and coy mistress. For her magnetized seekers, the world becomes a continually tragic love affair.

We do not conceive of this first-person speaker as a character with a detailed personal history, much less as Emily Dickinson of Amherst. The poem exemplifies exactly what Dickinson means when she calls her persona "the Representative of the Verse." The speaker is individuated just sufficiently to show that she is one of the "credulous," that in one way or another she has participated in the metaphysical design she proposes. She serves to charge hypothesis with feeling, to add a note of experiential authority to logic. The speaker of "Heaven—is what I cannot reach!" stands between the impersonal sage and the involved sufferer, as a wounded dialectician.

This third figure permeates the poems of renaming. It is his oddly unindividuated confessional tone which makes the word flesh. It is his implicit emotional response which separates Dickinson's poems of renaming from dictionary definitions and makes lyrical poetry of them. We see just how confessional the process of definition can become in a poem where the wound progressively overcomes the dialectician. It begins with an apparently absurd attempt to analogize mundane imagery into vision:

> What is—"Paradise"—
> Who live there—
> Are they "Farmers"—
> Do they "hoe"—
> Do they know that this is "Amherst"—
> And that I—am coming—too—

The childlike speaker proposes in question form an analogy between paradise and Amherst. The sweet child is totally confident that she will attain paradise and questions only its nature. This is one of Dickinson's typical poses: the child-persona who believes, and who believes with such passionate innocence that she must know exactly in what she places her faith. The result often proves embarrassing to the doctrinal faith itself, as the child unconsciously points out crucial inconsistencies.[4] That happens here. At first it seems the child wants to define paradise as a simple extension of our present surroundings. But as she goes on to ask whether it is "always pleasant—there" and whether "You are sure there's such a person / As 'a Father'—in the sky—," we begin to realize that the speaker desperately wishes to qualify the Amherst-Paradise analogy. Paradise had better differ in some ways from Amherst. It had better be more truly a pastoral community, a loving family which the persona lacks and needs. We begin to understand that the analogical vision, however naive its pantheism may be, is a serious cry of loneliness: "Won't they scold us—when we're homesick— / Or tell God—how cross we are—." The poem concludes by overtly revealing the analogical quandaries as an attempt to transform a pitiful reality:

> So if I get lost—there—ever—
> Or do what the Nurse calls "die"—
> I shan't walk the "Jasper"—barefoot—
> Ransomed folks—won't laugh at me—
> Maybe—"Eden" a'n't so lonesome
> As New England used to be!
>
> (215)

The poem defines itself finally as a deceptively tough-minded critique not only of New England coldness but of the Calvinist, terror-filled theology out of which such coldness grows. Life in "Eden," as it is explained to a child by his elders, is the exact obverse of the life those elders make for the child in Amherst. Appropriately, the poem reveals that its real analogy is not betwen Paradise and Amherst, but between Paradise and all the qualities so sadly absent from Amherst.

We find in this poem still another variation of the sage-sufferer compound. Our speaker begins as a rather silly sage, then she becomes a sufferer, and finally, unconsciously, she again becomes a sage in her very suffering. The poem is comparable to the version of "Holy Thursday" in Blake's *Songs of Innocence,* the version in which a child says more than he knows and thus implies a social complaint which is far more evocative than the "official" complaint of the "Holy Thursday" in the *Songs of Experience.* Just so, in "What is—'Paradise'—" Dickinson allows a social critique to grow naturally out of the speaker's innocent questions. (She knows of "death" only through her nurse's use of the word, a Blakean correspondence of coincidental and telling exactness.) Sage and sufferer become indivisible. As the final lines spread out to indict a culture, they nonetheless focus on establishing the emotional, if not the intellectual, dignity of the speaker's analogical wish-fulfillment. Here, the victims of Dickinson's irony exist outside of the poem.

The figure of the wounded dialectician can move as far toward the oracular as toward the confessional extreme. The process of definition can be humanized by joy as well as pain: the "wound" can be created by awe. We find this response in a variation on the naming process, the poems of unnaming. If the American writer finds his liberty in language, he must nonetheless admit the limits of his activity; otherwise, as Tanner says, he becomes an Ahab who subjugates and then replaces the world by the tyrannical self. To preserve the "other" and thus to allow for conversations with it, the American romantics typically stop naming long enough to admit "the futility of pretending that the putative exactness of words can ever measure up to the actual mystery of things. Along with this has gone a suspicion that there can be something damaging in confusing names and their referents."[5]

Oddly, this suspicion of her art's limit exists for Dickinson as a cause of joy; she celebrates her insufficiency. In her desire to establish the transcendent meaning of ever present realities, Dickinson takes the most commonplace phenomena out of the realm of the confidently known into a realm of evanescences. She removes their names because such names make dull those things which have a significance beyond the lexicon's reach. The look of death on a cheek is "the little Tint / That never had a name—" (559); the onset of night is "A Wisdom, without Face, or name" (1104); and "Exhilaration" is the breeze

> That lifts us from the Ground
> And leaves us in another place
> Whose statement is not found— . . .
> (1118)

Similarly, a poem which attempts to define "Nature" in terms of sight and sound ends by disqualifying itself:

> Nay—Nature is Harmony—
> Nature is what we Know—
> Yet have no art to say—
> So impotent Our Wisdom is
> To her Simplicity.
>
> (668)

Wisdom must submit to truth, the name must be removed. Dickinson stresses cognitive limitations in order to elevate experience, to make the world strange and new again.

In these poems, the persona is present only as an attitude of celebratory humility. The confessional voice is in service to the oracle: the admission of lexical limitation only heightens the claim being made for a transcendental reality. But a sad fate befalls the analogical process in these poems. It is so aligned with the mind's ordering impulse that it becomes a form of hubris. If analogical conjectures are not to be utterly negated, as they are in the examples above, the analogy must construct itself as a paradox:

> Hope is a subtle Glutton—
> He feeds upon the Fair—
> And yet—inspected closely
> What abstinence is there—
>
> His is the Halcyon Table—
> That never seats but One—
> And whatsoever is consumed
> The same amount remain—
>
> (1547)

"Inspected closely," the glutton Hope becomes a gastronomic paradox, for he can eat his cakes and have them too. His "Fair" fare, a vision of future possibilities, nourishes the soul; yet because reality never achieves the hopeful dreams of the imagination, hope's food supply remains constant. The poem dematerializes sustenance to suggest that hope depends on that which is not material, not present as an actual fact. The tenor "hope" gains status at the expense of its gluttonous vehicle, and the analogy survives by playing a trick on its own logic.

More often, Dickinson will increase the analogical discomfiture by attempting to describe qualities which simply cannot be named. In these poems, Dickinson does not wish so much to vivify what her culture considers commonplace as to capture those ephemeral realities which her culture neglects to consider at all. This process necessitates an analogical talking-around the unnamable noun. The sage becomes a sufferer in a new way. He cannot quite find a vehicle for his lonely tenor, and the tenor cannot quite be named in itself. The analogical quest always fails as we view the analogy's struggle, always unsuccessful, to be born. Consider this remarkable example:

> The Love a Life can show Below
> Is but a filament, I know,
> Of that diviner thing
> That faints upon the face of Noon—
> And smites the Tinder in the Sun—
> And hinders Gabriel's Wing—
>
> 'Tis this—in Music—hints and sways—
> And far abroad on Summer days—
> Distils uncertain pain—
> 'Tis this enamors in the East—
> And tints the Transit in the West
> With harrowing Iodine—

The "diviner" love cannot be stated but only exemplified in the widest and most evocative range of experience. It is a "thing" without a name whose presence, appropriately, is without definite shape or sound, a subliminal word which effects a subliminal difference throughout art and nature. The poem finally attempts to define the "thing" by its action and by its effect on the perceiver, but here too it is forced into a spectrum of statements:

> 'Tis this—invites—appalls—endows—
> Flits—glimmers—proves—dissolves—
> Returns—suggests—convicts—enchants—
> Then—flings in Paradise—
>
> (673)

Flings the speaker into a Paradise, by a sort of transcendental rough handling? Or, adds Paradise to its other effects? Either way, the poem admits its inability to say the "diviner thing," to explain a beyond-human evanescence by a human vocabulary. Yet, by her very failure to say the "thing," Dickinson re-creates the awe which every nature-lover, music-lover, and minimally imaginative human being has experienced. The poem is a very cagey failure.

The poems of analogical quest make most apparent an effect of all the poems. We are taken backstage to view in its very development the process by which thoughts find expression. We find that the process there itself reconciles opposing poses. It is another analogical quest—an even more futile attempt—which proves definitive of Dickinson's compound persona. The dialectician begins confidently with a multitude of temporal images which might serve as analogies to "Heaven." At first, she appears to be confused only by the luxury of choice:

> "Heaven" has different Signs—to me—
> Sometimes, I think that Noon
> Is but a symbol of the Place
> And when again, at Dawn,
>
> A mighty look runs round the World
> And settles in the Hills—
> An Awe if it should be like that
> Upon the Ignorance steals—

The poem continues to chase the "Heaven" which it already has transformed from a place to a symbolic idea. The appearances made in nature by times of day, "Noon" and "Dawn," seem to constitute a unity of imagery if not a temporal progression, and they are joined later by "The Rapture of a finished Day"; but in the meantime, a sunlit orchard, a birdsong of "Victory," and "Carnivals of Clouds" also are nominated. These most tangential associations at last suggest the randomness and futility of this analogical hunt. Simultaneously, they compliment those often unnoticed everyday natural phenomena which are so potentially stimulating to the spirit that they "remind us of the place / That Men call 'Paradise.' " The poem, even in the futility of its search, performs two functions which would seem at variance. Its images rouse our sleeping appreciation of life's commonplaces, while those quotation marks which surround "Heaven" and "Paradise" shock us out of a confident and vulgar visualization of heaven as a mere extension of earth's pretty places. It is the absurdity of a reverse pantheism which dooms the completion of the analogy. The failure is stated in a conclusion which brings "home" the issue of the unsuccessful analogical quest in a particularly discomforting way:

> Itself be fairer—we suppose—
> But how Ourself, shall be

> Adorned, for a Superior Grace,
> Not yet, our eyes can see—
> (575)

Since "Heaven" is like nothing we know, since our scene will be transformed, we will not be as we are; we too will find ourselves transformed, newly adorned. The first half of the logic creates expectation, but its extension is cause for fearful awe. In this figure of the poet trembling before her own conclusion, we see enacted what Dickinson elsewhere calls "the Art to stun myself / With Bolts of Melody!" (505).

2

The impersonal bard and the involved sufferer personify opposite desires: the one for order, for logic, for a clear view of things; the other for personal enunciation, for emotional catharsis, for comfort. What we have found to be particularly remarkable in the poems of naming is Dickinson's ability to include both of these desires, to combine them or to play one off against the other. When Albert J. Gelpi writes that Dickinson "was personally incapable of logical, not to say theological, thought," that "system and argument . . . were too hard and frigid for her," that she is saved as a poet by "the warm swelling, swirling notions of the Romantic poet-prophets,"[6] he denies exactly half of the qualities which make Dickinson's lyricism effective.[7] At the opposite extreme, when Dolores Dyer Lucas writes of Dickinson's poetry as an "intellectual exercise," as "deliberately obscure, having an element of conscious deception," and goes on to define that deception as a means for riddling,[8] she simply blinds herself to Dickinson's more "human" half. Head and heart coexist in Dickinson's poetic body.

It is Dickinson's desire to madden logic, to inject it with an individual sense of crisis. Yet it is equally her desire to create this sense of crisis without making the word or the world a mere extension of the self's emotional problems. At another level, the conflict is analogous: one aim is to dramatize the act of language-making, with all its difficulties, as emblematic of the struggle with human limits in general; another aim is not to allow the dramatization of this struggle to interfere with a produced effect, a deepening and expansion of the meanings of language. The subjective and the objective, spontaneity and craft—these are the contraries Dickinson sets out to compound and, by compounding, to destroy. In one poem she defines the ideal poet as "Exterior—to Time" (448); but the challenge was to discover presentational techniques that would not sacrifice either the poet exterior to time or the living woman to each other.

This is not primarily a stylistic study of Dickinson, for reasons of design and incapacity; but we can begin to understand Dickinson's response to the challenge of style by noting that the presentational form of the poems is very nearly epistolary. In reading her actual letters which incorporate poems, we often would experience great difficulty in deciding where the prose ends and the poetry begins were it not for indentation and, sometimes, metrics; in fact, scholars continue to dispute whether certain poems *are* poems. And Dickinson herself begins a poem on her poetic activity by describing that activity as "my letter to the World / That never wrote to Me." Lest the word "letter" and the second line's complaint be taken as a definition of a personal, sulky poetry, Dickinson states as the letter's content, "The simple News that Nature told—"(441). The question of whose "Nature" does the telling, the poet's or the world's, is deliberately made ambiguous; but either way, the phrase suggests a concern for truth which is not synonymous with public wailing. And in a letter which comments on itself, Dickinson goes further to stress the form's impersonal nature: "A letter always feels to me like immortality because it is the mind alone without corporeal friend" (L 330). Yet in the poems themselves we experience two minds, the analogical "mind alone" shocking its more involved and fearful, almost corporeal counterpart.

Of course, Dickinson's poems are only figuratively comparable to letters. But like the fictional letters of epistolary writers, the poems combine immediacy with reflection, involvement with objectivity. For instance, Dickinson's continual use of a subjunctive verb mediates between the present and the forever, just as her inexact rhymes mediate between artful and informal speech. They provide just enough of the "Bells, whose jingling cooled my Tramp" (L 265), just enough craft to insure that the poems will not be too spasmodically and selfishly emotional. Dickinson's quirky capitalizations of certain words actually do imitate nineteenth-century epistolary form, and they too achieve a letter-like merger of personality and objectivity. Dickinson takes over the ancient poetic habit of signifying the generality of importance of certain words by capitalization, but the words she *chooses* to capitalize are not usually the traditional ones. As an element of the confusion of categories, the capitalizations announce that a personality is deciding for itself the words that should be granted a philosophical stress.

In fact, the most controversial syntactical element of Dickinson's poetry, the dash, is borrowed from the common punctuation of nineteenth-century letters. These dashes have inspired such interest because they appear to afford Dickinson a freedom necessary to her unique syntax. For years, these simple little marks have engendered wild theories. Because Dickinson usually employs simple hymn meter and because her dashes in manuscript sometimes slant up or down, it has been suggested that the poems are to be spoken in sing-song with the dashes used as intonation marks. But even a Fischer-Dieskau would have trouble following the intonations of the fourteen dashes in the last stanza of "The Love a Life can show Below." We can rely on our natural sense of language to refute the idea that the poems are particularly mellifluous. At the other extreme, Ralph W. Franklin argues that the dashes should be eliminated and the punctuation regularized in modern editions of Dickinson's poetry. He notes that Dickinson used dashes even in recopying a recipe and goes on to state that "the dashes were merely a habit of handwriting. . . . Dickinson used them inconsistently, without system."[9] That is a pretty bad *non sequitur.* I might use commas or periods in writing both a recipe and a poem, but only in the poem would I consciously use them to signify anything. Furthermore, a great number of regularized editions of Dickinson's poetry have come out in the last hundred years, and their effect invariably has been to flatten the poetry.

Apparently then, the dashes work. How? They are a final, most iconic example of that merger between pure thought and individuated experience which we have traced throughout Dickinson's poetic strategy. On the one hand, they simply define syntax. They often display a word's dual relationship to what has gone before and what will come after it; and often, as David Porter suggests, they serve as "an admonition to the reader to allow every word to set apart its full measure of interpretation." On the other hand, as Porter also notes, the dashes denote "the presence of the creative impulse." They announce an authorial presence, though they do not always represent, as Porter claims, "the *spontaneity* of the emotional force that went into the composition."[10] Rather, they serve as another means by which Dickinson takes us backstage to view the struggle of poetic process, a struggle to find the right word, and they serve to represent a hesitancy, always defeated, to reveal the word which in turn reveals the poet's mind. The dashes are thus not only an instrument for clarification and elaboration of thought; they are also an anachronistic realization of a tenet of the modern projectivist poets set forth in 1950 by Charles Olson, as if it had not been done before: "Verse now, 1950, if it is to go ahead, if it is to be of *essential* use, must, I take it, catch up and put into itself certain laws and possibilities of the breath of the breathing of the man who writes as well as of his listenings."[11] Psychologically as well as syntactically, Dickinson's dashes create a pressure, a tension, a nervous breath which tells it own story.

These little dashes can serve as transition marks to our second problem, the conflict between spontaneity and craft. Dickinson's extreme economy of language not only is designed but appears so, and the dashes play a part in this effect. Dickinson's elliptical, progressively dwindling syntax depends on the dashes where periods, commas, and semicolons would be inappropriate and even confusing. The dashes serve as marks of ellipsis in the last two stanzas of an elegy on Mrs. Browning, as one great woman poet describes what it meant to read another's sonnets:

> 'Twas a Divine Insanity—
> The Danger to be Sane
> Should I again experience—
> 'Tis Antidote to turn—
>
> To Tomes of solid Witchcraft—
> Magicians be asleep—
> But Magic—hath an Element
> Like Deity—to keep—
>
> (593)

The reader may experiment by attempting to replace the dashes with more usual punctuations (exclamation mark, comma, space, period, space, space, comma, period). He will find, I think, that the dashes are far more suited to the subjunctive mood and to the tight "vertical" construction by which each line refers to preceding and subsequent lines to complete its syntax.

This brings us to the "spontaneous" syntactical function of the dash. (We have already considered one spontaneous function of the dashes, "breathing," as we considered the stylistic combination of the sage and the sufferer. Of course, spontaneity and craft, respectively, bear a connection to our earlier, personified dichotomy of the confessional sufferer and the impersonal sage.) The dash serves as a sort of hinge, sometimes to open out an apparently complete statement and expand it, sometimes to close a phrase and thus denote that a phrase

74

which at first glance appears incomplete is complete indeed. The hinge swings forward to create a fine ambiguity in the following poem:

> The One who could repeat the Summer day—
> Were greater than itself—though He
> Minutest of Mankind should be—
>
> And He—could reproduce the Sun—
> At period of going down—
> The Lingering—and the Stain—I mean—
>
> When Orient have been outgrown—
> And Occident—become Unknown—
> His Name—remain—
>
> (307)

Does "When Orient . . . And Occident" refer to the poet's "supernatural," artistic reproduction of the sun after it goes down and thus complete the second stanza, or do these lines lead toward the final phrase to suggest the poet's fame after his own final sundown, his death? Obviously the lines refer to both, though they are finally defined as most closely related (because syntactically necessary) to the poet's fame. Two day-night cycles, the one natural and the other human and synecdochic, are elegantly superimposed by the hinge technique as the lines refer back and forward.

An example of surprising closure occurs in the last stanza of another poem on fame:

> So let us gather—every Day—
> The Aggregate of
> Life's Bouquet
> Be Honor and not shame—
>
> (1427)

The first line becomes complete ("so let us gather our flowers of fame") once we see that the last line is in more desperate syntactical need of the middle lines to complete itself. A less complex illustration of closure occurs in the last line of the elegy to Mrs. Browning, where the final dash determines a particular meaning of "keep" which needs no completer, the meaning "remain fresh or vital."

The dash typically forces the reader continually to reinterpret meanings. It gives a quality of immediacy to the poems, makes them seem to develop before our eyes. Thus it not only condenses meaning almost scientifically; it also serves as a syntactical equivalent to Dickinson's dictum, "The Soul should always stand ajar" (1055). But what of the language itself? Dickinson's poetry is full of metaphors, and I suggested earlier that we could consider analogies as metaphors in the making and metaphors as completed, compacted analogies. Do not Dickinson's metaphors thus sacrifice spontaneity to elliptical craft? Not so, for Dickinson's metaphors implicitly reveal wih unusual fullness the analogical processes from which they originate. If Wordsworth's is the art of hiding his art, Dickinson's is the art of revealing her art. Consider just these four lines:

> How firm Eternity must look
> To crumbling men like me
> The only Adamant Estate
> In all Identity— ...
>
> (1499)

The lack of any scene except that created by the metaphor forces us to focus on the metaphoric transformations. We are made to re-create the confusion of categories by which the abstract ideal of Eternity, spatialized in Christian literature as heaven, is respatialized into the form of a solid architectural structure, "The only Adamant Estate." We also must re-create the process by which men are depersonified into crumbling buildings, and by which "Eternity" and "man" are suddenly made available to contrast, analogous in kind but not degree. From this necessary re-creation of the internal process of analogy, an outer analogy instantly develops: the "crumbling building" of time, the persona, desperately looking for "The only Adamant Estate" of timelessness as he crumbles in time. All this analogical action is presented as a speculation by a persona who makes himself a part of his completed metaphor. The act of creating the metaphor under the pressure of experiential necessity is made part of the drama. Thus, the history of a symbolic act, of an analogical development, announces its presence even in Dickinson's finished analogies, her metaphors.

We can conclude by adding another element to our explanation of the special attention we pay to Dickinson's language. Analogical action takes center stage because whatever else a poem is about, one of its subjects is always at least implicitly its own formulation. Dickinson's poems present us with a metapoetics, a poetry in the act of revealing its own creation.

3

We have gone looking for Emily Dickinson in her analogical strategies and we have found three versions of her, versions which often exist simultaneously. A bardic Dickinson creates her own symbols and molds language to the needs of her analogical visions. More modestly, Dickinson will dramatize herself as a mediator, a medium through which sublime experience passes:

> Pursuing you in your transitions,
> In other Motes—
> Of other Myths
> Your requisition be.
> The Prism never held the Hues,
> It only heard them play—
>
> (1602)

This Dickinson refuses to requisition images and falsify their life into brittle systems of belief. She will humbly chart the changes and follow where they lead. A third Dickinson actively suffers or exults over those changes and is "stunned" by her bardic alter-ego's "Bolts of Melody." Finally, then, a tripartite poet:

> A Mien to move a Queen—
> Half Child—Half Heroine—...
>
> (283)

The awed child of perception, the suffering heroine of experience, the contemplative queen of connective thought.

A Typology of Death, I: Dickinson in Black

I'd rather recollect a setting
Than own a rising sun....
(1349)

We must be less than Death
to be lessened by it—for
nothing is irrevocable but
ourselves.

(L 519)

1

A backward glance over the poems we have considered reveals an odd recurrence. Nearly every poem quoted in the first half of this study is a "death poem." In one sense or another, all these poems contemplate endings. Thoughts of death compel the life-gun persona of "My Life had stood—a Loaded Gun—" to recognize the ironic reality of her situation; "This is a Blossom of the Brain—" warns that failure to cultivate an inspired thought will result in "The Funeral of God"; constant attention to that ending of endings, Apocalypse, is the quality of thought which distinguishes the persona of "Sleep is supposed to be" from the "souls of sanity"; "Hope is a subtle Glutton—" denies an ending and the persona of "I started Early—Took my Dog—" runs away from one. Dickinson herself "started Early" on her contemplative journey toward death. At age twenty-one she tells her friend Jane Humphrey, "I think of the grave very often, and how much it has got of mine, and whether I can ever stop it from carrying off what I love; that makes me sometimes speak of it when I dont intend" (L 86).

I said earlier that nearly every poem Dickinson wrote contains an analogical transportation of meaning, and now I am saying that nearly every poem Dickinson wrote has to do with death, with endings. Is all this analogy-making thus a charade, a mask to disguise a grotesque obsession? To the contrary, death has a special epistemological status which necessitates analogy. Death is what we know least through direct experience. It is the "spacious arm... / That none can understand" (1625) and, more terrifyingly, "the Riddle" through which each of us must "walk" (50). Endings in nature are similarly confounding. "I'll tell you how the Sun rose—" one poem begins confidently, "But how he set—I know not—." Sunrise affords a multitude of seemingly ready-made synaesthetic images ("The Steeples swam in Amethyst—") but the description of the sunset must be framed by the tentative, qualifying verb "There seemed" (318).

Whether in relation to the sun, Christ, or one's Christian self, "To live, and die, and mount again in triumphant body," —now Dickinson goes beyond the sun— "and *next* time, try the upper air—is no schoolboy's theme!" (L 184). In a sense, death and its aftermath is not a theme at all, not so much a theme with assignable topics of rational discourse (this statement's assertion of resurrection will be questioned or denied in many poems) as a raw material for speculations, even for speculations about the limits of speculation.

Confronted by utmost mystery, Dickinson can proceed only by inference, and inference speaks in the language of analogy. Dickinson's considerations of endings are shaped by a particular analogical system, alternately named "figural" or "typological." Erich Auerbach defines this method of analogy in its broadest sense:

> Figural interpretation establishes a connection between two events or persons, the first of which signifies not only itself but also the second, while the second encompasses or fulfills the first. The two poles of the figure are separate in time, but both, being real events or figures, are within time, within the stream of historical life.[1]

In other words, a typology creates analogies grounded in real or projected experience, unequal analogies in which one of the terms (usually, but not always, the chronologically "later" term) completes and defines the meaning of the other. But the intent of a typological system goes beyond simple analogical usage in that it dictates a particular organization of time. Distinct from a common-sense, clock-time concept of events ("bottles in a row," as the linguist Benjamin Lee Whorf says) or a cyclical concept of progressive repetition, a typology posits a certain series of events at the center of time and views all other events as tending toward (or as emanating from) that center. It is this concept of time which informs Dickinson's poetry.

We are most familiar with typological thought in its Christian, Augustinian formulation. For Augustine, typology occurs in three stages: "the Law or history of the Jews as a prophetic *figura* for the appearance of Christ; the incarnation as a fulfillment of this *figura* and at the same time as a new promise of the end of the world and the Last Judgment; and finally, the future occurrence of these events as ultimate fulfillment."² As Christian typology progresses, it expands its terms. Not only the stories of the Old Testament but prior and subsequent historical events become "types" or "shadows" of New Testament characters and events, their "antitypes" or fulfillments (note that "antitype" here does not mean "the opposite type," e.g., Antichrist, but "the fulfilled type"); and crises in one's own experience come to be interpreted in relation to the various major moments of Christ's life. Another, more defensive change takes place in reference to the final antitype, the Apocalypse. Because frequently predicated "ends of the world" failed to materialize, the typology gradually became individualized; as Frank Kermode notes, "the type figures were modified, made to refer not to a common End but to a personal death or to crisis, or to epoch."³

Dickinson seizes upon this speculative expansion and personalization of the typology. She adopts Christian typology only to alter it for her own *ends*.⁴ She internalizes typological terms and subtly replaces the traditional antitypes with her own:

> One Crucifixion is recorded—only—
> How many be
> Is not affirmed of Mathematics—
> Or History—
>
> One Calvary—exhibited to Stranger—
> As many be
> As persons—or Peninsulas—
> Gethsemane—
>
> Is but a Province—in the Being's Centre—
> Judea—
> For Journey—or Crusade's Achieving—
> Too near—
>
> Our Lord—indeed—made Compound Witness—
> And yet—
> There's newer—nearer Crucifixion
> Than That—
>
> (553)

This poem takes us a long distance from the Augustinian typology. Dickinson does not value the crucifixion because Christ suffered it; rather, Christ is valued because he suffered crucifixion. No longer is "Our Lord" the center of time. His "Compound Witness" on the cross is unique only in that it made historically public the daily internal crucifixion all of us suffer. That "newer-nearer Crucifixion" which the poem finds most worthy of attention does not point to a more recent historical event but to the fulfillment of our deepest private selves, the "Being's Centre." Christ's agony in the garden at Gethsemane, his realization that he must suffer mortal destruction, is made universal. The pain of crucial life experiences affords each man a sense of his ending, a preview of his death. Yet our common agony, like Christ's, has a divine aspect; conversely, moments of awe as well as moments of despair are included in Dickinson's expanded notion of "agony": "I hope that nothing pains you except the pang of life, sweeter to bear than omit," Dickinson tells Maria Whitney in a late letter (L 815). And in a well-known poem, Dickinson considers "a certain Slant of light" as "An imperial affliction":

> Heavenly Hurt, it gives us—
> We can find no scar,
> But internal difference,
> Where the Meanings, are—

This "Hurt" foreshadows a personal ending (which may also be considered a new beginning) for

> When it goes, 'tis like the Distance
> On the look of Death—
>
> (258)

Death as antitype may be shaped variously—crucifixion is one possibility among many—but these poems define the crucial change in Dickinson's handling of typology. Personal death replaces Christ as the prime antitype; and personal states of consciousness, ecstatic or painful, replace historical events as the foreshadowing types. The self becomes type and antitype, its own future fulfillment.

Strangely, the vocabulary of Dickinson's typology is as conservative as its usage is audacious. In Christian typology, the antitypes are ready-made, defined by scriptural narratives; and the antitypes are often applied as propaganda, to subordinate competing myths and to borrow their power at once. This theological oneupmanship is perfectly

81

exampled in two stanzas of Crashaw's seventeenth-century translation
of St. Thomas's "Hymn for the Blessed Sacrament":

xii

Lo, the full, finall, Sacrifice
On which all figures fix't their eyes.
The ransom'd Isack, and his ramme;
The Manna, and the Paschal Lamb.

xiii

Jesu Master, Just and true!
Our Food, and faithfull Shephard too!
O by thy selfe vouchsafe to keep,
As with thy selfe thou feed'st thy Sheep.[5]

There is a hint here that the Old Testament types have been presump-
tuous and that Christian typology, by "fixing their eyes" to moments in
Christ's redemptive sacrifice, is putting them in their logical place. The
Old Testament images are treated almost as rudely as Crashaw's (and
Milton's) pagan gods who flee from Christ's incarnation. In short,
Christian typology, down to the expanded puritan version which often
subordinates all experiential life as well as other myths, settles questions. Dickinson's typology, varied and self-contradicting as its mani-
festations are, shapes questions out of many possible answers. She
cares little for scriptural authority and she exhibits no burning desire to
"spread the Word," especially since she often questions it. Death as
antitype can be structured in any way she chooses—and, remarkably,
she chooses to return to scripture. She coins no Emersonian "oversoul."
Crucifixion, the dust of the grave, resurrection, judgment, eternity,
immortality—the familiar language is sufficiently pliable to set up a
fruitful tension between traditional meanings and her own.[6]
   Dickinson herself stresses that the "chosen" nature of the return
makes all the difference:

I'm ceded—I've stopped being Theirs—
The name They dropped upon my face
With water, in the country church
Is finished using, now,
And They can put it with my Dolls,

> My childhood, and the string of spools,
> I've finished threading—too—

"Baptized, before, without the choice," Dickinson disowns the un-thinking "threading" assigned her by the culture into which she is born. That kind of belief is suitable to childhood, but the mature mind outgrows it:

> My second Rank—too small the first
> Crowned—Crowing—on my Father's breast—
> A half unconscious Queen—
> But this time—Adequate—Erect,
> With Will to choose, or to reject,
> And I choose, just a Crown—
>
> (508)

The mature mind does not necessarily choose a contradictory belief; yet if, with its newly "adequate, erect" self-conscious will, it returns to the old belief, that belief will not be the same, for it has been questioned and chosen. The mind has become large enough to contain the myth; the myth must become the supplicant. Thus, Dickinson can proclaim her spiritual sense as "Mine—here—in Vision—*and in Veto!*" (528, italics mine). To identify Dickinson's typology of death as Christian-derived in many of its aspects is less important than to identify its spirit as independent.[7]

Thus the old words take on a new status. They become stages in an extended quest of consciousness and as such they define the mental moods we live through. As Kenneth Burke argues,

> . . . whereas the words for the "supernatural" realm are necessarily borrowed from the realm of our everyday experiences, out of which our familiarity with language arises, once a terminology has been developed for special theological purposes the order can become reversed. We can borrow back the terms from the borrower, again secularizing to varying degrees the originally secular terms that had been given "supernatural" connotation.[8]

In Dickinson's typology, the "afterlife" is not only "after" but in, at least proleptically in, this life, this consciousness. The "afterlife" will not be absolutely new, but a fulfillment, a bared revelation. Death will reveal "How Conscious Consciousness—could grow—" (622). It is Dickinson's large idea of consciousness which enables the typology—otherwise type and antitype could not relate seriously:

Those not live yet
Who doubt to live again—
"Again" is of a twice
But this—is one—
The Ship beneath the Draw
Aground—is he?
Death—so—the Hyphen of the Sea—
Deep is the Schedule
Of the Disk to be—
Costumeless Consciousness—
That is he—

(1454)

If dissolution is the antitype, if the ship is finally grounded, then life is a type of meaninglessness and one never significantly lives. Yet Dickinson herself often "doubts to live" again, often wonders if the death of the grave precludes further consciousness. Late in her life, she questions her correspondent Charles Clark, "Are you certain there is another life? When overwhelmed to know, I fear that few are sure" (L 827). Dickinson can become one of the agnostics whom the persona of this poem disparages. The typology is based on an assumption of continuing consciousness which Dickinson herself can question. But one does not write poetry "when overwhelmed to know." The presence of a consciousness which will be revealed fully, costumeless, in death is Dickinson's chosen faith; nihilism is the alternative.

The poetic faith that "This World is not Conclusion," that "A Species stands beyond—" (501), that consciousness will continue in some increased form, shifts the question to the nature of the fulfillment. What will the newness be? Costumeless consciousness to be sure, but what will that mean? It is the very continuity of consciousness which makes its future a miracle and a fearful mystery:

This Consciousness that is aware
Of Neighbors and the Sun
Will be the one aware of Death
And that itself alone

Is traversing the interval
Experience between
And most profound experiment
Appointed unto Men—...

(822)

We do not know what will happen to that daily consciousness, "The Rumor's Gate was shut so tight" (1588). To Higginson, Dickinson writes, "we know that the mind of the Heart must live if its clerical part do not. Would you explain it to me?" (L 503). Higginson could not, of course; the question is rhetorical. "Philosophy—don't know—," Dickinson announces almost gleefully in "This World is not Conclusion." Neither does theology. That same poem which begins with such a buoyant statement of confidence in a continuing consciousness concludes with an eschatological version of Karl Marx's denunciation of religion as an opiate:

> Much Gesture, from the Pulpit—
> Strong Hallelujahs roll—
> Narcotics cannot still the Tooth—
> That nibbles at the soul—
>
> (501)

Even with the assumed given of a continuing consciousness, the typology of death appears doomed by an ignorance of the afterlife antitypes. But analogy, the language of surmise, can replace certitude:

> Of Paradise' existence
> All we know
> Is the uncertain certainty—
> But its vicinity infer,
> By its Bisecting
> Messenger—
>
> (1411)

The "Bisecting Messenger," death, blocks knowledge but spurs inference, and Dickinson's typology must be understood as analogical and inferential or else it will seem wild nonsense. Dickinson's typology constantly infers back and forth, from nature to the supernatural, from the supernatural to nature. That which is doubt when phrased conceptually provides a typological bonanza for poetic expression.

We have said what the typology is, but we have yet to explain why it is. What good does it do Dickinson or us? In its logical aspect, the typology fulfills a common human need, the need to organize and explain experience, to "get to the bottom" of things. Description does not fulfill this need. To get at a thing's "in itselfness," it must be defined by its substance, by what stands under it, the ground of its being. Paradoxically, one must explore what the thing is not. We are most familiar with familial definitions, definitions in which "the logically prior can be expressed in terms of the temporally prior."⁹ This "symbolic regression" is perhaps the prime technique of romantic definition, whether it takes the form of "the growth of a poet's mind" or of an orphan in search of a father, or of the beginnings of humanity, as in Byron's *Cain* and Keats's *Hyperion*. Familial definition is also a cornerstone of psychoanalytic theory. Freudians stress early experiences as formative; in fact one student of Freud, Otto Rank, organizes all psychological phenomena around the traumatic experience of birth. My point is that we are so used to definition-by-origin that we often neglect to see this kind of temporal definition as a cognitive choice, as one of many possibilities. For Dickinson, to whom "Adjourns—are all—" (L 229), familial definition is simply not appropriate. For her, end terms are central. Morning is apocalypse, noon is immortality, sunset confers "an ignorance... / Upon the Eye" like death (552), night is purgatory, sleep is Judgment. The second, defining terms of the metaphors are the "goals" of the first terms, temporally later and symbolically larger. Experiences are defined by what they lead toward. The present is defined by a projected future rather than a retrojected past. As Frank Kermode writes of supernatural fictions in general, "We project ourselves ... past the End, so as to see the structure whole, a thing we cannot do from our spot of time in the middle."¹⁰ Thus Dickinson's typology of death comforts "The Lonesome for they know not what" by the faith that our sense of a "missing something" is a temporary function of "middle time," that the blank will be filled by death.

In fact, the very idea of an epistemological completion in the future of consciousness provides a poetic ethic:

> The Province of the Saved
> Should be the Art—To save—
> Through Skill obtained in Themselves—
> The Science of the Grave
>
> No Man can understand
> But He that hath endured
> The Dissolution—in Himself
> That Man—be qualified
>
> To qualify Despair
> To Those who failing new—

Mistake Defeat for Death—Each time—
Till acclimated—to—
(539)

Only the man who has suffered the despair which foreshadows the death of the grave can differentiate between type and antitype, can convincingly give assurance of recovery, of "resurrection"—if only because he knows from his own painful experience that many terrible typological "endings" will precede the final death. Oppositely, and more positively, the typology vitalizes the daily life by constantly reminding consciousness of death's proximity. The dictum that "Each Second is the last / Perhaps" (879) is a goad to experience every second as fully as if it were the last.

There is one other reason for Dickinson's typology of death, and it has nothing to do with fears or ethics. Very simply, the typology provides an analogical playground for a connective mind. Whether a particular poem celebrates the link between nature and the supernatural or mourns the gulf between the two, whether the typology serves Dickinson's transcendental or skeptical thought, an element of wit remains constant and brings to mind the original meaning of "figura"—"something living and dynamic, incomplete and playful. "[11] This playfulness may seem to contradict Dickinson's avowal that death and resurrection constitute "no schoolboy's theme" just as it contradicts the earnest motivation of typological symbols as defined by Vico: "Their characteristic feature is that the thing represented must always be something very important and holy for those concerned, something affecting their whole life and thinking."[12] The contradiction is only apparent. It is resolved in Nietzsche's statement, "I know of no other way of coping with great tasks, than play."[13]

2

In a quasi-chronological manner, we are going to follow the course of a Dickinsonian death. At each stage of the death, we shall consider the emotions in Dickinsonian experience which foreshadow the antitype. While earlier we concerned ourselves with how Dickinson makes connections, now we will be concerned with what she connects and why.

We begin the narrative with the persona in black, standing at the grave to mourn the death of a loved one. Though Dickinson's truncated elegies do not often include such elegiac conventions as the invocation to the muse, the critique of the clergy, or the sympathetic lament of nature,

87

they do continue one great elegiac tradition: the focus of interest is on the mourner rather than on the mourned. In fact, Dickinson usually does not name, even by conventional epithets, the particular friend who has died.

The euphemism for "died" is "gone away"; Dickinson's type for the death of a friend is the geographical separation of friends in life. In itself, the equation of separation and death is hardly surprising. The fear that a loved one with whom we cannot communicate is in dire straits is a commonplace irrationality. The Civil War, which took place during Dickinson's most prolific years of creation, could only exaggerate the fear that "going away" was a preparation for death, since many Amherst friends did "go away" and then "were gone" forever. But Dickinson's equation of separation and death, of missing and mourning, begins much earlier, at age twenty in a letter to her close friend Jane Humphrey: "When I knew Vinnie [Lavinia, Emily's sister, who was away at school] must go I clung to you as the dearer than ever friend—but when the grave opened—and swallowed you both—I murmured—and thought I had a right to—I hav'nt changed my mind yet—either" (L 30). Dickinson here insists that, for all practical purpose, leave-taking *is* death; at least, it appears so to the one left behind, desolate. "I would have you here, all here," Dickinson tells another youthful friend, Abiah Root, "where I can *see* you, and *hear* you, and where I can say 'Oh, no,' if the 'Son of Man' ever 'cometh'!"(L 39). Jesus as the "Son of Man," as a symbol of mortality, here precludes the thought of Christ as the resurrected Son of God, and the mourner of absences is afflicted with the same helplessness and guilt that we usually associate with the elegiac mourner.

The surprising aspect of this equation between geographical and eschatological separations—one must imagine the great appeal the pun had for Dickinson in closing such a gap of meaning—is the extraordinary versatility Dickinson develops from it. We can infer the range of its applicability from this enigmatic linking:

> The Days that we can spare
> Are those a *Function* die
> Or *Friend* or *Nature*— ...
> (1184, italics mine)

Leaving aside for a moment the meaning of that odd word "function," we can focus first on the way "friends" die in the poetry. Here, usually, Dickinson begins by thinking of death as a special kind of absence.

88

Then, in a self-criticism typical of her skeptical world, she will criticize the figure of separation as absolutely insufficient. For instance, the comfort given a child by the euphemism "gone away" itself gives way to fear and awe as the journey is reinterpreted:

> I noticed People disappeared
> When but a little child—
> Supposed they visited remote
> Or settled Regions wild—
> Now know I—They both visited
> And settled Regions wild.
> But did because they died
> A Fact withheld the little child—
> (1149)

The substitution of the fact "died" for the surmised "disappeared" changes the sense of the journey so completely that Dickinson has only to repeat the exact words which describe a pioneer adventure to describe a vision of Eternity. Here the antitype is the grown-up version of the child's type, but elsewhere innocence may be retrieved in maturity as a rationalization to deny the "Fact":

> We'll pass without the parting
> So to spare
> Certificate of Absence—
> Deeming where
>
> I left Her I could find Her
> If I tried—
> This way, I keep from missing
> Those that died.
> (996)

The willfully delusive speaker not only wishes to deny the antitype; she wants to pretend that the absence is on her part, that she has put away her friend like a discarded doll which can be found and picked up once more. This refusal to write an elegy, to acknowledge the special nature of this absence, is so self-consciously transparent that it only emphasizes the absolute finality it pretends to deny. "There must be both similarities and differences between a type and its antitype," writes the Milton scholar William G. Madsen.[14] It is the emotional difficulty of admitting

89

the difference between separation and death, missing and mourning, that Dickinson here dramatizes.

Occasionally, in order to negate that emotional difficulty, Dickinson will evolve a traditional Christian consolation. Since the absent return in life, these poems reason, why not those who are absent because of death? To her absent brother Austin, Dickinson writes, "none of us are gone where we cannot come home again, and the separations *here* are but for a little while" (L 104). The death-separation, she implies, is only longer. By extension, since the dead are only somewhere else, why will I not rejoin them when I die? Dickinson thus projects a heaven of restored personal relations. "Fleshless Lovers" meet for a "second time" before "the Judgment Seat of God" and, this time, they wed (625). Unfortunately, when such a poem asks, "Was Bridal—e'er like This?" we are all too tempted to answer in the negative. Likewise, in "There Came a Day at Summer's full," a single day of love, a summer day so "full" that it is described as a form of immortality in time, ends in a separation whose finality is denied:

> And so when all the time had leaked,
> Without external sound,
> Each bound the Other's Crucifix—
> We gave no other Bond—
>
> Sufficient troth, that we shall rise
> Deposed—at length, the Grave—
> To that new Marriage,
> Justified—through Calvaries of Love—
>
> (322)

There is nothing inherently wrong with this fiction. I do not wish to deny Dante his vision of Beatrice, or Goethe's Faust his reunion with the soul of Gretchen. But what works in fleshed out, expansive epics does not work well in Dickinson's tight and tough lyrics. We do not experience, as in Faust, final triumph at the end of an arduous, tragic journey. We feel only that Dickinson is ignoring the questions she has posed, that she is eschewing the grief which is "so appalling—it exhilarates—" for an easy, opulent truth, a rationalization stated as a doctrine. Dickinson here resembles Dante less than Dante Gabriel Rossetti at his worst.

Nonetheless, this too-easy denial of death's terrifying finality can create powerful poems when it is not allowed to become a flat-footed article of faith. It can become a proud and fierce assertion of human over supernatural values:

> God is indeed a jealous God—
> He cannot bear to see
> That we had rather not with Him
> But with each other play.
>
> (1719)

God as a lonesome Nobodaddy kills us for company, and Dickinson's revenge is to create a supernatural fiction in which we continue to play with each other. Her bereft robin does not fly into the unknown expressly to reach paradise but what paradise may contain:

> She does not know a Route
> But puts her Craft about
> For *rumored* Springs—
> She does not ask for Noon—
> She does not ask for Boon,
> Crumbless and homeless, of but one request—
> The Birds she lost—
>
> (1606)

The robin heads for rumored eternal springs not to gain happiness or immortality but to get back what has been taken from her, the objects of her greatest affection in life. The poem presents an earned heterodoxy, earned through desolation. It is less a critique of God than a hymn to love.

In other words, this vision of an immortal family reunion becomes powerful when it is stated not by Dickinson's oracular bard but by her confessional sufferer. As a consolatory fib, the reunion fiction leads away from Dickinson's serious thought. But when the sufferer voices the fiction as a desire, as a means to express grief rather than to negate it by projecting an overly fleshy fleshlessness, then it reflects back on the separation-death typology and reminds us of the passionate feelings of loss contained in that intellectual equation. At such times, it expresses the immortal "mind of the heart."

The extension of the typology to nature is easy, though it involves a paradox:

> There comes a warning like a spy
> A shorter breath of Day
> A stealing that is not a stealth
> And Summers are away—
>
> (1536)

91

Both death and separation are figurative here. Days begins to die as daylight dwindles, and their "shorter breath" (a nice pun on "breadth") synecdochically warns that summers are departing. Of course, it is a stealing-away which literally is not a stealth, for, unlike the dead departed, seasons will return. The cyclicity of nature thus may raise the specters of absence and death only to deny them.

The typology's application to "functions" is more intricate. If we take "functions" to mean not physical capabilities but relational emotions, we discover Dickinson's social definition of absence. The type of separation takes another antitype, the death of affection:

> Now I knew I lost her—
> Not that she was gone—
> But Remoteness travelled
> On her Face and Tongue.
>
> Alien, though adjoining
> As a Foreign Race—
> Traversed she though pausing
> Latitudeless Place....
>
> (1219)

The persona mourns the loss of a friend, a loss manifested in neither absence nor death but in a new and dismaying loss of feeling for the speaker on the friend's part. We can pity that middle term of "separation" almost as much as we pity the persona of this poem. We have seen the separation typology skillfully employed only to be subsequently criticized for its rationalization of the "fact" of death; now it is employed with great concision—"Remoteness travelled" is as neat a paradox as any of Donne's, with the nominative quality of absence actively absenting itself in the verb—only to be criticized for its literal, spatial rendering of a change from one to another emotional, and thus nonspatial, "Latitudeless Place." The ending of a relationship in indifference, like the ending of life in death, is more totally devastating than mere physical separation. "Love's transmigration," as the poem goes on to term the antitype, is as final as the transmigration of souls.

This use of the typology to characterize an alteration of feeling suggests a more metaphysical reason for Dickinson's equation of separation and death. The dead are separate not only in that they are gone but in that they are terribly incommunicative, gone beyond what we can know. When the loved one's "Clock stopped," he became unknowable in temporal, human terms:

> Decades of Arrogance between
> The Dial life—
> And Him—
>
> (287)

If we adopt a "supernatural" belief, we can know only that the dead are metaphysically powerful; but from a natural point of view, their "sea change" is simply grotesque and negative. The dead are separate in that they can participate no longer in human life, they are "dead" to common joys. In a poem which begins "As far from pity, as complaint," the metaphysical distance traveled is from, not to, the most highly valued condition:

> To eyelids in the Sepulchre—
> How dumb the Dancer lies—
> While Color's Revelations break—
> And blaze—the Butterflies!
>
> (496)

Here the dead are simply petrified. They create no awe for themselves but only for what they lack, the resplendent, dynamic life of nature. In these opposing visions of the dead, we see most clearly the typology's function. It does not solve the impossible problem, but it raises and shapes the issue: "of the Separated Parties / Which be out of sight?" (1061). Life or death—which is the supreme term? Dickinson's poems can be thought of as conflicting answers to an unanswerable question.

This "certain uncertainty" makes a final extension of the separation-mourning typology all the more surprising. Metaphysical self-debates may yet issue in a single-minded social criticism. Dickinson's ironic view of the funereal honoring of the dead is based on her idea of the dead as metaphysically gone. It makes little difference whether the dead are too buried or too lifted; they no longer can be helped by human affection. Worse, the attention paid the corpse is often an attempt to make up for past neglect of the living body. "I fear my congratulation, like repentance according to Calvin, is too late to be plausible," Dickinson writes to Mrs. Edward Tuckerman in reference to an unknown occasion (L 406). Love for the dead suffers from the same bad timing:

> 'Tis easier to pity those when dead
> That which pity previous
> Would have saved—
> A Tragedy enacted—

Secures Applause
That Tragedy enacting
Too seldom does.

(1698)

If, as I have suggested, the separation-death typology stems from a common neurosis, it grows into a fully rational ethical strategy: to imagine those near and alive always about to leave so as to give the tender elegiac consideration to those who most need it, to ourselves who are "dying in Drama" (531) all our lives.

3

It is the middlemost moment in her narrative of doom, the very act of dying, that most fires Dickinson's imagination. From that moment evolve two great and troubled masterpieces: "I heard a Fly buzz—when I died" and "I felt a Funeral, in my Brain." To get at these crucial poems, we must consider a group of lesser, but fully remarkable, poems which form a bridge between the elegiac analogy of separation and death and the analogy which informs the two masterpieces, an analogy between psychological pain and one's own death.

These are "Hamlet" poems, in which the mourner typologically leaps into the grave. That is, the mourner, by a psychological metaphor, imitates the death of the loved one; and, like him, the mourner achieves a completed understanding through an intensity of pain. We die only once, but before that we project ourselves into death many times, whenever another "leaves" or dies: "Parting is one of the exactions of a Mortal Life," Dickinson writes to Mrs. Holland. "It is bleak—like Dying, but occurs more times" (L 399). The distance between the type of separation and the antitype of death—now, one's own death—is closed.

There is nothing luxuriously altruistic in this extreme empathy; it is based on the fact of mortality, the fact that the mourner, too, will die. Thus in one poem Dickinson has us peer into an "Ebon Box" filled with mementos of the dead—withered flowers, yellow letters, antique trinkets, a curl. Symbols of dead nature, dead youth, dead affections, and human death itself are contained in that box, and yet we shut it again, "As if the little Ebon Box / Were none of our affair!" (169). As if . . . and yet that box both contains our past and foreshadows our fate, when we too will be placed in a larger ebon box. The persona who typologically dies in contemplating actual death represents Dickinson's attempt to make the ebon box her affair.

In short, "Looking at Death, is Dying—" (281). Yet, however ghastly this magical equation appears, it allows an opportunity for Dickinson's oracle as well as for her sufferer. Identification in itself is a triumph of thought. At first, the mourner feels stranded and cheated, for the dead may be beyond, as well as beneath, nature:

> I had no Cause to be awake—
> My Best—was gone to sleep—
> And Morn a new politeness took—
> And failed to wake them up—
>
> . . . .
>
> I looked at Sunrise—Once—
> And then I looked at Them—
> And wishfulness in me arose—
> For Circumstance the same—. . .

We seem to have a classic case of the death-wish, and finally the wish seems to be fulfilled: "I struggled—and was There—." Our speaker appears to have chosen death over life, to be speaking back at us from the beyond. But I have omitted two lines which change the poem's meaning entirely:

> Sweet Morning—When I oversleep—
> Knock—Recollect—to Me—
>
> I looked at Sunrise—Once—. . .
>
> (542)

The whole point is that in the life, the "Sweet Morning," of thought, one does not have to die to put oneself in the death condition. The persona asks the morning to remind him of an ability which allows thought to go beyond its condition. In one aspect, the poem is an argument against suicide. The typology makes suicide superfluous.

More specifically, the imitation of the dead allows for an epistemological expansion:

> There is a finished feeling
> Experienced at Graves—
> A leisure of the Future—
> A Wilderness of Size.

95

By Death's bold Exhibition
Preciser what we are
And the Eternal function
Enabled to infer.

(856)

Here the language which describes the dead one's "finished" condition
also describes the mourner's new sense of things. His woe equally
plunges him into that "Wilderness of Size" experienced in journeying
other worlds; and that submission of will, that "leisure of the Future,"
allows him to see both this world and the whole with a more detached
and daring intelligence.

The dead are both cold and transcendent, under the ground and
beyond the sky. The imitative mourner undergoes a similarly mixed
fate. His woe paralyzes and enlarges him. In "A Coffin—is a small
Domain," Dickinson plays not only on this compound of loss and gain
but also on the likeness of the mourner and the mourned:

> A Grave—is a restricted Breadth—
> Yet ampler than the Sun—
> And all the Seas He populates
> And Lands He looks upon
>
> To Him who on its small Repose—
> Bestows a single Friend—
> Circumference without Relief—
> Or Estimate—or End—
>
> (943)

Dickinson's syntactical shock-tactic here is to set up the earlier stanza
as though it refers to the body in the coffin and then to disclose in the
final stanza that she is describing instead (or in addition) the condition
of the mourner who places the friend on the coffin-bed. The coffin's
narrow space nonetheless contains the largest possibility, an immortality which dwarfs nature. Just so, thoughts of the coffin on the
mourner's part give him the largest range of speculation—too large,
"without Relief," to be suitably comforting. Even the enlargement of
consciousness may be more torturous than benevolent. Dickinson
reaches the only possible conclusion about this identificatory, typological death of the mourner in a poem which recalls the death of two
friends. It begins, in absolute identification, "My life closed twice
before its close—" and concludes,

> Parting is all we know of heaven,
> And all we need of hell.
>   (1732)

In these poems, a hell of woe is the only way to a heaven of thought. The pain of the mourner is only one of many psychological "dyings." To Mrs. Holland, Dickinson writes, "I suppose there are depths in every Consciousness, from which we cannot rescue ourselves—to which none can go with us—which represent to us Mortally—the Adventure of Death" (L 555). Any depth in consciousness whose exploration pains and yet enlarges the persona may be considered a type of dying.

The equation of an enlightening anguish and actual death depends on a simple pun of logic which results from what Kenneth Burke calls "the temporalizing of essence." That which is beyond experience, afterlife, also may be considered life's essence, the non-being which creates being. It may be spatialized as another world, but that other world need not take the form of a Christian heaven. Richard Poirier has written in detail about the quest of American romantics to find other worlds *in* experience.[15] That is, essence can be detemporalized and respatialized, within consciousness:

> I like a look of Agony,
> Because I know it's true—
> Men do not sham Convulsion,
> Nor simulate, a Throe—
>
> The Eyes glaze once—and that is Death—
> Impossible to feign
> The Beads upon the Forehead
> By homely Anguish strung.
>   (241)

Both agony and death eliminate facade, and that link permits Dickinson to modulate almost imperceptively her descriptions of the two states. Since dying is regarded primarily as a moment in consciousness, death may be regarded as merely an external show of agony. The capitalization of "Agony" reminds us of the word's biblical sense, Christ's foreknowledge of his crucifixion, and thus emphasizes the link between a present psychological condition and a future physical correlative.

Crucifixion, with its edifying pain, becomes a plural event, even a continuing condition of life; and death may be regarded variously as its fulfillment or as just another version of it. In the latter case, type and antitype exchange positions, as in a poem where the persona tells a master-figure why she will not die for him:

> The Dying, is a trifle, past,
> But living, this include
> The dying multifold—without
> The Respite to be dead.
>
> (1013)

The typological fulfillment of dying leads to relief, while the endless type of daily anguish demands continual self-sacrifice.[16]

One final point before we consider the two great poems. Dickinson's emphasis on pain has nothing to do with a willed masochism. Whatever oracular benefits accrue as a result, self-crucifixion is not chosen; it is a condition of being alive, a law of life, possibly even a divine intention:

> He fumbles at your Soul
> As Players at the Keys
> Before they drop full Music on—
> He stuns you by degrees—
> Prepares your brittle Nature
> For the Ethereal Blow
> By fainter Hammers—further heard—
> Then nearer—Then so slow
> Your Breath has time to straighten—
> Your Brain—to bubble Cool—
> Deals—One—imperial—Thunderbolt
> That scalps your naked Soul—
>
> When Winds take Forests in their Paws—
> The Universe—is still—
>
> (315)

In this analogical collection, the master-figure is deliberately ambiguous, because his—or His—identity doesn't matter. Dickinson does not worry the cause but the experiencing of the terrible moment. The master-figure is pianist, smithy, Thor, and wind; the self is the pounded piano, the tempered metal, scalped tree, and wind-pawed forest. Active terms develop out of each other (pianists and smithies are both "pounding" forces, and in the poem both begin their action quietly and then decisively crescendo) and passive terms fade into each other (brain, soul, and forests somehow equate as the "preparation" continues). But the poem achieves its effect by maintaining a clear distinction between active and passive terms. If Whitman's persona is Walt, the personified walker down open roads, dream-visitor and flower-plucker, Dickinson's persona is contrastingly passive and synecdochic, a supersensitive *soul* whose destiny is not to be achieved but suffered.

In "He fumbles at your Soul," it is difficult to decide whether the active force's preparatory visits are benevolent foreshadowings of a final transcendent anguish or extended tortures progressing to a cruel climax. Images of creation and destruction alternate, and the final term in the coda is silence. Once again, we are faced with Dickinson's double vision. Anguish is defined by the actual horror of dying consciously, and yet this horror is a grace, an agonizing growth.

Dickinson's two finest poems of dying emphasize different aspects of this compound of pain and power along with a double sense of loss and gain. In "I heard a Fly buzz—when I died," we are placed at the pole of the antitype; there is no ostensible suggestion that the poem is describing anything "earlier" than how the mind feels when it dies. Yet the scene of this "last onset" is so exclusively the mind that it cannot help suggesting figural, experiential states of consciousness. Thus Dickinson insists that the posthumous voice can remain to speak with us, though logically it should be gone and silent. Her justification is that the voice, by hyperbole, speaks to our living condition.

The voice begins by attempting to define the peculiarity of its moment:

> I heard a Fly buzz—when I died—
> The Stillness in the Roon
> Was like the Stillness in the Air—
> Between the Heaves of Storm—
> (465)

We know nothing about the fly's buzz yet except that its sound stands out against a background of silence.[17] The room is silent because the persona is nowhere—this is a special moment between the "heave" of life and the renewed "heave" of whatever lies beyond. If death is but "the Hyphen of the Sea," this slowed moment is the experiencing of that hyphen. However sanguine consciousness has been and will be, this is a painful moment of suspense, of a suspense "hostiler than Death—" (705), as Dickinson elsewhere says. We may visualize this moment by its description in an analogous poem:

'Tis Miracle before Me—then—
'Tis Miracle behind—between—
A Crescent in the Sea—
With Midnight to the North of Her—
And Midnight to the South of Her—
And Maelstrom—in the Sky—
(721)

This very serious and very playful parody of Tennyson's "Charge of the Light Brigade" similarly creates a frozen moment of crisis. "Myself— the Term between—" is compared to a waning moon fallen into the sea which is confronted by a maelstrom risen into the sky. With the help of this gaudier, nearly surreal imagery, we can predict two aspects of "I heard a Fly buzz" from its first stanza: an idea of dislocation, both sensory and metaphysical, as the persona is stalled between worlds; and a stress on what is being lost rather than on what is to come, since neither the psychological realism of the presentation nor the oppressive closeness of the moment it presents will allow for speculations on the "thereafter."

In the second stanza, this world seems to be coming apart for the persona:

The Eyes around—had wrung them dry—
And Breaths were gathering firm
For that last Onset—when the King
Be witnessed—in the Room—

The mourners are seen by the dying persona in synecdoche and metonymy. They are eyes that act like hands or towels, breaths that "gather firm" like a phalanx of soldiers. The shaken persona sees a mechanical world part by part. Her crisis is all the more evident in distinction to the onlookers' ability to collect themselves, their luxury to be philosophical.

While the onlookers "collect," the persona gives away:

I willed my Keepsakes—Signed away
What portion of me be
Assignable—and then it was
There interposed a Fly—

The willing of parts of the self as keepsakes suggests a preparation for the meeting with God, for that moment described by another poem:

Typology of Death, I: Dickinson in Black

When the Judged,
His action laid away,
Divested is of every Disk
But his sincerity . . . .
(1671)

At this point in the poem, all is going according to plan. The mourners
are consoled and rewarded, the dying one is prepared to die. But as
everyone waits for the king, "There interposed a Fly—"

With Blue—uncertain stumbling Buzz—
Between the light—and me—
And then the Windows failed—and then
I could not see to see—
(465)

The functions of the fly are so various that one is tempted to imitate
J. L. Lowes's *Road to Xanadu* and write *The Flight of the Fly*. First, the
fly is a dramatic disappointment. We expected a king, and so the
passage from the world becomes pathetic in a macabre way.[18] However
royal one may yet become through death, its onset is purely physical
and negative. (The world will end not with a bang but with a buzz.) In
addition, though the fly seems to bring or at least focus death, its
buzzing flight represents natural vitality and thus emphasizes the
persona's paralysis.[19] Finally, this fly is a past and future annoyance.
Dickinson does not like flies in her life, and when she wishes to suggest
doubt about an afterlife, insects often come to mind.[20] This fly's very
buzz is "uncertain," and since the persona is frantically externalizing
her experience in the final stanza, the uncertainty may be her own.[21]

We should consider that externalized failure of sight more fully. The
fly's "blue buzz" simply continues the poem's synaesthesia, a synaesthesia which is equally a sign of Dickinson's brilliant, and her persona's
confused, perception.[22] But it is when phenomena begin to fade that we
fully realize Dickinson's audacity in placing the voice within the dying
process, in seeing the change of phenomena from inside the victim.
Pathetically, the victim pretends it is "the windows" that are failing.
The final admission, "I could not see to see," is a direct refutation of
the "compound vision" Dickinson elsewhere imagines for the dying
one:

'Tis Compound Vision—
Light—enabling Light—

101

Chapter Five

The Finite—furnished
With the Infinite
Convex and Concave Witness—
Back—toward Time—
And forward—
Toward the God of Him—

(906)

'Tis compound blindness here. Instead of seeing both worlds linked, the persona in "I heard a Fly buzz" sees neither. The voice stays with the body electric as the electricity shuts off. The poem ends and we are left, quite literally, in limbo.

Why would Dickinson write such a poem? Granted that the moment of dying is of interest, does it deserve a poem quite so good as this one? The answer, of course, is that the poem concerns more than that moment. It is one of Dickinson's attempts to take account, to force her otherworldly imagination to admit earthly realities.[23] Paradise may or may not be achieved, but the wall of death first intercedes and a functioning nihilism is not pleasant. It is not intellectually pleasant either, for the poem admits the uncertainty of those supernatural inferences on which Dickinson's entire typology is built. We earlier qualified the poet's statement, "When overwhelmed to know, I fear that few are sure," by saying that poetry, after all, is not "overwhelmed to know." But in this poem Dickinson deliberately creates a persona who is so overwhelmed and who gains no certainty. I hesitate to read this poem more typologically, as a description of the onset of anguish, because such a reading seems too inferential for a poem which implicitly criticizes inference. But we may speculate that Dickinson is simultaneously dramatizing experiential pain and loss.[24] Perhaps anguish will prove edifying, but at its first moment it simply swamps consciousness. "I heard a Fly buzz" stresses the hurt of pain, the finality of death, the blank of uncertainty. It is the climactic poem of Dickinson's world of veto.

It is strange to say that a poem which begins "I felt a Funeral, in my Brain," will prove relatively optimistic, but such is the case. The typology is in full play here; in fact, the poem depends on a total merger of the type of anxiety and the antitype of actual death. This procedure is established in the first line. "Felt" is a sensory reaction, "Funeral" is a public ritual not usually "felt" and certainly not "in my Brain," which in any case we do not usually think of as a "feeling" instrument. The way in which we read this first line determines the way we read the strangely literal yet internalized burial which follows, though the confusions of categories in the first line refuse to provide us with a single situation. Who is this "I"? Is he himself dead? Is he attending the funeral of a loved one? Is he simply creating an extended analogy for a crucial change in his consciousness? For years, critics have argued the merits of these "solutions" while the real solution is in the problem. A major alteration in consciousness *is* death, an ending and a beginning; differentiations are irrelevant. Whether this "death" is caused by a physical change, by sorrow for another's death, or by a terrible, unspecified event in one's own emotional life, the result "in my Brain" is identical. The technique is Dickinson's version of solecism, that willful jumble of words and tenses which Sir Thomas Browne considered the only proper way to describe eternity.

Given this ambiguous funeral which is a burial service both for the physical body and for ordinary, reasoning consciousness (the mind's more "material" part, perhaps), the poem can be literal and surreal at once:

> I felt a Funeral, in my Brain,
> And Mourners to and fro
> Kept treading—treading—till it seemed
> That Sense was breaking through—
>
> And when they all were seated,
> A Service, like a Drum—
> Kept beating—beating—till I thought
> My Mind was going numb—
>
> And then I heard them lift a Box
> And creak across my Soul
> With those same Boots of Lead, again,...

All of the poem's confusions of categories tend to destroy the dichotomy between an inner psychological event and an external social ceremony. The treading of the mourners, so real that it is onomatopoetically repeated, is like sense breaking through. Typologically, just as mourners and the funeral service attempt to bring reason to bear on the unreasonable, so the consciousness which has been jolted in some way by experience tries, with equal futility, to hold itself within bounds, to dam the flood tides of its irrational thoughts.[25] If that procedure fails, the mind attempts the defense of thought-canceling denial. And in the second stanza the insistently dull service plays this role "on the outside." But these tactics pain more than they comfort. The grotesque image of a corpse which is still conscious, perhaps more conscious than ever before, as it undergoes its own funeral is yet another imaging of the maelstrom-moment "Between the Heaves of Storm," the moment when it is "too late for Man— / But early, yet, for God—" (623). This corpse *connaissant* serves as an antitype for a consciousness prepared to go beyond itself but stranded, restricted by its own rational part. Thus the soul—the floor of the church and the substance of the mind— is pounded by those "Boots of Lead" which the mourners wear as they carry the body to the grave. We noted earlier Dickinson's sense of the inappropriateness of funeral ceremonies. Here the funeral, linked to the rationalizing tendencies of the mind, is so inappropriate as to become a torture. Comfort is excruciating. This body can be physical no longer, let it go; this consciousness can reason no longer in its old way, let it let itself go.[26]

As the serious inappropriateness of the funeral reaches a climax, the stranded consciousness is finally freed:

> Then Space—began to toll,
>
> As all the Heavens were a Bell,
> And Being, but an Ear,
> And I, and Silence, some strange Race
> Wrecked, solitary, here—
>
> And then a Plank in Reason, broke.
> And I dropped down, and down—
> And hit a World, at every plunge,
> And Finished knowing—then—
>
> (280)

First, the persona's alienation from life becomes absolute. In a letter to Mrs. Holland, Dickinson describes "Memory" as "a strange Bell— Jubilee, and Knell" (L 792). But in the poem the dying persona has gone beyond such an act of ordinary, if heightened, consciousness. All experiential space is a bell, all experiential being is the ability to hear, while the stranded consciousness is suited only to a nonspatial realm of silence. The conclusion of another poem which conceives of the grave as the antithesis of sound and time (and therefore space) can amplify this situation:

> By Clocks, 'twas Morning and for Night
> The Bells at Distance called—

But Epoch had no basis here
For Period exhaled.

(1159)

The metaphysical indecorum of the funeral threatens to leave the corpse in even a worse limbo than that in "I heard a Fly buzz." But then, almost luckily, "a Plank in Reason," the floor or ground of sequential being, breaks. The coffin is lowered into a grave with no bottom; the mind falls through ontological realms until mentality itself is left behind. The journey becomes inexpressible because it goes beyond conceptualization. Beyond, above, beneath the floor of reason, somewhere else, the persona travels through realms of silence; wherever those realms are and whatever values are attached to this journey, the persona is being transported to a final eschatological place and to a final circumference of expanded or violated consciousness.

It is essential not to attach values to this finale because the poem is saying that any human values are simply inapplicable. Clark Griffith attempts to read the poem as a description of approaching insanity and to consider the final chaotic fall as the descent of the mind into madness. It is possible, typologically, to think of the finale as a descent into the unconscious, so long as we remember that "the unconscious" did not exist as a connotative word for a pre-Freudian romantic like Dickinson, and that the mind's most buried self can be conceived of, by Freudians and romantics alike, as destructive *and as creative*. But it is more helpful not to color the finale in pejorative terms at all. The final "—then—" after the mind finishes knowing, as Griffith argues, "marks off the communicable part of the process" but not "from an aftermath which could be expressed only through the shriek, or gibberish, or wild, undifferentiated raving."[27] The men in white coats are not coming to carry Emily away. Rather, the aftermath cannot be expressed by very definition, for it is absolute silence and any conceptualization of what comes after "knowing" is finished would be a falsification.

"I felt a Funeral, in my Brain" is a particularly bare poem. As a psychological poem, it will tell us nothing about the situation which causes the funeral. The cause, after all, may be joyful:

Since Grief and Joy are done
So similar—An Optizan
Could not decide between.
(329)

105

Characteristically, Dickinson is more interested in how the emotion is "done" in consciousness than in its specific origin. It is intense and that is enough. Similarly, the final fall *could* be glossed as a climax of triumphant joy as well as a climax of horror. A sense of the bottom falling out from under is often a sign of terrifying joy rather than of grief:

> I can wade Grief—
> Whole Pools of it—
> I'm used to that—
> But the least push of Joy
> Breaks up my feet—
> And I tip—drunken—...

And though we cannot ignore the pain expressed in the poem, "Power is only Pain—" (252). The final fall may be glossed by other poems which stress either pain or power,[28] but the end of "I felt a Funeral, in my Brain" is free of the judgments these poems make. Only one other Dickinson poem is comparable but more explicit. Its opening, "It was not Death, for I stood up," more explicitly merges an experiential state of consciousness with dying. The basic question—am I alive or dead?— suggests a confusion caused by an extreme psychological condition, that same condition which is suggested more elliptically by the phrase "I felt a Funeral in my Brain." Likewise, the ending of "It was not Death," in which another burial occurs, simply restates the conclusion of knowing in "I felt a Funeral" and more overtly criticizes attempts to define this condition:

> But, most, like Chaos—Stopless—cool—
> Without a Chance, or Spar—
> Or even a Report of Land—
> To justify—Despair.
>
> (510)

Here, too, the persona is reporting only the impossibility of describing in notional, experiential terms a state which is sub- or super-notional. Likewise, human emotions like despair are irrelevant in a realm of chaos, for despair depends on expectation, and expectation depends on a possible ordering of events. In "I felt a Funeral, in my Brain," the dying mind falls into neither a heaven nor a hell but into a somewhere which is beyond the realm of language. The poem is not more optimistic than "I heard a Fly buzz" because it projects a sublime paradise, real or psychological; its silence criticizes such predictions, at least when a first-person speaker within the drama is "overwhelmed to know." It is a more optimistic poem only in that it affirms a continuing adventure of consciousness. Its limbo, at least, is vital.

This minimal, hard-won belief, often interrupted by doubt but always reasserting itself, that vitality continues, transformed, after death, and in life increases through awe and pain, is sufficient. It is sufficient to keep Dickinson on the path of discovery, even when that path leads beyond the known and the mind transgresses the bounds of safety. It is this willingness to persevere in danger which earns Dickinson's quest toward silence the spiritual-sounding name she once gave it, "the White Exploit" (922).

6

A Typology of Death, II: Dickinson in White

Earth *is a merry damsel, and* heaven *a knight so true*
And Earth is quite coquettish, and beseemeth in vain to sue.
—From Dickinson's first poem

1

The narrative of death can continue after "knowing" is "finished"
only by contemplating that ending within endings. The typology again
transforms its terms. After death, the grave; "After great pain, a
formal feeling comes—":

> The Nerves sit ceremonious, like Tombs—
> The stiff Heart questions, was it He, that bore,
> And Yesterday, or Centuries before?
>
> The Feet, mechanical, go round—
> Of Ground, or Air, or Ought—
> A Wooden way
> Regardless grown,
> A Quartz contentment, like a stone—
>
> This is the Hour of Lead—
> Remembered, if outlived,
> As Freezing persons, recollect the Snow—
> First—Chill—then Stupor—then the letting go—
>
> (341)

The antitype of the grave fulfills two interconnected types. Its psychological type is the aftermath of pain, when the whole physical system goes into a state of paralyzed shock. The pain has been too great, it has burned out the body electric. The entombed, silenced consciousness affords rest, but only the rest of final failure and indifference. "Anguish has but so many throes—," Dickinson once wrote in a note to herself, "then Unconsciousness seals it" (L, p. 922). Time does not expand to timelessness for the living dead; it simply becomes meaningless. All meanings, all aspirations, all duties (a loose translation "Of Ground, or Air, or Ought") become "regardless," indifferent.

Thus the grave houses not only a frozen, unresponsive non-person but also a destructive skepticism. For Dickinson, the grave represents both emotional fatigue and spiritual doubt. But the grave has a beneficent underside. In "I heard a Fly buzz" and "I felt a Funeral, in my Brain," knowing stops at the grave. The grave may create and represent doubts, but in doing so it reminds the imagination of its limitations. It pulls back the arm of an overreaching fiction and makes it earn its way. More positively, the grave may not be a final failure at all; the type of anomie may be "outlived" just as "The Dust—connect —and live" in resurrection (515). "Christ robs the Nest" of death (153); the grave has a "Tunnel" (1652). The grave and the paralyzed consciousness constitute Dickinson's vision of what Christians have called purgatory and existentialists the void. (Interestingly, Dickinson's grave is at once more otherworldly than the Christian purgatory of lifelike tortures and more existentially real than the existential void.) The purgatorial grave, if permanent, becomes Dickinson's vision of hell, a permanent end to consciousness. And the grave, if only temporary, must yet be passed through; its types of limitation, doubt, and emotional paralysis must by taken into account as qualificatory notes, even if those notes head toward a supreme fiction.

Dickinson's two great visions of the grave have suffered more misreadings than nearly any of the other poems. The first, which frequently has been interpreted as almost excessively pious, is instead a terrifying vision of the grave as a possibly permanent hell.[1] "Safe in their Alabaster Chambers" questions the certainty of the Resurrection and thus many of the assumptions on which the later, "immortal" stage of Dickinson's typology rests:

> Safe in their Alabaster Chambers—
> Untouched by Morning
> And untouched by Noon—

Sleep the meek members of the Resurrection—
Rafter of satin,
And Roof of stone.

Light laughs the breeze
In her Castle above them—
Babbles the Bee in a stolid Ear,
Pipe the Sweet Birds in ignorant cadence—
Ah, what sagacity perished here!

(216, first version)[2]

This first version of the poem is simple, ironic, and horrifying. Of the first verse, Dickinson's future sister-in-law, Susan, tells her, "I always go to the fire and get warm after thinking of it, but I never *can* again."[3] These are cold saints indeed. Their purity is surpassed only by their deafness to nature. "Alabaster" implies purity but "Chambers" suggests ponderous stolidity and the "Rafter of satin," of luxurious warmth, is topped, literally, by the "Roof of stone."[4] They are "Safe," but such safety is hardly desirable, for they are safe only from the splendors of the world—and perhaps, in the words "Morning" and "Noon," from a personal apocalypse and the splendors of paradise. Perhaps the sun is kept out to keep these sleepers from knowing that a cosmic joke has been played on them. In "How dare the robins sing,"

Insulting is the Sun
To him whose mortal light
Beguiled of immortality
Bequeaths him to the night.

(1724)

Here "Sleep the meek members of the resurrection," but why are they sleeping? Why have they not risen? The conclusion of "A long—long sleep" raises these skeptical questions more explicitly:

Was ever idleness like This?
Upon a Bank of Stone
To bask the Centuries away—
Nor once look up—for Noon?

(654)

Mustn't they look up in despair once for the noon that fulfills nature and forms a link with immortality?

110

The second stanza even more aggressively suggests that these "meek members" have been beguiled. We see the warm and vital world that these sleepers have sacrificed for a hope which remains unfulfilled. The only "stolid" image in nature is the "stolid Ear" of the flower in which the bee babbles—a lovely vegetative stolidity in contrast to the marble deafness of the sleepers.[5] Could it be that the "ignorant cadence" of the "Sweet Birds" is far wiser than the religious sagacity of the ages? The direction in which the poem has tended gives a sarcastic ring to the final line, "Ah, what sagacity perished here!" The line does not mean, "Oh, imagine with respect the great wisdom of those now dead" but "All their wisdom and faith are unavailing here." Another interpretive possibility provides the more brutally ironic paraphrase, "How fortunate that these foolish sages have been silenced, that nature's sounds need compete no longer with theological mumblings." In either case, Dickinson is not denying resurrection so much as she is criticizing pompous statements of its certainty. This particular grave *may* be an eschatological ending, but it is definitely a cognitive ending; "through a Riddle, at the last— / Sagacity, must go—," and here we see sagacity stranded within that riddle.

The second version of the poem repeats the first stanza almost exactly,[6] but the second stanza becomes more complex in its attitude:

> Grand go the Years—in the Crescent—above them—
> Worlds scoop their Arcs—
> And Firmaments—row—
> Diadems—drop—and Doges—surrender--
> Soundless as dots—on a Disc of Snow—
> (second version)

Now we have a vision of life which is as pessimistic as the vision of death. Life seems a pompous and idiotic show, at least when viewed from the grave. The cosmic life cycles on to no apparent purpose while the rich and powerful end their delusion of self-sufficiency in death. The first stanza now may be reinterpreted in two ways. It is possible to see the meek members as secretly better off than the doges. Such is the attitude of another poem:

> It is an honorable Thought
> And makes One lift One's Hat
> As One met sudden Gentlefolk
> Upon a daily Street

Chapter Six

That We've immortal Place
Though Pyramids decay
And Kingdoms, like the Orchard
Flit Russetly away
(946)

Perhaps now the sleep of the grave pictured in stanza one is merely a confident preparation for immortality, perhaps we have a valuation of the sleepers at the expense of cyclical nature and temporal human life. Perhaps, as Ruth Miller says of the meek members, "it is their *inaction* that has purpose, in contrast to the forceful active change but without goal of the non-dead."[7] Perhaps, but such a reading neglects too much. Even the gloss we employed to support this reading is problematic, for the idea of an immortality simplistically contrasted to life is framed as quaint and gentlemanly—honorable, a nice way to look at things, but perhaps not quite true. More directly, there simply is no sense in which the sleepers of the first stanza appear purposive; the stanza's irony cannot be dismissed. And though we have no direct statement of Dickinson's intention in the revision, a subsequent revision of the second stanza which Dickinson sent to Susan is prefaced by the question, "Is this frontier?" The version of the second stanza which we are now considering is not designed to soften the poem's critique of faith but to increase the poem's vision of despair. The revised poem is designed to make both life and death condemn themselves and each other. The dynamic crescents, arcs, dynasties, and firmaments stress, by contrast, death's finality. In the more explicit language of another poem, "All but Death, can be adjusted"; "Dynasties" may be repaired or "Citadels—dissolved," but "Death—unto itself—Exception— / Is exempt from Change—" (749). The sleepers of the first stanza appear even more granite-like in contrast to the revised second stanza. And yet life comes off poorly too. Impersonal cosmic space is the cold setting for furious and futile human desires. The humility of the "meek members" implicitly criticizes the "Doges" and in any case, as "Diadems and Doges drop," the royalty become members of this meek group. In fact, the only pretty image in the entire revision is the final line's description of silent destruction. No other poem Dickinson ever wrote toys more intimately with nihilism than this revision.

The final nomination of a second stanza could be no frontier, but it is more pointed in its critique of faith.[8] Life is not judged here at all, except as that sunny springtime from which death is locked out.

Springs—shake the Sills—
But—the Echoes—stiffen—

> Hoar—is the Window—and numb—the Door—
> Tribes of Eclipse—in Tents of Marble—
> Staples of Ages—have buckled here.
>
> (third version)

The grave stiffens and silences all dynamic and evocative phenomena. The faithful who are contained in these "Tents of Marble" deserve their eclipsed fate, at least epistemologically. Dickinson writes to Higginson of her family, "They are religious—except me—and address an Eclipse, every morning—whom they call their 'Father' " (L 261). Those who take too-easy consolation from a hidden but confidently assumed presence may find themselves finally within the eclipse, for all past wisdom, "Staples of Ages," are themselves stapled, "buckled" together in defeat at the grave. The brush with nihilism in the second version is averted in this final version only by an all-out attack on fatuous faiths. Dickinson is willing to admit that the traditional faith is an "honorable Thought," the "Gentlefolk" of speculation, but she questions whether it will not collapse "when overwhelmed to know":

> "Faith" is a fine invention
> When Gentlemen can *see*—
> But *Microscopes* are prudent
> In an Emergency.
>
> (185)

If Dickinson is unwilling to grant Christian faith an authority any greater than her own typology, she is equally hard on her invention. "Because I could not stop for Death" (712) stands alongside Whitman's "As I Ebb'd with the Ocean of Life" as a prime example of self-correction in American poetry. Once again, speculation will be made to "pause" by the grave, but first it is "stopped for" by death itself:

> Because I could not stop for Death—
> He kindly stopped for me—
> The Carriage held but just Ourselves—
> And Immortality.

The first few lines create the same range of ambiguity we found in "I felt a funeral, in my Brain." In their simplest sense, the opening lines say that the living cannot will themselves to die, they must be "stopped for" if they are to stop. But there is another sense in which the lines can be taken. Dickinson is fond of naming in letters what her ever expanding thought cannot stop for. For instance, in reference to mockery she writes, "Perhaps you smile at me. I could not stop for that —My Business is Circumference—" (L 268). In our poem, the persona's thought cannot stop for death, or *would* not, but the thought of death will stop for her. Again, Dickinson is erasing the distinctions between type and antitype, in this case between thinking about death and its physical realization. And, again, the resultant terror is expressed in totally collected language, so cool in tone that it italicizes the fear it pretends to repress. The developing analogy of an amatory carriage ride with the gentlemanly suitor Death is secretly fraught with danger; why would immortality (or Dickinson's inner sense of immortality)[9] serve as a chaperon if not to hinder the overzealous lover from making a final claim of what should be only a temporary liaison, ending in resurrection?[10]

The poem's second stop is not actual but logical:

> We slowly drove—He knew no haste
> And I had put away
> My labor and my leisure too,
> For His Civility—
>
> We passed the School, where Children strove
> At Recess—in the Ring—
> We passed the Fields of Gazing Grain—
> We passed the Setting Sun—
>
> Or rather—He passed Us—. . . .

The death-thought is in no hurry. He forces his mistress to "pass" all life—the playful striving of childhood activity, the growing reflection ("Gazing Grain") of maturity, the sunset of seniority—to review it in passing, for this is what she will lose and what she will go beyond. Then comes a crucial correction. The carriage does not pass the sun, the sun passes by it. The correction does far more than to insist on the mimetic accuracy of the analogical setting.[11] That minor insistence on astronomical accuracy is only part of a greater reality principle. Had the carriage passed the sun, it would have passed out of time, to that place where all time could be viewed from a timeless height. The suitor Death would have been spurned for the chaperon Immortality. In fact, Dickinson writes some poems in which the persona, a compacted version of Goethe's Faust or Byron's Cain, gains such a high, holistic perspective—and without Satanic aid.[12] But this death vision is more solidly grounded. Life is not risen above, but lost. In a passage from an analogous poem, a persona bemoans a similar mistake which in this case goes uncorrected:

> The single Flower of the Earth
> That I, in passing by
> Unconscious was—Great Nature's Face
> Passed infinite by Me.
>
> (978)

Dickinson wants us to recognize the value of life, the cost of death: vitality, nature. A greater existence eventually may be gained, but the stress here is on what must be given up and what must be "passed through" first, both in the life of the body and the stages of thought.

Before the dawn, then, night:

> The Dews drew quivering and chill—
> For only Gossamer, my Gown—
> My Tippet—only Tulle—
>
> We paused before a House that seemed
> A Swelling of the Ground—
> The Roof was scarcely visible—
> The Cornice—in the Ground—

This is a night dew, giving off the cold that emanates from that "frigid zone," the grave. The crucial moment is near, and yet the tone of sociality persists. "The only Ghost I ever saw," Dickinson says in another poem, "Was dressed in Mechlin—" (274). The persona's sole worry seems to be that she will be dressed indecorously to assume the role of ghostly corpse. Even the grave is curiously domestic, simply a "house." Yet it is enough to make the "passing" carriage "pause," for this is a house with a difference. This house has the "civility" of the suitor Death, and its civility, like his, is cunning.[13] The cornice is the gravestone, the roof is the coffin lid; this house is not constructed on the ground by men, but seems "A Swelling of the Ground," an unnatural growth of natural dust. And, of course, it has no door, a fact which suggests the true reality of this house. From another poem:

> Doom is the House without the Door—
> 'Tis entered from the Sun—

And then the Ladder's thrown away,
Because Escape—is done—. . .
(475)

Escape is not necessarily "done" in "Because I could not stop," but the veneer of civility is wiped away. The persona must admit the full force of the experience:

Since then—'tis Centuries—and yet
Feels shorter than the Day
I first surmised the Horses' Heads
Were toward Eternity—
(712)

John Lynen argues that the time since that day "feels shorter" because the realization of that final destination, "Eternity," creates an eternal moment in thought.[14] This is part of the explanation, but we should remember that "the Horses' Heads" point down as well as forward. The poem's greatest surprise, in fact, is the white space between stanzas five and six, in which the grave is not gone beyond and immortality does not replace death as a point of view. To combine Lynen's idea and mine, "Eternity" will be achieved only through its opposite, the grave with its indifference to (rather than expansion of) time. Time may "feel shorter" because the persona is no longer riding through time. She has been in pause ever since, either in terms of her thought or her physical reality, at or in the grave, pondering the gruesome timelessness of the grave and the sublime timelessness of a potential paradise. The "Day's surmise" is a question, next to which other questions shrink. The persona may be left, like the persona of "Our Journey had advanced," at the edge of "The Forest of the Dead," looking through it to the far "God at every Gate." Alternately, the persona may be pictured within the grave, in that "Forest of the Dead," in full confrontation with the thought of nothingness. Her attitude then can be expressed by another posthumous voice:

Were it a Witchcraft—were it Death—
I've still a chance to strain

To Being somewhere—Motion—Breath—
Though *Centuries beyond,*
And every limit a Decade—
I'll shiver, satisfied.
(1046, italics mine)

In either case, there is no final loss of faith in "Because I could not stop," but Dickinson's imagination receives a dual setback. The imagination is forced to stop for a terrifying thought, which then forces the imagination to admit that this thought constitutes its circumference of certitude. We are ready now to answer more fully the question of why Dickinson makes us (and herself) confront these poems of dying and the grave. Dickinson's poetry shows her to be as enamored of Emersonian idealism as Emerson himself; but the realist in Dickinson fights off the bardic seer, and the poems we have just considered represent the realist's thrust. Like Emerson, Dickinson can say that "Paradise is of the option" (L 319), but she has a greater concern than Emerson for blocking forces, psychological and natural. She, too, sees thought as a process of constant expansion, but Emerson's circles become Dickinson's circumferences. That term, "circumference," is often overrated and made the key to an understanding of Dickinson. Thus it becomes mysterious. Simply put, "Circumference" may denote an ultimate, totally inclusive vision, but more often it is a name for the boundaries of thought and suggests exclusion as well. Dickinson strives to measure the imagination rather than to claim everything for it, and she wants it to earn its way, by suffering. Dickinson implies that a transcendental vision is hers for the asking, but

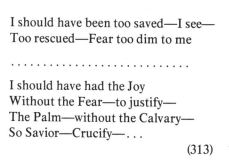

> I should have been too saved—I see—
> Too rescued—Fear too dim to me
>
> . . . .
>
> I should have had the Joy
> Without the Fear—to justify—
> The Palm—without the Calvary—
> So Savior—Crucify—. . .
>
> (313)

The death of the grave and its equivalents of emotional paralysis and cognitive limitation are not morbid concatenations. They constitute an attempt to ground ideal fictions in common experience, to force those fictions to keep in touch with the nerves. The grave is the antitype of circumference in its limiting sense. But the grave is not the final term in the typology. "The power and the glory are the post mortuary gifts" (L, p. 920), Dickinson writes in direct rebuttal of Emerson, but it is important to remember that often in Dickinson's typology "the post mortuary gifts" are available in experience as well as after.

This brings us to a more biographical defense of Dickinson's grave of skepticism. The American romantic typically begins his career with a comic vision and ends his career in tragedy. Emerson may speak of his writings as "a sort of Farmer's Almanac of mental moods" but the general weather gets wintry as he ages; Emerson's career, chronicled as "Freedom and Fate" by Stephen Whicher,[15] moves away from idealism toward necessity. The more skeptical Hawthorne suffers the same change artistically; once the master of playing with and merging diverse genres, his last four romances are botched, stranded, left unfinished. And Melville, once almost joyful in his relativity and skepticism, completes *The Confidence Man* and lapses into decades of nihilistic silence. This is melodrama and oversimplification, of course, but it suggests a pattern which is at once human and peculiarly romantic and American. Dickinson beats the system by her system. She "buries"— not hides but ostensibly inters—her fears, doubts, and frustrations *within* the typology of death. She mingles her pain with her power and joy, and conquers skepticism by making it a constant pressure on all her thoughts.

2

Judgment Day is the traditional notion which Dickinson's typology most completely transforms. A moment of individual judgment based on standards the living cannot fully comprehend, with its puritan concomitants of original sin and constant guilt, is clearly absurd and hateful to Dickinson:

> "Heavenly Father"—take to thee
> The supreme iniquity
> Fashioned by thy candid Hand
> In a moment contraband—
> Though to trust us—seem to us
> More respectful—"We are Dust"—
> We apologize to thee
> For thine own Duplicity—
>
> (1461)

If we are dust, Dickinson asks in this militant satire, what does that make our "Father"? For Dickinson, God is either a loving father or a metaphysical essence, but he is not a stupidly intolerant parent or an abstracted superego. When Dickinson allows for individual evaluation as spiritual at all, she replaces Judgment and its type of guilt with an ethic of self-realization, of sincerity and circumference:

> Obtaining but our own Extent
> In whatsoever Realm—
> 'Twas Christ's own personal Expanse
> That bore him from the Tomb—
> (1543)

Even Dickinson's satire on "Soft—Cherubic" gentlewomen makes its criticism in terms of artificiality and powerlessness. They will be shut out of paradise not because their cruelty will be punished but because their cruelty is the result of their failure to live in the spirit, to seek the "heaven below." They will not receive grace because they will not sue for glory.

One of the chief qualities of romanticism is its struggle with guilt, and of New England romanticism this is particularly true. When sin is translated into guilt, the villain is no longer the sinner but his crippling emotion of remorse. The community's code of ethics becomes suspect and the penitent, a long way from Mary Magdalene, becomes a victim of masochism and a scapegoat for sadism. Thus, in part, Dimmesdale and Hester. Emerson looks around him at a society of men crippled by guilt and self-degradation and attempts to abolish those terms of understanding.[16] Dickinson more closely resembles a confessional version of Hawthorne. She looks inside herself and mourns the "Disease" which cannot be banished:

> Remorse is cureless—the Disease
> Not even God—can heal—
> For 'tis His institution—and
> The Adequate of Hell—
> (744)

Dickinson cannot eliminate remorse or its antitype of negative Judgment, but she can ignore guilt and transform the meaning of Judgment in her typology. The "sinner" comes to judge his maker. The question "Am I inexcusably guilty?" becomes "Is this life a constant negative Judgment, its condition a continual repulse from paradise, or can this life, at least potentially, become its own antitype of immortality?" Judgment becomes a question of the relations between the natural types and the supernatural antitypes, between time and eternity. The "final" terms in our pseudo-chronology inform all the others.

Two excellent modern theoreticians of literary time have found in Dickinson this same question: whether life precludes an infinite perspective or whether such a perspective is so available in life that a chronological "afterlife" is superfluous. The two critics, Georges Poulet and John Lynen, arrive at opposite and conflicting conclusions. For Poulet,

> . . . each time Emily reflects on her existence, she sees it begin with a grand victory immediately followed by a bitter defeat. All her spiritual life and all her poetry are comprehended only in the interpretation given them by two initial moments, one of which is contradicted by the other, a moment in which one possesses eternity and a moment when one loses it. . . . All duration is made to be the eternal exclusion of an instantaneous eternity. . . . this consciousness would continue indefinitely to prolong its monotonous contemplation over this extent, if finally at the end of it, at the extremity of the future, there were not, as at the extremity of the past, a supreme instant which forms the transcendent termination of the level plain. That termination is death. [17]

We can say that Poulet reads Dickinson's poetry as a huge extension of T. S. Eliot's complaint of duration at the conclusion of "Burnt Norton": "Ridiculous the waste sad time / Stretching before and after." Poulet suggests for Dickinson a tragically inconstant typology, an early experience as the figural foreshadowing of a transcendent death with a stretch of boredom between.

Lynen agrees that Dickinson dramatizes an opposition between experience and eternity. But he sees her poems as attempts to find the eternal in the present moment and to so intensify the duality of a particular and a universal that they become one:

> The self stands within the present yet in eternity also; for one aspect of its identity is that of a transcendent spectator, who stands outside of every experienced moment and takes all epochs into account. This self, which plays God and, in a sense, is God, is manifest in the mind's general concepts, for such ideas make reference to any and all times. [18]

Lynen makes Poulet's single past ecstasy a constant. If true, Lynen's interpretation negates the typology I have proposed, for it suggests that figura and fulfillment *always* are contained within the figural experience.

It would be easy, too easy, to say that Lynen's version of Dickinsonian time fits inside Poulet's version, as extended descriptions of moments which are invariably lost. Lynen allows for no "plain of duration" and Poulet allows for no such multiplicity of ecstatic instants. Furthermore, Lynen's idea of Dickinson's happiness concerns artistic and metaphysical fulfillment, while Poulet's idea of Dickinson's melancholy concerns personal, emotional disappointment. The two theories are in absolute disagreement even as to the general nature of the poetry. Yet both fit inside Dickinson's pluralistic typology of death as it reaches its own final and definitive antitypes of judgment and immortality. I said earlier that Dickinson's typology is designed not to insist on the superiority of one set of answers (one doctrine) but to dramatize various and conflicting answers. When we come to the supreme typological equation, the type of experience in general and the antitype of an afterlife immortality, we receive two distinct answers, one corresponding to Poulet's idea of Dickinsonian time and one to Lynen's: life as negative judgment and life as its own fulfillment, the only paradise. Though type and antitype are set at war at this crucial point—Poulet's idea of Dickinsonian time devalues typological experience while Lynen's devalues any fulfilling antitype which is not "now"—the two answers, like all of Dickinson's self-debates, may be seen finally as one answer, variously viewed from incongruent perspectives.

We can begin to build a bridge between these two ideas by reshaping Poulet's sense of Dickinson's tragic time, a sense of time which obviously belongs to Dickinson's world of veto. Poulet errs by stating a phenomenology in uncomfortably biographical language: "Such is Emily's lot: Condemned all her life to unhappiness in order to pay the price of a single instant of happiness."[19] But Dickinson's idea of experiential life as negative judgment, as an expulsion from a beheld heaven, is not framed as a biographical wound peculiar to Emily Dickinson of Amherst. It is a large law of nature and humanity. One of Dickinson's most effective poems exemplifies Poulet's idea of Dickinsonian time perfectly, yet its tone is not confessional in a self-pitying sense and its object of contemplation is, at least explicitly, independent of the poet's psychological set:

> At Half past Three, a single Bird
> Unto a silent Sky
> Propounded but a single term
> Of cautious melody.
>
> At Half past Four, Experiment
> Had subjugated test
> And lo, Her silver Principle
> Supplanted all the rest.

Chapter Six

At Half past Seven, Element
Nor Implement, be seen—
And Place was where the Presence was
Circumference between.

(1084)

This drama of ecstatic truth and its subsequent loss within four early morning hours has nothing to do with Emily Dickinson's "single instant of happiness." It is as daily and universal as the dawn. Dickinson juxtaposes casual "half pasts" with scientific and metaphysical terms to emphasize both the common occurrence of the phenomenal bird song and the uncommon, unnoticed significance of it. The investigative bird issues a nervous prolegomenon, then more confidently states herself as the essence of the world, and then disappears, leaving a world devoid of her "silver Principle." The poem is a comment on human reason as well as nature. Revelatory "Presence" becomes dull "Place" at the moment humanity awakes. Circumference intrudes not only because the sun is risen and the bird's rite completed but also because man's dreamy intelligence has given way to his daylight perception, practical and limited. Only the early riser, with his awakened imagination, catches the bird, and only he can recognize and mourn the inevitable escape of this compound tenor and vehicle, this "Element" which is its own "Implement." Paradise is lost every morning as nature and men become busy.[20]

In brief, Dickinson is attempting a universality of meaning for which Poulet's biographical terms do not allow. Even when a poem's thrust is explicitly psychological, the psychology is general. In "The Soul has Bandaged moments—," Dickinson classifies three states of the soul. The first is roughly equivalent both to Freudian anxiety and subsequent repression and to typological dying and the subsequent death of the grave:

The Soul has Bandaged moments—
When too appalled to stir—
She feels some ghastly Fright come up
And stop to look at her—

Salute her—with long fingers—
Caress her freezing hair—
Sip, Goblin, from the very lips
The Lover—hovered—o'er—
Unworthy, that a thought so mean
Accost a Theme—so—fair—

Typology of Death, II: Dickinson in White

We cannot but feel the pressure of experience behind this gothic psychology, but the analogical collection prevents a particularity of situation. The soul is an injured paralytic, a frozen flower, a fair theme in ruin. The "fright" is a monster, a goblin, an icy replacement of the bee-lover, a mean and demeaning thought. Dickinson casts about furiously to describe the horror of these moments, not their cause, and their stated plurality, like the plurality of analogous images, tends toward law and away from situation. Somewhat sequentially—the poem, like many of Dickinson's best, compounds sequential narrative and classificatory explication—a second kind of moment is described, a moment roughly equivalent both to Joycean epiphanies and typological resurrection:

> The soul has moments of Escape—
> When bursting all the doors—
> She dances like a Bomb, abroad,
> And swings upon the Hours,
>
> As do the Bee—delirious borne—
> Long Dungeoned from his Rose—
> Touch liberty—then know no more,
> But Noon, and Paradise—

The Soul "bursts," like "Christ's personal expanse," from a tomb—from the dungeon of fright if we wish to stress the poem's narrative progress, but more generally from the limitations of life's body. It achieves timelessness in time as it "swings upon the Hours." Again, the analogical collection creates its precise imprecision, but joyfully now. No longer a victimized flower in winter, the soul is a bee as spring renews nature. The lover supplants the goblin who supplanted him. The soul itself is now active and even dangerous, a dancing bomb of ecstatic power. The soul again reaches that "know no more" state of the first stanzas of this poem but now its journey beyond knowledge ends not in paralysis but in "Noon, and Paradise—."

Like the dawn of "At Half past Three," this noon must pass, and when it does a third kind of moment occurs, similar to (but worse than) the first:

> The Soul's retaken moments—
> When, Felon led along,
> With shackles on the plumed feet,
> And staples, in the Song,

123

Chapter Six

The Horror welcomes her, again,
These, are not brayed of Tongue—
(512)

The full horror consists in a torturously belated negative Judgment. The living soul is allowed to pass through the paradisiacal gates. It not only gains an idea of immortality but fully experiences it and begins to think of it as a constant. Only then is it thrown out, thrown back to temporality and its victimizing horrors and mean thoughts. The persona who suffers this negative Judgment is essentially passive, acted upon; his dynamic transports, where he feels himself master of his own fate, are quickly negated and punished by a renewed sense of helplessness. This second dungeon—and it is only now that the jail images of the earlier stanzas gain full expression—is darker than the first because the "retaken" soul now recognizes its possibilities, its lost freedom and power. It knows of its "plumed feet" and triumphant "Song," and its knowledge is what makes particularly intolerable the "shackles" and "staples" of experience. The dungeon is darker now because the soul's Indian summer of ecstasy has been experienced as an alternative. This is the payoff of the poem's odd mixture of exposition and narrative sequence: though the soul may escape again and again, by the end of the poem we know that it *always* will be recaptured, that internment is its regular condition.[21] These "retaken" moments also lead beyond knowledge. The poem ends by invoking silence—the last two lines of the poem are purposely left unwritten. Silence is Dickinson's chief symbol of extra-experiential truth, but this particular silent truth is of the nihilism of the grave, unambiguously disastrous. That these moments are less exclusively personal and more recurrent than Poulet's theory would suggest simply spreads the disaster around.

If Poulet neglects Dickinson's extrapersonal interest in how the world works and how we put it together, he nonetheless presents an accurate picture of Dickinsonian pessimism. He makes conceptual sense of what earlier critics vaguely called Dickinson's complaints of "flux." In a poem like "The Soul has Bandaged moments," Dickinson complains not merely that bliss does not last, but that it is given and then taken away. This apparently slight semantic difference creates a great difference in attitude. If "flux" were the problem, the poet's task would be to achieve resignation, while this belated negative Judgment creates resentment and demands cosmological jusification from God. That is, the tone is angry because the God of experience becomes Satan:

> Perfidy is the virtue
> That would but he resign
> The Devil—without question
> Were thoroughly divine
> (1479)

It is a bully-God who allows "Old Moses" to "See—the Canaan— / without the entering—" (597). Whether the persona is passively visited by an Angel whom "God calls home" (231), or actively transported to where "those Jasper Gates / Blazed open—suddenly—" only to be subsequently banished (256), the complaint is not of a mechanical, meaningless universe but an actively demonic one: "Why the Thief ingredient accompanies all Sweetness Darwin does not tell us" (L 359). The "Thief ingredient" proves the existence of a Supreme Power, but this Power is a morbid trickster, not the benevolent God of orthodox anti-Darwinians. Life under him becomes a series of delusions, and yet it is the persona's sublime gullibility which receives greatest scorn. "It would never be a Common—more—," a speaker announces as he achieves a paradise, but when "suddenly—my Riches shrank," Dickinson records an awful return to the common state with almost gleeful, self-hating furor:

> I clutched at sounds—
> I groped at shapes—
> I touched the tops of Films—
> I felt the Wilderness roll back
> Along my Golden lines—. . .
> (430)

God as Satan, the persona as Faustian *alazon*—this is not a complaint of flux but of false and revoked Election.

Yet Poulet's second error is his failure to notice the potentially *redeeming* aspects of this apparently ironic pattern. The Election was not delusory, only its permanence, and

> If I'm lost—now
> That I was found—
> Shall still my transport be—. . .
> (256)

This is, after all, a "sumptuous Destitution" (1382), an intimation of a future immortality which will not be revoked, a comfort and a goad to the spirit:

> To help our Bleaker Parts
> Salubrious Hours are given
> Which if they do not fit for Earth
> Drill silently for Heaven—
> (1064)

"The Soul's Superior instants" are types in experience, and if we remember that they are not their own fulfillment, they become reliable types:

> Eternity's disclosure
> To favorites—a few—
> Of the Colossal substance
> Of Immortality
> (306)

Dickinson's point, like Eliot's later in the *Four Quartets*, is that the great expanded moment is not in itself sufficient; mysticism is not a sustaining faith. If accepted as all-inclusive, the moment, when lost, will leave only the anger against heaven of a Gloucester. If taken as less inclusive, as types, these moments do not make life a prolonged negative Judgment but a meaningful postponement in an eventful quest toward a final Election. The moments can become permanent in thought if not in experience, and thus can provide the raw materials for a more satisfactory and permanent hope:

> I had the Glory—that will do—
> An honor, Thought can turn her to
> When lesser Fames invite—
> With one long "Nay"—
> Bliss' early shape
> Deforming—Dwindling—Gulfing up—
> Time's possibility.
> (349)

What Poulet calls "the level plain" need never exist if the supreme instant can be kept alive in cognition, as a perspective on life's end and potential. The tragedy of life as negative judgment, revoked Election, is what Dickinson sets as her challenge.

It is at this point where meditation resurrects a lost heaven that

Poulet's and Lynen's ideas of Dickinsonian time meet. The mind's task is to expand the temporary, always lost moments of grace into a constant perspective:

> Not "Revelation"—'tis—that waits,
> But our unfurnished eyes—
>
> (685)

We must strain to see. The mind must make its own mountains on the "level plain." (In fact, of course, there is no "level plain" as Poulet describes it in Dickinson's poetry. Dickinson's typological interpretations transform the most complete boredom—"After great pain, a formal feeling comes"—into a duration of excruciating importance, equally beyond experience in its negative fulfillment as the ecstatic moment in its positive antitype.) The persona of temporal eternality is active and victorious in contrast to the struggling and always defeated sufferer of negative Judgment because it is a different, more immediately cerebral function of the self which Dickinson here personifies.

In some few poems, Dickinson focuses on a moment in which the experiential, confessional persona is transformed into a seer of immortality. In "To the bright east she flies," the bereft persona conquers the "level plain" by filling experiential time with thoughts of time past and future:

> Fashioning what she is,
> Fathoming what she was,
> We deem we dream—
> And that dissolves the days
> Through which existence strays
> Homeless at home.
>
> (1573)

Such a victory must be partial, as the downturning last lines suggest. The "days" in themselves will remain days of loss, and did the persona neglect to convert them, to "dissolve" them into a cognitive dream, she would wander dissolutely in a level forest of horror. But dream-thoughts do replace the days. The mourner creates fictions, a "fashioning" of her lost friend's present, and her own future, sublimity; and the mourner seizes on memories, a "fathoming" which recovers a past glory. That is, the mourner is able to think into immediate existence a "beyond" and a "past" which are utterly unavailable to the present days when unadorned by imagination. If we can say that the idea of revoked Election

127

"contains" the idea of temporal eternality as a canceled moment of transcendence, we also can say that the idea of temporal eternality contains and conquers the disappointment of revoked Election as the mind surrounds experience.

In its dramatized development, Dickinson's experiential eternity makes the most extravagant claim for the typological imagination. To think of immortality allows the persona to adopt a timeless perspective toward experiential time; that perspective in turn becomes the chief reality; the persona achieves a permanent immortality in life, at least in the life of thought; and the type verges on its own fulfillment. A poem begins,

> I think just how my shape will rise—
> When I shall be *"forgiven"*—
> Till Hair—and Eyes—and timid Head—
> Are *out of sight*—in Heaven—

In anguish, which in itself is a type of the grave, the persona remembers that some earlier sorrows were relieved:

> *Some* drifts were moved away—
> Before my simple bosom—broke—
> And why not *this*—if *they?*

Why should not the greatest anguish, the worst foreshadowing of death, lead to the greatest transport? Thinking makes it so. The persona seizes on the two expectations, of heavenly resurrection as the antitype, of recuperation as heaven's type in life, makes the two expectations one, and bursts from the tomb:

> And so I con that thing—*"forgiven"*—
> Until—delirious—borne—
> By my long bright—and *longer—trust*—
> I *drop* my Heart—*unshriven!*
>
> (237)

The long and longer trust, with recovery and heaven as its dual object, enables the persona to forgo the purgatory of confession and rise above the conditions of life. In fact, the future becomes the present, the contemplated antitypes are actualized by contemplation. Recovery is no longer desired; the organ of physical existence, of the ordinary existence that includes guilt, is "dropped" for a better, more delirious existence which has been discovered. It is difficult to say whether the typology still exists as it achieves its final triumph. Clearly, the typology begins to totter as the idea of the expectation begins to make unnecessary the expectation's supernatural fulfillment. When Dickinson speaks from the end of the transformation and does not indicate the cognitive struggle to achieve it, the afterlife is abolished, its antitypes transported to experience. Transcendence becomes a matter of will, and sometimes simply a matter of acceptance. In a remarkable letter to Higginson, Dickinson admits that immortality is "the Flood subject" which "I explore but little since my mute confederate";[22] but as for the earthly, paradisiacal representation of immortality, "the 'infinite beauty'—of which you speak comes too near to seek." She continues aphoristically,

To escape enchantment, one must always flee.
Paradise is of the option.
Whosoever will [may] Own in Eden notwithstanding Adam and Repeal.
                                                                    (L 319)

In a letter to her close friend Elizabeth Holland, written seven years later, in 1873, Dickinson renews this idea in a shockingly casual manner: "Vinnie says you . . . dwell in Paradise. I have never believed the latter to be a superhuman site. Eden, always eligible, is peculiarly so this noon" (L 391). We have traveled a long way from that equally bardic statement, "The Power and the Glory are the post-mortuary gifts." Only the substitution of the word "Paradise" for "Immortality" prevents an overt denial of the typological idea of experience as *heading toward* a great end and of death as boundary and entrance. The typology is nearly inoperative here, and it is only a short journey from its neglect to a direct repudiation of the antitypes. In a fragment, Dickinson weighs life and afterlife and arrives at a surprising conclusion: "to know whether we are in Heaven or on Earth is one of the most impossible of the minds decisions but I think the balance always leans in favor of the negative—if Heaven is negative" (L, p. 928). In its form as extreme law rather than dramatized development, Dickinson's idea of experiential eternity leaps over the grave, negates Judgment, and insists that the mind's circumference *is* the ultimate circumference. The typology of death seems to become a blunder:

The Blunder is in estimate
Eternity is there
We say, as of a Station—
Meanwhile he is so near
He joins me in my Ramble—
Divides abode with me—
No Friend have I that so persists
As this Eternity.

(1684)

Eternity as a constantly felt possibility replaces a naive spatialization. This consciousness contains all possibilities. The level plain has become a level apex.

Life as immortality and life as negative Judgment are attitudes which Dickinson holds concurrently. They may be separated in conflict or made to compete and transform one another. Just as thought can convert experience into living immortality, experiential pain, always linked to death, can shrink that immortal vision into time, involvement, doubt:

The vastest earthly Day
Is shrunken small
By one Defaulting Face
Behind a Pall—

(1328)

Viewed as one extreme of a range of answers to a crucial question, the most bardic statements of time as immortality participate in the typology they appear to negate. The chief paradox of Christian typology, as stated by Auerbach, equally applies to Dickinson's typology of death:

> . . . every future model, though incomplete as history, is already fulfilled in God and has existed from all eternity in His providence. The figures in which He cloaked it, and the incarnation in which He revealed its meaning, are therefore prophecies of something that has always been, but which will remain veiled for men until the day when they behold the Savior *revelate facie*, with the senses as well as the spirit. Thus the figures are not only tentative; they are also the tentative form of something eternal and timeless; they point not only to the concrete future, but also to something that has been and will always be . . . to something which is in need of interpretation, which will indeed be fulfilled in the concrete future, but which is at all times present, fulfilled in God's providence, who knows no difference of time.[23]

In Dickinson's more personal typology, the antitype of immortality is both foreseen in the concrete future and present in life. The persona who suffers negative Judgment takes a historical, experiential point of view from which the immediate fulfillment of the antitype is impossible. The persona of temporal eternality adopts a godlike perspective, a perspective which "knows no difference of time," and thus can infuse the experiential moment with the concrete future which exists the other side of death's door. Denials of the typology occur only when the persona adopts a supreme epistemology by which types are not interpreted but immediately realized. The typology's negation is equally its climactic affirmation.

"There is no first, or last, in Forever—," Dickinson writes to her sister-in-law. "It is Centre, there, all the time—." How can this "Centre" be achieved in time? "To believe—is enough, and the right of supposing" (L 288). Life as negative Judgment with the mind as insufficient circumference, and Life as potential Immortality with the mind as "Centre," are both suppositions, and Dickinson claims the right to suppose either and both. The choice almost seems to depend on the commonplace Dickinson challenges. Metaphysical modesty results when Dickinson confronts facile versions of Transcendentalism, but faced with doctrinal statements of the Christian afterlife afterplace, Dickinson will claim all for this life and the mind of this life.[24] Conceptually, at least, the conflict between the two views of life and immortality becomes a complex cooperation. But poems are individual as well as parts of a life *oeuvre* and we do not want to discount too much the apparent conflicts which result from the choices of attitude and voice taken by various poems. Dickinson's typology of death is less a fiction than a system that generates fictions. It molds the questions and thus defines the shape of Dickinson's imagination. The final question of the typology, the question we have considered in this section, can be stated simply: is experience, is the experiential self, its mind and language, all-sufficient? From the affirmative answer of temporal eternality stems the fiction we will consider next, a fiction which asks whether the potentially immortal self *should* be activated; from the negative answer of revoked Election stems the fiction we will consider last, a fiction which asks whether the limited self can somehow capitalize on its frustrations.

As for the underlying question we have considered here, Dickinson would have it both ways. She would will herself into one or another mode of expression—the one corresponding roughly to what we earlier called the bard, the other to the sufferer—and deliver the appropriate answer. Dickinson's deathbed statement, in which we might expect a final choice, appears deliberately problematic. In her last few months,

Dickinson was seriously ill. A few days before her death, she scribbled her last, most terse and ambiguous note. To her "little cousins," the Norcross sisters, she wrote two words: "Called back" (L 1046). The title of a Hugh Conway novel she had recently read, the words also announce a reply, the act itself without any enumeration. But what is their deeper meaning? "Called back" to what? Had Dickinson awakened from a coma, partially recovered, as some biographers believe, and written the note to announce that she had once again returned to this life with "Odd secrets of the line to tell"? Or, as seems more likely, was Dickinson foreseeing her death? If so, is she called back "home" to a more fulfilling existence and a wider circumference, or has the great adventure of life been revoked, canceled? Is the greater "Home" within the circumference of this consciousness or beyond? Emily Dickinson leaves life with a question. Yet this constant questioning is an intrinsic element in a life which exemplifies and expands Plato's advice in the *Phaedo*: "Practice dying."

7

Poetry from the Power Station: A Regulation Fiction

> The mind is the terriblest force in the world, father
> Because, in chief, it, only, can defend
> Against itself. At its mercy, we depend
> Upon it.
>
> —Wallace Stevens

1

Essence can be personified as well as "temporized," and personified not as an exterior god or master but as a property of the self. Contemplated further, a statement quoted in my first chapter becomes the basis for Dickinson's primarily Transcendentalist fiction: "Had we the first intimation of the Definition of Life," Dickinson writes to Mrs. Holland (L 492), "the calmest of us would be Lunatics!" It is this "Definition of Life," tantamount to immortality, which Dickinson's seer elsewhere celebrates as an eternal moment; but it is also this "Definition" which imposes itself on the unwelcoming victim who feels a funeral in his brain. Who would not attempt such a definition, were it in his grasp? And yet, who would trade the unexamined certainties of the "Daily mind" (1323), the blinkered calm which enables consciousness to survive the onslaughts of phenomena, for a wild, lunatic knowledge of the real? Consider the quandary of an imagination which is convinced of its potential to achieve a "further heaven" in experience and which is equally convinced that, since a thing must be defined by what it is not, the achievement of this definition, the experiencing of self and nature in their undiluted power, will cancel the conditions of existence. This is the quandary Dickinson chooses to confront in poems

133

which, taken together, constitute a regulation fiction. An electric reality lives within us and abroad. Survival depends upon its denial, but a life of power depends on its actualization. The voice of these poems must decide whether to risk destruction of the common self in order to achieve a royal perspective.

We may envision the human organism which must mediate these rival claims through the analogy of a power station. A modern power station receives electrical energy produced elsewhere. It runs this energy through a transformer which boosts or diminishes the power so that the circuits for which it cares will be amply supplied but not overloaded. Finally, it transmits the energy outward. In addition, larger power stations (and Dickinson is a very large power station) contain generators which create their own energy. Our analogy, if anachronistic, is fortunate, for Dickinson herself often images the "Definition of Life" in terms of a timeless electricity:

> The Lightning playeth—all the while—
> But when He singeth—then—
> Ourselves are conscious He exist—
> And we approach Him—stern—
>
> With Insulators—and a Glove—...
>
> (630)

Here, the lightning charge creates awe and fear and a technique of self-protection. But the decisions of our power station are inconsistent. Elsewhere, it eagerly embraces the charge:

> But I would not exchange the Bolt
> For all the rest of Life—
> Indebtedness to Oxygen
> The Happy may repay,
> But not the obligation
> To Electricity—
> It founds the Homes and decks the Days
> And every clamor bright
> Is but the gleam concomitant
> Of that waylaying Light—
> The Thought is quiet as a Flake—
> A Crash without a Sound,
> How Life's reverberation
> Its Explanation found—
>
> (1581)

This bolt is the substance and significator of life, the founder of "Homes," of final fulfillments. It is praised as far superior to "Oxygen," the atmosphere of mere existence. The only regret here is that the power station, the poet's thought, cannot "repay" this electricity. It can transmit only a like but diminished charge. In the first poem we cited, the body protects itself; in the second, the mind tries to take full account of the stimulus but cannot do any better than an explanatory reverberation—and this alone causes a threatening "Crash." Both poems assume a special reality which, when confronted without psychic insulation, carries utmost meaning in a creative but dangerous force to the shocked persona.

The self is an electrical circuit with a regulator which decides to accept, reject, or alter its charged load. But sometimes there is no opportunity for choice. The "Heavenly Hurt" inflicted by "a certain Slant of light" is not chosen or denied; the poet must wait passively until it leaves with the departing look of death, and then can only examine the "internal scar" for its hieroglyph of meaning. Sometimes, then, to quote Stevens's electrical vision in "The Auroras of Autumn,"

> ...The scholar of one candle sees
> An Arctic effulgence flaring on the frame
> Of everything he is. And he feels afraid.

For Dickinson, there would be no proof of the electrical reality, no real challenge to the lowly love of oxygen, were the regulator not periodically surprised and wrecked.

This particular imagery of lightning, which is only one name among many for Dickinsonian Spirit, should not blind us to what is, in large measure, a humanizing of essence. We see this more clearly if we place the regulation poems in their romantic context. When self-generated, as it most often is, Dickinson's "Bolt" is the "Central Man" of Emerson and Stevens and Whitman's "real ME."[1] For Emerson, this figure is the source of humanity, buried as a potential within his every fragmented expression, you and me; the "great secular personalities" —Socrates, Shakespeare, Michelangelo, Saint Jesus—"were only expressions of his face chasing each other like the rack of clouds."[2] All of these expressions are "below us," below our highest destiny, which is to become the central man complete. Stevens is more willing to posit him as an unattainable ideal, "The impossible possible philosophers' man, / ...Who in a million diamonds sums us up."[3] Whitman is less sanguine. The idealized Walt's crippling moment of humility in the early stages of "As I Ebbed," where Walt is "baffled, balked, / Bent to the very earth," provokes the "real ME" of the poet's distant depths to scold and torture the poet for his earlier pretensions (specifically, we can suppose, for the boasts of "Song of Myself"):

> . . . before all my insolent poems, the real ME
> still stands untouched, untold, altogether
> unreached,
> Withdrawn far, mocking me with mock-congratulatory
> signs and bows,
> With peals of distant ironical laughter at every word
> I have written or shall write,
> Striking me with insults till I fall helpless upon
> the sand.[4]

The "real ME" scourges Walt with the lesson that its special, essential selfhood, that deepest individuality which is paradoxically coequal with the essence of everything, is so separate from the fallen personality of daily experience (and even its most heroic idealizations) that it can seem a separate character, the antithesis as well as the origin of the "Daily mind." Distinct from the actual self but buried within it, the "real ME" goads Emerson, Stevens, and Whitman into the wild and the sincere.

Amid all the attempts to see American romanticism as a prelude to contemporary literature, this central man stands as a conservative resistant. He is based on that belief in depths of character and hidden meanings which the avant-garde novelists of the last twenty years have tried to destroy.[5] Among Dickinson's contemporaries, only Melville, with one foot firmly planted in the great Nothing, would dispute the existence of the "real ME." The narrator of *Pierre* cries that the world is "nothing but superinduced superfluities," that "appallingly vacant as vast is the soul of a man." Yet even the ferocity of this attack on deep meaning depends on the equally strident claims for the fecund vastness of a hidden selfhood that had been made by Melville's contemporaries. If romanticism, and American romanticism in particular, has a calling card, it is what Georges Poulet terms "the God more interior to ourselves than ourselves and more central than we could ever become."[6]

Dickinson is one with the party of optimism, though her personalization of essence differs in important respects. Most superficially, her self-contained "Definition of Life" is less codified than Emerson's or Whitman's. Ever changing images replace the single concept of a central man: lightning, a glowing substance such as phosphorus, secret streams and wells, and "soul," "spirit," or "brain" in opposition to body.

As this list suggests, Dickinson often emphasizes the special nature of the deepest human self by borrowing spectacular images from nature. This transference suggests three more substantive aspects in her model of meaning. The first alone is predictable. Given the idea of man as his own potential God, we should expect an internalization of values and conflicts, and Dickinson does not disappoint us. "The Battle fought between the Soul / And No Man" (594)—that is, the struggle of the soul to realize itself—is the only battle worth considering; "A soul admitted to itself" is the definition of "Finite infinity" (1695); if you wish to find "The 'Undiscovered Continent,' " Dickinson tells De Soto, "Explore thyself!" (832); the "reticent volcano" of man is silent, but then "The only secret people keep / Is Immortality" (1748).

The narrative of a soul struggling against its own blocking forces, with its attendant internalizing of myth and image, is *the* romantic narrative.[7] Dickinson conforms to this pattern. But it is more interesting to note what she does not subordinate to her "real ME." Public events, manners, in fact the whole of history is easily subordinated— "How dimmer than a Saturn's Bar / The Things esteemed, for Things that are!" (1086)—but nature, however often it is drawn upon for internal images, retains its essential facticity. An effect of tooth-pulling always accompanies the admissions of Emerson and Whitman that consciousness and nature share a hidden source of meaning; Dickinson, as enthusiastically as Thoreau, posits a model of nature corresponding to her model of man. There is also a "real Nature," deep under sanguine appearances, and it also subsumes history: could you comprehend "the Battle of Burgoyne" within every sunset, "You would chastened stare—" (1174). It, too, is overpowering: to meet "The last of Summer" without "celestial Mail" is "Audacious as without a Knock / To walk within the Veil" (1353). It, too, lies like a sleeping volcano, ready to erupt: "A Bird came down the Walk" with comic practicality, bisecting an angleworm and dodging a beetle in Darwinian style, until the persona, shyly seeking to know this diminished Chanticleer,

> . . . offered him a Crumb
> And he unrolled his feathers
> And rowed him softer home—
>
> Than Oars divide the Ocean,
> Too silver for a seam—

Or Butterflies, off Banks of Noon
Leap, plashless as they swim.

(328)

The pedestrian bird suddenly becomes pure spirit and the persona's mockery turns to awe. Often, in fact, it is the breaking out of "real Nature" that ignites the "real ME." Bird songs of a summer morning "stab my ravished spirit / With Dirks of Melody" to create a "Joy of so much anguish" (1420). The first robin of the new spring (348), "The Tint I cannot take" (627), "A something in a summer's Day" (122), and, of course, "a certain Slant of light, / Winter Afternoons" (258)—all these sudden and evanescent spectacles of nature create dread, a moment when the perceiver's full soul threatens to burst its fleshly bounds. In Dickinson, then, the essential is not made human as often as it is made private. It is a matter of the soul unto itself, or of the secret sky unto the solitary retina.

The final step in Dickinson's model of meaning comprises a reversal of sorts. If the events of the historical world are replaced by the interior actions of a "real ME," that "real ME" so vehemently opposes the poem's regulatory voice that it becomes part of the oppressive beauty of the not-me. God is placed within only to be flung out again, transformed. "I am constantly more astonished that the Body contains the Spirit—," Dickinson writes late in her life to Maria Whitney. "Except for overmastering work it could not be borne—" (L 643). Sometimes it cannot be borne, and the Spirit is dramatized as an antagonistic, "out there" agent. Dickinson's "real ME" makes itself known in alienation, as a departed part of the self threatening to return and take over the territory of the damped "Daily mind." This externalization often expresses itself in psychological terms:

Presentiment—is that long Shadow—on the Lawn—
Indicative that Suns go down—

The Notice to the startled Grass
That Darkness—is about to pass—

(764)

"Presentiment" here is not so much a representative of the "real ME" as a shield against it, a prefigural lesser shock to the nerves. It presses its late-afternoon shadow on "the startled Grass" of the mind to prepare the grass for the total darkness of night, to defend the mind against the shock of unmediated experience. Even so, it is distinct from and external to the grass which it startles: the "instinctive" form of consciousness cannot but startle its passive counterpart. For a more exact paraphrase, we must turn to modern experimental biology. In *Man Adapting*, Rene Dubos writes that human response

> is determined not only by the nature of the stimulus itself but also by the indirect reactions that it mobilizes in them [the nerves]. This chain of indirect response is of greatest importance in man because of his propensity to symbolize everything that happens to him, and then to react to the symbols as if they were actual environmental stimuli.[8]

"Presentiment" here is experienced by the grass, the "mere humanity" with which the poem's voice sympathizes, as if it were an environmental stimulus.

In "One need not be a Chamber—to be Haunted—," the well-known poem on the brain as a chamber haunted by partially repressed memories, we find Dickinson's full spatial sequence. First, the chief objects of terror are redefined as interior:

> The Brain has Corridors—surpassing
> Material Place—
>
> Far safer, of a Midnight Meeting
> External Ghost
> Than its interior Confronting
> That Cooler Host—
>
> Far safer, through an Abbey gallop
> The Stones a'chase—
> Than Unarmed, one's a'self encounter—
> In lonesome Place—

This parody of a cheap gothic ballad attempts to rescue Burkean sublimity from the genteel shudder.[9] It internalizes "haunting" and devalues external horrors in comparison to self-inflicted ones. But this bisection of the self into victim and specter demands a casting-out of uncontrollable, truth-inflicting thoughts into the frightening environment:

> Ourself behind ourself, concealed—
> Should startle most—
> Assassin hid in our Apartment
> Be Horror's least.

139

> The Body—borrows a Revolver—
> He bolts the Door—
> O'erlooking a superior spectre—
> Or More—
>
> (670)

The body can protect itself from the external "assassin" but he cannot shut the door on that inner externality, that spirit of memory which is the "superior spectre / Or More," not a specter at all but the chief reality. One might still utilize the revolver, but only in the sense that

> No Drug for Consciousness—can be—
> Alternative to die
> Is Nature's only Pharmacy
> For Being's Malady—
>
> (786)

The gothic physicality of "One need not be a Chamber" and other poems—Dickinson can report coolly that "A Thought went up my mind today" (701)—indirectly suggests the most important difference between Dickinson's "real ME" and that figure as envisioned by the other American romantics. For Dickinson, the "real ME" is very real. It is not an idealization, not even a state of consciousness to be quested toward and achieved. It is ever present, an almost physical entity ever ready in hiding to ambush the "Daily mind" and assassinate sanity. Repeatedly, Dickinson insists on the secret imminence of the "real ME":

> On my volcano grows the Grass
> A meditative spot—
> An acre for a Bird to choose
> Would be the General thought—
>
> How red the Fire rocks below—
> How insecure the sod
> Did I disclose
> Would populate with awe my solitude.
>
> (1677)

And again:

Though the great Waters sleep,
That they are still the Deep,
We cannot doubt—
No vacillating God
Ignited this Abode
To put it out—

(1599)

If anything, the "real ME" is all too imminent. Of the American romantics, only Dickinson (with the possible exception of Poe) could fear the "Over-soul" and consider it a threat as well as a glorious potentiality. The Transcendentalists seek to unite the two selves, John Lynen writes, but "the union is never achieved, except faintly, as an intuition glimpsed, a momentary insight." No need to fear the "real ME" since "there is no more danger of losing one's personal identity than of achieving perfect consciousness."[10] Dickinson, who on occasion makes even the early Emerson appear restrained, can think of the achievement and the danger as natural and unavoidable, though what she fears is not the subsuming of individuality into the primordial sludge of Poe's *Eureka* but simply the battering of the nerves unto death. She is not so anxious for the still, sleeping waters to rise because she knows they will rise and because she knows they will be destructive as well as creative. In *Walden*, Thoreau prays for a flood:

> The life in us is like the water in the river. It may rise this year higher than man has ever known it, and flood the parched uplands.

In *Nature*, Emerson mourns the flood's absence:

> Man is the dwarf of himself. Once he was permeated and dissolved by spirit. He filled nature with his overflowing currents.... But having made for himself this huge shell [man's model of the cosmos], his waters retired; he no longer fills the veins and veinlets; he is shrunk to a drop.

Thoreau places the flood in an ideal future, Emerson in an ideal past. Each lavishes uncritical approval on it, perhaps because of its unreality. Dickinson thinks of such a flood as an habitual expectancy—"Fathoms are sudden Neighbors" (L 804)—and her attitude toward it is far more mixed:

The Brain, within its Groove
Runs evenly—and true—
But let a Splinter swerve—
'Twere easier for You—

141

Chapter Seven

To put a Current back—
When Floods have slit the Hills—
And scooped a Turnpike for Themselves—
And trodden out the Mills—

(556)

The mechanically grooved brain is hardly admirable, and there is an obvious degree of relish in the description of its wreckage. But there is also a horror at the destructive aggressiveness which slits, scoops, and treads and a despair at its finality. The fragility of the grooved brain lends it some value. Ernest Lowrie paraphrases the puritan theologian Samuel Willard to the effect "that to know God directly would be 'altogether destructive'; that a mere glimpse of God's most glorious and illustrious 'face with its dazzling Oriental Brightness' would obliterate man's creatureliness."[11] Dickinson expresses the same reticence toward the internalized God, and for the same reason: she has some fondness for her creatureliness and does not wish it to end prematurely.

In the figure of "The Brain, within its Groove," the "Daily mind," Dickinson has the courage to include within her poetry the anti-heroic, perhaps anti-poetic tendency of recalcitrance. Harold Bloom calls recalcitrance "the final enemy" of the romantic quester[12] and H. J. C. Grierson names the enemy of romantic imagination as "reason, not the scientific reason which has thought out the matter and attained conviction, but reason in the sense of what the society in which a man lives deems reasonable."[13] Dickinson recognizes the dangers of recalcitrance. The soul cannot be destroyed by external forces; it is invincible "Except Thyself may be / Thine Enemy—" (384). When the "Daily mind" interferes with an expansion of consciousness out of a solipsistic love of comfort, when it becomes a thorough attitude toward life, it is bitterly despised. The earl who will not risk all for the pearl and the "soft, cherubic ladies" whose precious decorum robs them of their souls suffer Dickinson's most withering glare. With Dickensian intonations she writes to her brother, " 'Mrs. Skeeter' is very feeble, 'cant bear Allopathic treatment, cant have Homeopathic'—dont want Hydropathic—Oh what a pickle she is in—should'nt think she would deign to *live*—it is so decidedly vulgar!' " (L 82). "The Ditch is dear to the Drunken man," begins a poem which reimages the *grooved* brain with intentional vulgarity, "Oblivion bending over him / And Honor leagues away" (1645). A love of comfort creates a distorted, static pleasure principle "Impeding navigation bright":

142

> A stagnant pleasure like a Pool
> That lets its Rushes grow
> Until they heedless tumble in
> And make the Water slow...
>
> (1281)

Opposed to an adventuresome soul, the "Daily mind" offers only conventionality and a stifling security. It is only when the "Daily mind" is dramatized as a survival principle that it is grudgingly valued, most often as a necessity rather than as a glory. "What is called real is too often an exhausted phantasmagoria," Bloom writes, "and the reality principle can too easily be debased into a principle of surrender, an accommodation with death-in-life."[14] To justify itself, the "Daily mind" must prove it is not that. In Dickinson's words, " 'tis when / A Value struggle—it exist—" (806) and the "Daily mind" must struggle more than most. If we wonder why it is justified as often as it is, we should remember the intimate connection of torture and transcendence in Dickinson: "Power is only Pain—" (252); "All— is the price of All" (772); "A *Wounded* Deer—leaps highest—" (165). Often, Dickinson will urge on this bursting of joy's grape against a palate of melancholy and even death. She will say that "Ecstasy is peril" (L 989). Yet in the face of death, recalcitrance is not always seen as cowardly. Its prudence may disclose a fierce love of life:

> Crisis is sweet and yet the Heart
> Upon the hither side
> Has Dowers of Prospective
> To Denizens denied...
>
> (1416)

In fact, as a temporary respite from the volleys of the real, the blinkered brain may encourage the now-exhausted nerves to greater adventures. Of "Dull days," Dickinson tells Joseph Lyman:

> I specially love them because, [by] the kindly thirst they give, I can drink deeper from the sun: just now for instance I would be glad of a little mist, a furlough, for June has been bombarding us, boom after boom of summer glory—a very cannonade of splendors.[15]

If a value must struggle to exist, that law applies equally to the hypervital real, and the dull days of the blinkered brain are necessary for dialectical opposition. And should the "real ME" emerge as a result of extreme anxiety or sorrow, the unglorious "Daily mind" is often granted the more positive value of life-saver:

> Floss won't save you from an Abyss
> But a Rope will—
> Notwithstanding a Rope for a Souvenir
> Is not beautiful—
>
> But I tell you every step is a Trough—
> And every stop a Well—
> Now will you have the Rope or the Floss?
> Prices reasonable—
>
> (1322)

The darker Dickinson paints the abyss, the better the rope looks and the more reasonable the price of recalcitrance seems. By such a process does Dickinson's confessional voice of limitation get a hearing in a fiction dominated by a Transcendentalist tone.

2

The struggles between Dickinson's "real ME" and her "Daily mind" are waged on various grounds, with various weapons, to conflicting conclusions. The regulation fiction is Promethean. It helps to form the greatest and most minute questions.

Often the conflict is ontological:

> We never know how high we are
> Till we are asked to rise
> And then if we are true to plan
> Our statures touch the skies—
>
> The Heroism we recite
> Would be a normal thing
> Did not ourselves the Cubits warp
> For fear to be a King—
>
> (1176)

This Emersonian poem converts the single, postmortem act of resurrection into a perpetual process of growth in life. We are not suddenly raised from the grave but gradually raise ourselves to heaven. God is

implied not as an external agent but as an internal principle, the "real
ME." Sadly, the second stanza must admit that this is only a vision,
made unreal by what here is a thoroughly despicable recalcitrance. The
blinkered brain triumphs but Dickinson treats the victory with the
same disdain by which Shelley treats "The Triumph of Life."

The conflict may be restated in terms of moral courage. Not
surprisingly, "real ME" is favored here. Dickinson's bardic voice
proclaims, "If your Nerve, deny you— / Go above your Nerve—"
(292).[16] It is the rising above fears that endears others to us:

> Sweet, to have had them lost
> For news that they be saved—
> The nearer they departed Us
> The nearer they, restored,
>
> Shall stand to Our Right Hand—
> *Most* precious and the Dead—
> Next precious
> Those that rose to go—
> Then thought of Us, and stayed.
>
> (901)

This poem, which plays on the separation-death analogy of the typology
of death, stresses the importance of leaving. Those who rise above their
nerve, their human sentiments, to risk transport are dearer than those
who stay, even if they stay because of affection. Whether the travelers'
return is actual or metaphorical (resurrected in memory or in heaven),
they will stand at "Our Right Hand"—and at God's. Unfortunately,
the intentional choice of the "real ME" is infrequent. Consider this
explicit contest:

> Is Bliss then, such Abyss,
> I must not put my foot amiss
> For fear I spoil my shoe?
>
> I'd rather suit my foot
> Than save my Boot—
> For yet to buy another Pair
> Is Possible,
> At any store—
>
> But Bliss, is sold just once.
> The Patent lost

145

None buy it any more—
Say, Foot, decide the point—
The Lady cross, or not?
Verdict for Boot!

(340)

The verdict is a surprise. In the first stanza, the foot represents the usually adventuresome spirit, the boot the usually reticent body. The persona seems ready to risk death to gain bliss, ready to sacrifice the common oxygen for the uncommon lightning—and yet the foot decides in favor of the boot, its antithesis. The point is that too much questioning negates the opportunity, that the will must not abdicate its power of choice. When the foot is allowed to make the choice, it loses its symbolic identity to become a mere part of the comfort-seeking body.

Not only large issues but also the most common occurrences may be dramatized in terms of the regulation fiction. The simple act of crying to express joyful gratitude for a kind act is expressed in such a way:

To try to speak, and miss the way
And ask it of the Tears,
Is Gratitude's sweet poverty,
The Tatters that he wears—

A better Coat if he possessed
Would help him to conceal,
Not subjugate, the Mutineer
Whose title is "the Soul."

(1617)

A better coat would not negate the soul of sincerity; but it would hide true feeling entirely from view. Dickinson here gives thanks to the tattered covering of the "Daily mind" which allows the "real ME" (not a cosmic, abstract figure in this case, but simply honest emotion) to show through.

While the regulation fiction itself shows through an endless variety of "topics," it is most often and most effectively dramatized in psychological terms. The idea of the "Daily mind" is transformed into a theory of repression and defense mechanisms which strikingly anticipates the scientific investigations of Sigmund and Anna Freud. We like the "Daily mind" better in these instances because its protection is not chosen but automatic:

There is a pain—so utter—
It swallows substance up—
Then covers the Abyss with Trance—
So Memory can step
Around—across—upon it—
As one within a Swoon—
Goes safely—where an open eye—
Would drop Him—Bone by Bone.

(599)

Sometimes, there is nowhere to go "above your Nerve." The involuntary nature of repression is made strikingly apparent by the ascription of its cause to the very pain that is repressed. Of course one does not wish to trade consciousness for a swoon, but when the alternative is a gruesome self-destruction the swoon becomes the lesser of two negations. The poem's final phrases constitute one of many examples in which Dickinson's apparent hyperboles have come to be taken literally: psychoanalysts contend that if one's repressed thoughts suddenly surfaced, the result might be actual and immediate death. (This is not to say that we must value Dickinson because modern science "proves" her, but that her hyperboles have a more exact intent than we often credit to them.)

This swoon, this "Doubt if it be Us" as we undergo anguish, is the negation "that makes the living possible / While it suspends the lives" (859). In many of these directly psychological poems, the blinkered brain's immediate forgetfulness becomes an agent of mercy. Its meddling "Grass" which once covered the gravestone "Of All Conceived Joy" is saluted as a principle of perseverance in " 'Tis good—the looking back on Grief—" (660). But such gratitude should not disguise the dark, necessitarian look of the regulation fiction as it becomes psychological. The further repression spreads its net of negations, the more tragic its necessity becomes. We saw in an earlier chapter how the very thought of death can become a typological death in good and bad senses. As a psychological occurrence, it is seen in its worst aspect:

I never hear that one is dead
Without the chance of Life
Afresh annihilating me
That mightiest Belief,

Too mighty for the Daily mind
That tilling its abyss,

147

Had Madness, had it once or twice
The yawning Consciousness,

Beliefs are Bandaged, like the Tongue
When Terror were it told
In any Tone commensurate
Would strike us instant Dead

I do not know the man so bold
He dare in lonely Place
That awful stranger Consciousness
Deliberately face—

(1323)

The only way in which the total consciousness of the "real ME" can be achieved in the face of the fact of death is by a surprise attack, dramatized here in the first three lines, before the "Daily mind" can protect itself. The subsequent bandaging of beliefs is every bit as instinctual as its opposite, the desire to live intensely, for a full recognition would burn out the power station. No one would be bold enough to face "That awful stranger Consciousness" when that stranger contains a realization which leads not to "transport" but to instant dissolution. And yet "boldness" and "consciousness" have an intrinsic value whose denial is simply another kind of death. The poem leaves us with a choice of defeats. The two extremes are clearly stated and each is an abyss: one is the "Daily mind's" negation of significance, the other is the annihilating fall into "yawning Consciousness." The poem is yet another statement of the regulation fiction's central paradox: self-maintenance and self-realization deny each other. The extinguishing ultimate reality both attracts and repels until, by the natural and unavoidable process of death, it gains victory.

3

The sense we get from the conflict of the "real ME" and the blinkered, grooved brain is of the extreme perilousness of existence, in which "each step is a Trough." We are in a pit with "Heaven over it" and "fathoms under it." "To stir would be to slip—" (1712) and yet how else can we rise from the lowly groove? It is in this quandary that our third character, the voice of the poem, exists. Because of the externalization by which the brain, the soul, and even the tender nerve ends of the "Daily mind" are components of what the voice speaks

148

about, we may wonder who the voice is, or, more properly, what human function it bespeaks. The closest we can come to describing it in established nomenclature is by the term "Freudian ego." Most simply, the ego plays off instinct against conscience to keep the human machine functioning. But we must find a more original term for Dickinson's voice in these poems for, while the "real ME" may bear some resemblance to the Freudian id, the grooved brain (except in its most debased form) does not resemble the implanted standards of a society (the superego) so much as the survival-minded ego itself. Our early analogy of the power station suggests a more accurate name for the typical persona of the regulation fiction. Call him the voice of the transformer, for the voice mediates between the overload of total consciousness and the cowardly retreat of the "Daily mind" to meaningless activity.

In all, the voice represents a regulatory agency. I take the word "regulation" from "The last Night that She lived," a poem in which the persona is one of several observers at the death of a friend. (In fact we can think of this persona as the alter-ego of the "dying voice" in "I heard a Fly buzz when I died—," as one of the mourners who wring their eyes dry.) The death occurs and the mourners must find a way to consider it:

> And We—We placed the Hair—
> And drew the Head erect—
> And then an awful leisure was
> Belief to regulate—
>
> (1100)

To regulate! Not only does the word suggest the boosting of faith to a power adequate to dispel doubts, but also a stepping-down of that too powerful typological faith which would demand the psychological equivalent of death on the part of the mourner. In this especially terrible situation, the transformer seems to retreat to orthodoxy; elsewhere, as we have seen, its judgment is more bold. Of course, this voice is not apart from the struggle; it is not objective in unconcern about it. The regulatory voice does not take the stance of the speaker in meditative poetry where, as Louis L. Martz comments, "the self casts itself upon a mental stage for critical examination."[17] No such fiction of self-distancing is available to Dickinson's voice, for her fiction stresses that the self which criticizes lives intimately with the self which acts. In her first letter to Higginson, she asked him to judge her poems because "The Mind is so near itself—it cannot see, distinctly—and I have none to ask—" (L 260).

But, the reader may complain, the transformer's decisions are all too various. Sometimes it cheers on the "real ME," sometimes it cautiously advises retreat into the "Daily mind," and sometimes it simply bemoans the paradox of its situation. Granting the dramatic necessity of an ethic-in-situation and the apparent contradictions that must accrue, will Dickinson never stand still long enough for us to know her position? In the case of the regulation fiction, she will. Dickinson here posits a definite life-ethic, though she usually dramatizes disruptions of the balance she advises. This balance does not transcend the conflict of "real ME" and "Daily mind"; instead it makes a compromise—a compromise which distinctly favors one of the disputants. We can get at this ethic in a poem which disguises it as a preordained law:

Crisis is a Hair
Toward which the forces creep
Past which forces retrograde
If it come in sleep

To suspend the Breath
Is the most we can
Ignorant is it Life or Death
Nicely balancing.

Let an instant push
Or an Atom press
Or a Circle hesitate
In Circumference

It—may jolt the Hand
That adjusts the Hair
That secures Eternity
From presenting—Here—

(889)

The forces of the "real ME" creep toward eternity, the forces of the blinkered brain push us back, and our duty is to keep a delicate balance upon the hair of crisis. It is a hair at the edge of the territory of death and eternity but not in it. The slightest further movement of the mind will allow eternity to present itself in the realm of this life. Life at the hair is not a comfortable situation and the daring involved may be foolhardy; but another poem which draws out other connotations of this odd image of hair argues that such daring is the only alternative to a living death. In "We like a Hairbreadth 'scape," Dickinson parodies pulp romances for the serious purpose of explaining the benefits of a crisis-bound life:

> If we had ventured less
> The Breeze were not so fine
> That reaches to our utmost Hair
> Its Tentacles divine.
>
> (1175)

Only by tempting death are we put in touch with divinity. Only as a "Hairbreadth 'scape" from the death involved with an activation of the "real ME" do the common pleasures of the "Daily mind" take on vitality. Similarly, in "These are the Nights that Beetles love—," Dickinson considers threatening thunder as a vitalizing danger:

> A Bomb upon the Ceiling
> Is an improving thing—
> It keeps the nerves progressive
> Conjecture flourishing—
> Too dear the Summer evening
> Without discreet alarm—
> Supplied by Entomology
> With its remaining charm—
>
> (1128)

Charm and alarm are rhyming synonyms. If we cannot have the harrowing storm, let us have the harrowing fly. Dickinson views ideal man as a living dialectic between life and death, dull reason and annihilating madness.

But the hair leans toward the "real ME." Furthermore, the nature of any moderation principle depends on the subtle choice of the extremes which are to be avoided, and Dickinson's choice creates an extremely immoderate moderation principle. It is an ethic of "power at all costs, almost." Despite the qualification afforded by the blinkered brain, this leaning toward the realization of a true self makes Dickinson's ethic liable to all the enraged attacks on Emersonian Transcendentalism. Yvor Winters, whose condemnation of Emerson has somewhere been described as the act of a static square attempting to capture a dynamic spiral, stated the obvious but well-taken objection that such an ethical system is amoral, that it offers no restraints whatsoever in man's relation to his fellows—or to himself. Winters especially condemns Emerson's euphemism, "if I am the Devil's child, I will live then from the Devil"[18] and he goes on to charge Emerson with murder in the suicide of Hart Crane, whose poetry was influenced by Emerson. This outrageous charge is easily refuted by W. J. Bate's argument against blaming originals for the faults of their imitators. To blame poor romantic art on Wordsworth, Hazlitt, or Keats (or Nazism on Nietzsche or Crane's suicide on Emerson) "is almost as weak a generalization as to say that in Aristotle are the inevitable seeds of Thomas Rymer."[19] Furthermore, when Emerson puts himself in possible league with Satan, he is not saying that he is willing to do evil but that natural impulses must be good and that any idea of God or good which denies those impulses must be wrong—so wrong that the villain of such an idea must be the true God. If the ideal of power is sadly and even viciously redefined by Emerson late in his career, in its more important earlier formulations it is equated with virtue, just as virtue etymologically derives from *virtus,* manliness and power.[20] In Dickinson, we find a similar trust in Rousseau's natural man:

> A Counterfeit—a Plated Person—
> I would not be—
> Whatever strata of Iniquity
> My Nature underlie—
> Truth is good Health—and Safety, and the Sky.
> How meagre, what an Exile—is a Lie,
> And Vocal—when we die—
>
> (1453)

I will not argue for the absolute truth of such a doctrine. Sincerity is not safe: Dickinson has suffered a century of ridicule for the social quirks created by her sincerity and late in her own life suffered a breakdown which she herself blamed on her intense mode of life. Some people find the idea of "real ME" naive and injurious and a life in quest of that phantom obsessive and self-deluding. Others find the idea and the life which springs from the idea heroic and exemplary. We are not arguing a philosophy so much as an attitude; and one cannot prove or disprove it but only approve or condemn it by one's own lights.

But there is more to say on Dickinson's behalf in this matter. The "real ME" of her regulation fiction may be shaped to approve simple kindness as well as wild force:

To do a magnanimous thing and take oneself by surprise, if one is not in the habit of it, is precisely the finest of joys. Not to do a magnanimous thing, notwithstanding it never be known, notwithstanding it cost us existence, is rapture herself spurned.

(L, p. 913)

Anyone who has read her letters will conclude that Dickinson's devotion to the "real ME" is a benevolent attention to the deepest feelings not only of herself but of anyone with whom she came into the slightest contact. And however much Dickinson wishes to do away with a censoring and recriminatory conscience, she cannot. She will say with her puritan forefathers that conscience is a part of the natural man. She includes it as memory in her regulation fiction, as a function of the blistering real, not of the blinkered brain:

> The Past is such a curious Creature
> To look her in the Face
> A Transport may receipt us
> Or a Disgrace—
>
> Unarmed if any meet her
> I charge him fly
> Her faded Ammunition
> Might yet reply.
>
> (1203)

Shame as memory is described in the same images as the last of summer or the soul *"at the White Heat"* (365).[21] It, too, brings forth a recommendation which, issued by Dickinson, means that the great challenge is to unarm, remain, and confront the unbidden reality. If, then, Winters is right to believe that the doctrine of power may lead to exclusive self-concern and devastating failure, we can respond only that Dickinson's shaping of that doctrine actively prevented these solipsistic evils.

To return to the life-ethic of the regulation fiction in itself, we can trace its influence on widely diverse aspects of Dickinson's thought. Translated into an aesthetic, and given the built-in distancing provided by art, Dickinson usually opts for a total activation of the real—within limits. Poetry is the activity in which one should dare to overwhelm oneself:

> Dying at my music!
> Bubble! Bubble !

153

Hold me till the Octave's run!
Quick! Burst the Windows!
Ritardando!
Phials left, and the Sun!

(1003)

This may be the worst of all kinds of poems, unintentional self-parody, but for all its bubbles it suggests the suitability of art to an overdaring temperament. A poem or a piece of music must end, and thus the development of the destructive real can be timed to reach past the hair to death just as the "music" ends. The "Daily mind" whose "forces retrograde" has its say in the silence of the "Ritardando." The musician-poet barely survives, but survives in such a way that the sun's warmth is newly, more intensely appreciated. The reader is to imitate this process. Higginson reports that Dickinson told him:

> If I read a book [and] it makes my whole body so cold no fire ever can warm me I know *that* is poetry. If I feel physically as if the top of my head were taken off, I know *that* is poetry. These are the only way I know it. Is there any other way?
>
> (L 342a)

Yes there is, we are tempted to answer. But Dickinson, playing the innocent, is simply approving the wholehearted response teachers demand of students, though in striking physical imagery. Hidden within the approval of direct response is the blinkered brain's sophisticated recognition that art affords an innate "feel as if" which makes an overpowering neurological response less dangerous than in direct experience.[22]

Besides explicit applications to poetry, the regulation fiction affords poems which *may* be read as justifications of Dickinson's poetic peculiarities. In "A nearness to Tremendousness," Dickinson offers a (potential) justification for a poetry deliberately out of strict control. "Laws" are for the "Daily mind":

Vicinity to Laws

Contentment's quiet Suburb—
Affliction cannot stay
In Acres—Its Location
Is Illocality—

(963)

The poem may be read psychologically, in tandem with Freud's definition of anxiety as a general dis-ease which cannot be isolated, but it also may be read in tandem with Emerson's "Merlin":

> Great is the art,
> Great be the manners, of the bard.
> He shall not his brain encumber
> With the coil of rhythm and number;
> But leaving rule and pale forethought
> He shall aye climb
> For his rime. . . .

Yet if Dickinson indirectly approves direct expressions of thoughtful passion (and the contradiction suggests the partiality of the approval), we may return to the image of the hair for a justification of her frequent double-mindedness:

> Staking our entire Possession
> On a Hair's result—
> Then—Seesawing—cooly—on it—
> Trying if it split—
>
> (971)

We are to give our all to an idea, but we are then to challenge it with pretended unconcern, rocking back and forth on the value to make it struggle to exist. (In our next chapter, we shall see the entire regulation fiction so challenged.)

The regulation fiction affords an ideal even for Dickinson's admittedly pessimistic psychological poems, though here it is not so much a compromise which is recommended as a risky sequence. We know that the "Daily mind" is brought into play automatically by strong, potentially destructive reactions to experience, but too much repression creates its own danger. Inevitably, the self will revolt against overly tight restrictions on self-realization and become uncontrollable:

> The Life that tied too tight escapes
> Will ever after run
> With a prudential look behind
> And spectres of the Rein—. . .
>
> (1535)

Do not underrate the strength of the mind's resilience, Dickinson commands. Do not deny what the self can withstand:

> There is a strength in proving that it can be borne
> Although it tear—
> What are the sinews of such cordage for
> Except to bear
> The ship might be of satin had it not to fight—
> To walk on seas requires cedar Feet
>
> (1113)

First, experience the reality; if it is too terrible, it will contain its own opiate, but perhaps it can be defeated through confrontation: "Despair's advantage is achieved / By suffering—Despair—" (799).

I will seem now to run my own embargo on biographical interpretation by reading the psychological ethic of the poems into the life. But I warned earlier against reading any particular poem too literally according to a biographical event, while here I simply want to claim that the pattern of Dickinson's poems as a whole corresponds to some of the self-stated patterns of her life. It does no harm to the truth to identify *this* speaker with its creator:

> I lived on Dread—
> To Those who know
> The Stimulus there is
> In Danger—Other Impetus
> Is numb—and Vitalless—
>
> As 'twere a Spur—upon the Soul—
> A Fear will urge it where
> To go without the Spectre's aid
> Were Challenging Despair.
>
> (770)

Dread, in different forms, is the highest value of the typology of death and the regulation fiction. (Of course, these two organizations are not separate but overlapping.) In the most general terms, I would argue that this is a triumphant, comic dread, a barbed hymn to the power of life. And dread appears to be the uncomfortable but productive ruler of Dickinson's personal existence. The oddest quirk, say Dickinson's reluctance to greet visitors in the last several years of her life, becomes dignified and admirable when considered in terms of the regulation fiction. At first, this habit of speaking to guests from a hiding place, behind a door or in the hall, appears ludicrous, coy, and life-denying. We can see it now as a protective function of the blinkered brain, as the protection of a sensibility so open and intensely cultivated that the merest meeting would issue in significant disturbances.

Am I romanticizing? Dickinson met with Higginson face to face and this is part of his report to his wife:

> I never was with anyone who drained my nerve power so much. Without touching her, she drew from me. I am glad not to live near her. She often thought me *tired* & seemed very thoughtful of others.
>
> (L 342b)

Perhaps her occasional solitudes were to protect others as well as herself from her own intensity.

Clearly, as to her own regulation, Dickinson overindulged her "real ME." That, of course, is the condition of the ethical "compromise" in the poems. In June 1884, while Dickinson was baking a cake, she became delirious. "I saw a great darkness coming and knew no more until late at night," she explains to her "little cousins," the Norcross sisters. The balancing upon the hair, the varied psychological imitations of death were taking their predictable toll. "The doctor calls it 'revenge of the nerves'; but who but Death had wronged them?" (L 907). It isn't that I have lived too intensely, Dickinson implies, but that I have lived attentively at all. Singularly missing from this note is any indication of regret. Apparently, Dickinson still believed in her dark summer what she had written to Maria Whitney in the spring of the previous year: that "the pang of life" is the pain "sweeter to bear than to omit" (L 815).

8

The Necessary Veil:
A Quest Fiction

> *Hope never knew Horizon—... Moving on in the Dark like Loaded Boats at Night, though there is no Course, there is Boundlessness—*
>
> (L 871)

1

Dickinson's bardic pronouncements are countered by her confessions of failure and suffering; her belief that each earthly moment contains a potential paradise is countered by her belief that this heaven is always lost as time runs on. Just so, the poems of the regulation fiction are countered by the poems of epistemological quest. In the regulation fiction, God (and again I will insist that we not identify Dickinson's God-term completely with the God of orthodox Christians, but define it simply as the prime source of meaning and power) is within as well as abroad, always threatening to overflow the grooves of sense. In the quest fiction, God is not only separate from the first-person speaker; he is hidden and possibly absent, the power behind the cloud "If any Power behind it, be" (293). The quester need not fear involuntary transport and the mind's abundance of wild power in this fiction, but involuntary stoppage and the mind's limitations.

We can exemplify the crucial differences between these two fictions by recalling the image of the "hair." In the regulation fiction, the hair symbolizes the delicate balance which the persona must maintain between his temporal and eternal self; he seesaws giddily upon it. In the quest fiction, the hair remains in the same position, but it has become

158

an absolute barrier. It prevents the persona of "I had not minded—Walls—" from reaching the object of her desire, an object which may be considered as either a departed lover or a godlike personification of self-completion, or both. Were the barrier a wall and all the universe a rock, the persona proclaims, "I'd tunnel—till my Groove / Pushed sudden 'thro to his—." It is the barrier's insubstantiality, as an invisible law of life, which makes such a tunneling impossible:

> But 'tis a single Hair—
> A filament—a law—
> A Cobweb—wove in Adamant—
> A Battlement—of Straw—
>
> A limit like the Veil—
> Unto the Lady's face—
> But every Mesh—a Citadel—
> And Dragons—in the Crease—
>
> (398)

This hair, like the "Forest of the Dead" in "Our Journey had advanced—," signifies the limit of the mind's knowledge. It establishes a territory for the unknown and protects that territory with the dragons of Spenserian romance. So near and yet so far, the great mystery tantalizes but remains ungraspable. The quester, however persistent, never will bypass this hair; it dooms him, as another poem expresses it, to inhabit only "The Suburbs of a Secret" (1245). He will never penetrate the inner city. How can one penetrate a hair?

If the regulation fiction, with its self-frightened insistence on the boundless possibilities of the self, illustrates Dickinson's relation to (and her reaction against) Emersonian Transcendentalism, these poems of frustrated quest may be considered Dickinson's puritan fiction, her humble vision of a profoundly dependent self striving to reach the object of her faith. That goal is never achieved, not in the life of this consciousness; yet the crux of this fiction, the event of this quest which most deserves explanation, is Dickinson's transformation of a tragic-seeming vision of limitation and necessity into a hope-filled vision of opportunity and will.

To begin our own quest toward this explanation, we first must wade the turgid waters of philosophical debate. It is widely held, especially among her most ardent admirers, that Dickinson is naive in philosophical matters—this, always with the addendum that formal philosophy has little to do with poetic expression. Such a generalization is too vague to mean anything, though in one respect it is itself hopelessly naive. H. J. C. Grierson insists that Plato, "despite his condemnation of poets, effected that inter-relation of philosophy and poetry which has characterized every great romantic movement."[1] The nineteenth-century romantics, with the exception of Coleridge, may not have studied every document of the epistemological debate which began with Descartes. Nonetheless, its resolution in the German idealism of Kant permeated the romantic air. Most simply put, this debate concerns the relationship of the human agent and his scene, the world, and the specific issue of whether mind or matter is prior and creative. Such a statement of the problem, with its either/or formulation, simply annoys Dickinson. She responds to it with a pair of hilariously contradictory poems, obviously designed to dismiss the question. The first asserts that the effect of an oriole's song depends on its hearer's state of mind. It concludes:

> The "Tune is in the Tree—"
> The Skeptic—showeth me—
> "No Sir! In Thee!"
> (526)

The second proceeds from an assumption exactly opposite: "Split the Lark—and you'll find the Music— / Bulb after Bulb, in Silver rolled—" (861). Not only do the poems cancel each other, but each expresses such an extreme and simplistic view that it deliberately parodies itself and argues for the opposite view. Dickinson cannot take seriously the all-or-nothing question of whether the internal or the external is the source of the other. In the regulation fiction, the problem is that they can combine to become all too real; and, as we have seen, Dickinson's poetic techniques generally put the question aside to examine things-as-they-are, a procedure which anticipates modern phenomenology.

Yet, characteristically, Dickinson is willing to consider the question, and even to worry it over and over again, once it is formulated less dogmatically. I do not wish to picture Dickinson poring over the *Critique of Pure Reason*, but she shares Kant's sense of the futility of the prior debate and reaches toward the same conclusions. Bertrand Russell neatly summarizes Kant's resolution:

> According to Kant, the outer world causes only the matter of sensation, but our own mental apparatus orders this matter in space and time, and

160

supplies the concepts by means of which we understand experience.
Things in themselves, which are the causes of our sensations, are
unknowable; they are not in space and time, they are not substances, nor
can they be described by any of those other general concepts which Kant
calls "categories." Space and time are subjective, they are part of our
apparatus of perception.[2]

As Kenneth Burke notes, human perception becomes "a questionnaire
with a set of blanket questions to be filled in differently in the case of
each object, but with the whole set of questions requiring some kind of
answer in every case."[3] Our perceptual grid of time and space prohibits
a pure knowledge of absolute realities yet that grid is a trustworthy
human reality which allows for a relationship to things-in-themselves.[4]
Dickinson expresses this very notion in a poem which thoroughly
disproves the opinion that she is philosophically naive:

> Perception of an object costs
> Precise the Object's loss—
> Perception in itself a Gain
> Replying to its Price—
>
> The Object Absolute—is nought—
> Perception sets it fair
> And then upbraids a Perfectness
> That situates so far—
>
> (1071)

Denis Donoghue believes that in this poem "the dualism of subject and
object is, in a flash, consumed,"[5] but the poem expresses no such facile
merger. Rather, dualism is replaced by an idea of imperfect, partial
relatedness. As soon as the absolute *Object* is perceived, it becomes a
mere object. Gain and price: human perception is necessary for any
comprehension of the real, but through it we lose any hope of knowing
the real in its raw, unreduced state. As a final irony, only by the act of
our limited perception do we learn how limited it is, how far the real is
situated outside the mind's circumference.

The limited gift of the perceptual grid provides us a "why" for the
quest poems: why the quest is doomed to failure until death, when, it is
hoped, the subject-object opposition *will* be consumed in a flash; and
why the quest nonetheless is worth the undertaking, as a preparation
for perfection. In this life, mind is larger than matter but smaller than
matter's underlying reality. "The Brain—is wider than the Sky—,"
begins a poem which seems to claim all for consciousness; the brain is

also "deeper than the sea—." Nature, as appearance, is easily enclosed within circumference. The final stanza begins in the same vein (vain), but at the last moment enacts a quicksilver reversal:

> The Brain is just the weight of God—
> For—Heft them—Pound for Pound—
> And they will differ—if they do—
> As Syllable from Sound—
>
> (632)

We must take that qualifying "if they do" ironically. The difference of weight between "Syllable" and "Sound" is at once minute and absolute, the difference of a hair. It is the difference between the thing itself and its imperfect, itemized explanation. It is the difference, say, between paraphrase and poetry, poetry and thought. The brain is not quite and not at all the weightless weight of God.[6]

Dickinson's achievement in the quest fiction is to accept the mind's limitations without flinching, and to make the best of those limitations by recasting the role of the quester. Dickinson's poetic quester is heroic not because he succeeds in reaching his goal but because he is motivated to devote himself to this ungraspable goal. He is special only because he can intuit that which he, no more than another man, can rationally comprehend. This awareness is the function of Dickinson's sixth sense;[7] the quester alone possesses "The Ear / Susceptive" to "Reportless Measures" (1048). This sixth sense is fiercely opposed to analysis, for "Too much of Proof affronts Belief" (1228) and emphasizes the mind's limits in spite of itself.[8] "By intuition, Mightiest Things / Assert themselves—and not by terms—" (420). These intuitions become "The Pierless Bridge" of an inferential faith, "Supporting what We see / Unto the Scene that We do not—" (915) and interpreting "Apprehensions" as "God's introductions" (797).

But to infer a far reality is not to own it or know it satisfactorily, as we saw in Dickinson's poems on evanescences:

> Their Graspless manners—mock us—
> Until the Cheated Eye
> Shuts arrogantly—in the Grave—
> Another way—to see—
>
> (627)

Could we presume the pier "behind the Veil" to which the bridge of faith leads,

The Necessary Veil: A Quest Fiction

> The Bridge would cease to be
> To Our far, vacillating Feet
> A first Necessity.
>
> (915)

At best, the poetic quester is actively walking that bridge. To change metaphors, he is within a cocoon, no longer a caterpillar crawling from appearance to appearance, but not yet a butterfly able to soar to a final reality:

> My Cocoon tightens—Colors tease—
> I'm feeling for the Air—
> A dim capacity for Wings
> Demeans the Dress I wear—
>
> . . . .
>
> So I must baffle at the Hint
> And cipher at the Sign
> And make much blunder, if at last
> I take the clue divine—
>
> (1099)

The image of the cocoon, a three-dimensional circumference, serves both as a preventing veil and as a promise that the veil will finally be rent.

The cocoon, with its implication of a gradual metamorphosis, eases the quest fiction's terrible message, that the "divine" is achieved only by death, if then. More often, Dickinson fleshes out the poet's middlemost position in the person of the stranded quester. Throughout his life, he remains at the edge of the "Forest of the Dead," where advance is impossible and "Retreat—was out of Hope—" (615). At most, as in "Tho' I get home, how late—how late—," he can only prophesy his delayed, postmortem victory. Dickinson's quest is a long, arduous journey which must conclude in disappointment:

> Three rivers and the Hill are passed—
> Two deserts and the sea!
> Now Death usurps my Premium
> And gets the look at Thee.
>
> (1664)

The quester is stopped at the boundary of life and language; this is the point at which the voices of "I felt a Funeral" and "I heard a Fly buzz" can say no more. "The lonesome for they know not What" are never envisioned possessing the "What" they have lost "ever since—the purple Moat / They strive to climb—in vain—" (262). The sunset sky cannot be climbed. The final reality, like the dead loved one in the early stages of the typology of death, is beyond the grasp of the living mourner. The same model persists even when the sought goal is not outside the quester, but within. In "Each Life Converges to some Centre—," Dickinson comforts herself with the belief that there "Exists in every Human Nature / A Goal—." But the question of achieving the goal of self-fulfillment in this life is cause for grief:

> To reach
> Were hopeless, as the Rainbow's Raiment
> To touch—. . .
>
> (680)

However "converged" the center becomes, it will seem as diffuse as the prismatic rainbow. The "real ME" here becomes an unexplored and forbidden territory, sadly contradicting the regulation fiction's idea of a real self that is all too available.

It would seem sufficiently frustrating that the quester cannot achieve his goal. Yet, in addition, the quester lacks an exact idea of that goal: "Our Port a secret / Our Perchance a Gale" (1656), the gale of real or figural death. Even when the barrier suddenly and mysteriously disappears, the goal refuses to present itself:

> I saw no Way—The Heavens were stitched—
> I felt the Columns close—
> The Earth reversed her Hemispheres—
> I touched the Universe—
>
> And back it slid—and I alone—
> A Speck upon a Ball—
> Went out upon Circumference—
> Beyond the Dip of Bell—
>
> (378)

Even when life opens up to hurl the quester out upon the circumference of his globed mind, out beyond his limitations, the quest is not yet completed and the goal is not yet known. The quester's middlemost position, his extreme alienation from both the mundane and the spiritual, the before and after, is simply redefined.

The Necessary Veil: A Quest Fiction

When Dickinson compares her questing self to "the Seed / That wrestles in the Ground," hoping to push through hard-packed soil but unsure of how this penetration will be achieved or what the achievement will mean, "The Hour, and the Clime— / Each Circumstance unknown," we must agree with her conclusion: "What Constancy must be achieved / Before it see the Sun!" (1255). This is a quest which demands utmost patience and the daring of a faith unsure of its object. Amazingly, many, even most, of these poems of quest are avowals of purpose rather than plaints of frustration. Such plaints do surface occasionally. It is a bitter reassurance that "I shall know why—when Time is over— / And I have ceased to wonder why—." When Christ explains "each separate anguish / In the fair schoolroom of the sky," Dickinson implies that the explanation will be a large bit tardy: "I shall forget the drop of Anguish / That scalds me now—that scalds me now!" (193). This exclamatory repetition shrieks that present harms cannot be satisfied by postponed cures.⁹ The hidden God's "fond Ambush" is a pleasant joke only if he does not carry it too far:

> Should the glee—glaze—
> In Death's—stiff—stare—
>
> Would not the fun
> Look too expensive!
> Would not the jest—
> Have crawled too far!
> (338)

If the goal is hidden and unknown, who is to say that it exists at all? And if it does not exist, then the quester himself ceases to exist as a hero and becomes a self-deluded fraud:

> Finding is the first Act
> The second, loss,
> Third, Expedition for
> The "Golden Fleece"
>
> Fourth, no Discovery—
> Fifth, no Crew—
> Finally, no Golden Fleece—
> Jason—sham—too.
> (870)

In such cryptic and emphatic language, Dickinson can call into

165

question the worth of her quester, the persona by which, as I shall show, she justifies her own mode of living. Yet I would see these poems of doubt in the same light as those poems of the regulation fiction which momentarily disown "transport" for the low comforts of the "Daily mind." In the quest fiction, recalcitrance comes to be defined as impatience and despair, and it must be eschewed for the travails of quest. "Out of sight? What of that?" Dickinson demands of her fears. "Better 'tis to fail—there— / Than debate—here—" (703). The quest fiction's ethic is, in part, a recapitulation of Dickinson's idea that a value must struggle to exist:

> What merit had the Goal—
> Except there intervene
> Faint Doubt—and far Competitor—
> To jeopardize the Gain?. . .
>
> (550)

But since the "far Competitor," death, will not only jeopardize but win the gain, the ethic must extend itself to justify hopelessness:

> The Service without Hope—
> Is tenderest, I think—
> Because 'tis unsustained
> By stint—Rewarded Work—
>
> Has impetus of Gain—
> And impetus of Goal—
> There is no Diligence like that
> That knows not an Until—
>
> (779)

The greatest diligence is to push forward the quest in spite of the strong suspicion that it is endless and fruitless. Success is irrelevant. Dickinson's quest fiction enacts a momentous change in the history of romance, a new emphasis on the hero's act of questing over against his successful completion of the quest. This theme has appeared so often in modern works that it has lost some of its moral surprise for us; the disruption of a convention becomes a convention in turn. But in Dickinson's poems of hopeless yet noble quest, as in Browning's "Childe Roland," we rediscover the passion, the thrill of discovery, that accompanies the restructuring of a narrative pattern at the moment of its disruption.

Dickinson is redefining values through an ethic which somewhat resembles the "purposiveness without purpose" by which Kant defines beauty. Dickinson's ethic, like Kant's formulation, is, in W. K. Wimsatt's apt words, "not a teleology toward a nameable further end." But whereas the purposive purposelessness of beauty for Kant consists in "a highly satisfactory fitting of experience precisely to our own faculty of experiencing, to the progress of our knowledge,"[10] Dickinson's "tenderest Service" consists in an invigorating and unsatisfying imbalance between imaginative desire and "our faculty of experiencing" which it outruns, again "to the progress of our knowledge." Dickinson's idea of beauty, her impossible quest, includes tragedy as an assumption and thus, on its own terms, becomes invincible to it. In its doomed failure, the quest fiction is profoundly comic.

A far more pragmatic belief couples with this Sisyphus-like heroism to cheer the quester. Richard Wilbur names this belief, in Dickinson's own phrase, "sumptuous destitution." It is the law that "once an object has been magnified by desire, it cannot be wholly possessed by appetite," and further that "food, or victory, or any other good thing is best comprehended by the eye of desire from the vantage of privation."[11] The idea runs through hundreds of poems, as a fruitful investigation and enlargement of a statement credited by Dickinson to Charlotte Brontë: " 'Life is so constructed that the event does not, cannot, match the expectation' " (L 442). Dickinson has this principle connect and subordinate topics as she constantly reimages it: "Dominion lasts until obtained" (1257); "The moment that a Plot is plumbed / Prospective is extinct—" (1417); "How destitute is he / Whose Gold is firm" (1477); and even "Anger as soon as fed is dead— / 'Tis starving makes it fat—" (1509). "Sumptuous destitution" serves as a retrospective explanation for many of Dickinson's poetic habits. Its inverted formulation indirectly explains Dickinson's technique of making common phenomena strange:

> I had a daily Bliss
> I half indifferent viewed
> Till sudden I perceived it stir—...

To make the common strange so that it "Increased beyond my utmost scope" (1057) is to get it right. The inherent value of the ungraspable also explains Dickinson's constant interest in death and the formulation of the separation-death typology in particular. And it is in this idea of sumptuous destitution that the fictions of regulation and quest combine. The regulation fiction's approval of dread may be interpreted in terms of the quest's approval of impossible desire:

> Expectation—is Contentment—
> Gain—Satiety—
> But Satiety—Conviction
> Of Necessity
>
> Of an Austere trait in Pleasure—
> Good, without alarm
> Is a too established Fortune—
> Danger—deepens Sum—
>
> (807)

Thus, paradoxically, the regulation fiction's "transport" may be found in the quest fiction's unfulfilled "expectation," the very frustration of transport.

Though the principle of sumptuous destitution affords these new perspectives on a range of Dickinson's poetic concerns, its major effect is on the quest fiction in itself. Its demand for the imagination to outrace reality transforms the quest's failure into a self-willed predicament. The forbidding hair may be erected not by a God who wishes to remain hidden but by the self's "Sweep Skepticism of the Heart," which

> Invites and then retards the Truth
> Lest Certainty be sere
> Compared with the delicious throe
> Of transport thrilled with Fear—
>
> (1413)

The quester here chooses to be balked, to become passive. The Veil becomes the lady's own, and she refuses to lift it "Lest Interview— annul a want / That Image—satisfies—" (421). The will's denial of itself is nonetheless an act of will. Because "It's finer—not to know—," Dickinson tells God to keep his secret:

> I would not—if I could,
> Know what the Sapphire Fellows, do,
> In your new-fashioned world!
>
> (191)

Once again, we view Dickinson in the act of converting a law of necessity into a necessary choice and working that conversion in such a way that it is no mere rationalization. Once again, the voice of the lowly sufferer modulates into the voice of the divine bard: "Consummation is the hurry of fools, but Expectation the Elixir of the Gods—" (L, p. 922). The necessary veil does not replace the veil of necessity, except in the progression of our argument. In the poetry itself, the quest as deliberately self-doomed simply alternates with the quest as doomed by life, another example of Dickinson's agile ability to allow two conflicting visions their appropriate moments of insight. Yet this prismatic effect of the poetry is itself an aesthetic borne of the principle of nonattainment. When Dickinson asks the Moon "Which is the best— the Moon or the Crescent," the Moon refuses to choose. "That is best which is not—Achieve it— / You efface the Sheen" and "Transport's decomposition follows— / He is Prism born" (1315).

2

If Dickinson "Invites and then Retards" any number of truths, the possibility of self-willed incompletion nonetheless has mighty effects. For one, it creates a renunciatory ideal which we can state in positive terms as the maintenance of the ego's freedom. The quest fiction's psychological ethic is simple and terrible: do not tie your entire self to any earthly object, for that would be to worship a false God:

> Enchantment's Perihelion
> Mistaken oft has been
> For the Authentic orbit
> Of its Anterior Sun.
>   (1299)

We must not attribute ideal qualities to real entities, for disappointment must follow and that disappointment will cause us to discard both the imagined ideal and the reality which cannot measure up:

> Taking up the fair Ideal,
> Just to cast her down
> When a fracture—we discover—
> Or a splintered Crown—
> Makes the Heavens portable—
> And the Gods—a lie—...

The "Heavens" are not "portable." We are here and they are there, beyond our reach. Keep the realms separate, Dickinson advises; cherish the ideal as a nonreality

> Till the broken creatures—
> We adorned—for whole—
> Stains—all washed—
> Transfigured—mended—
> Meet us—with a smile—
> (428)

It is only "the hurry of fools," exemplified by the poor persona of "My Life had stood," which can prevent a final, postmortem marriage of the real and its ideal mate.

No lover, no friend, no worldly ambition deserves dominion over the soul. A failure to recognize Dickinson's insistence on this point has created countless difficulties for interpreters of her poetry and her life. The chief victim, perhaps, has been this poem:

> The Soul selects her own Society—
> Then—shuts the Door—
> To her divine Majority—
> Present no more—
>
> Unmoved—she notes the Chariots—pausing—
> At her low Gate—
> Unmoved—an Emperor be kneeling
> Upon her Mat—
>
> I've known her—from an ample nation—
> Choose One—
> Then—close the Valves of her attention—
> Like Stone—
>
> (303)

This is the poem invariably invoked when a biographer wishes to nominate a new candidate as Dickinson's secret lover, the "One" chosen by Dickinson's feminine soul before she closes "the valves of her attention." But if we read the poem without the intention of pimping, we see that the second stanza rules out worldly suitors, emperors, and their chariots. The chosen "one" is a "what," not a "who," unnamed

because its only name is "Mystery"; as a Grecian bard Dickinson
writes,

> Lad of Athens, faithful be
> To Thyself,
> And Mystery—
> All the rest is Perjury—
> (1768)

The soul must attend to itself and its furthest goal; everything in
between is perjury. Less censoriously, Dickinson tells Higginson, "To
live is so startling, it leaves but little room for other occupations though
Friends are if possible an event more fair" (L 381). More fair, perhaps,
but less essential: "The Missing All—prevented Me / From missing
minor Things" (985).

Only in contrast does the quest fiction's psychological ideal relate to
Freud's more familiar theory of the ego. J. H. Van den Berg, in a wild
though engaging attack on Freud, demands that we recognize the
pessimism of Freud's models, especially his model of the object-seeking
libido:

> What prompts the libido to leave the inner self? In 1914 Freud asked
> himself this question—the essential question of his psychology, and the
> essential question of the psychology of the twentieth century. His answer
> ended the process of interiorization. It is: the libido leaves the inner self
> when the inner self has become too full. In order to prevent it from being
> torn, the I has to aim itself on objects outside the self; ". . . ultimately man
> must begin to love in order not to get ill." So that is what it is. Objects are
> of importance only in an extreme urgency. Human beings, too. The grief
> over their death is the sighing of a too far distended covering, the groaning
> of an over-filled inner self.[12]

Van den Berg wishes to see the ego's object-finding as ugly, and he
locates this ugliness in the "interiorization" begun by Rousseau and
concluded by Freud. The idea of object-finding (and even the actuality,
for Van den Berg is one of those scholars who assumes that the psyche
changes every few years, with each new cognitive theory) is blamed on
romanticism and its "interiorization" (for which, in truth, romanticism
is not a cause but an antidote). Dickinson would agree that object-
finding is ugly, but not because it is the function of an overstuffed
selfhood. She denies herself object-finding so that the self's circumference can expand continually as it takes account of that mystery

which it cannot, or will not, wholly contain. The self is never "over-filled" because it is constantly expanding. It is not worried about ego-affiliations because, in one sense, the self is a "Nobody":

> I'm Nobody! Who are you?
> Are you—Nobody—Too?
> Then there's a pair of us?
> Don't tell! They'd advertise—you know!
>
> How dreary—to be—Somebody!
> How public—like a Frog—
> To tell one's name—the livelong June—
> To an admiring Bog!
>
> (288)

For Dickinson, the simple desire for a private life contains, by implication, the life-principle of a protean ego, free to identify with its moving thoughts as they move forward (not to) the mystery behind the veil. She will sacrifice fame for immortality since "One's—Money—One's—the Mine—" (406); again, this is the difference between "Syllable" and "Sound." Dickinson's persona forsakes the frog-like certainty of a public Somebody to become a voyaging epistemology, voyaging in the hope of finally achieving the status of a Somebody at the Source, an Everybody-Everything with yet—chief paradox of hope—an individual identity, the carpetbag of the ego. It is, essentially, an isolated quest; "Growth of Man—like Growth of Nature— / Gravitates within—" by "the solitary prowess / Of a Silent Life—" (750), though "friends if possible are an event more fair." This very growth, borne of longing, will substitute for social relations as a source of present joy. It is a joy "edible to longing, / But ablative to show"; if Freudian anxiety is a dis-ease without an object, the quester's joy is "The joy that has no stem nor core, / Nor seed that we can sow" (1744).

Dickinson names this quest "the White Exploit" (922). The "White" is a symbol for the ego's pure devotion to the Ultimate. It is a borrowing of Mary's "blameless mystery" (271), a denotation of chosen "Tribulation" (325), a substitution of low joys by "that White Sustenance— / Despair—" (640), and a futile portrayal of "This limitless Hyperbole / Each one of us shall be—" (1482). In her maturity, Dickinson identified with her fictional quester by constantly wearing the white robes which symbolized both the nature and the unattainable object of the quester's faith. We should not be surprised by this direct transference of a poetic idea to Dickinson's life. Romantic poetics, with its avowal of sincerity, makes demands on the poet's life which an aesthetic stressing impersonal craftsmanship might find absurd. Romantic poets, Harold Bloom writes, "provide both a map of the mind and a profound faith that the map can be put to a saving use."[13] In Dickinson's phrasing, "For Pattern is the Mind bestowed"; by "imitating her" our lives will "Exhibit worthier" (1223).

Dickinson's pattern is in her poems, and they are a more reliable map to her life than the abstract psychological theories frequently and ruthlessly applied to her. Her isolation (which, in any case, was not so complete as her early biographers believed—as witnessed by the *Letters*, friends were frequently "possible") and her resultant failure to marry cease to vex us once we comprehend the quest's renunciatory ethic. In fact, the real problem becomes Dickinson's three apparent lapses, including her two verifiable romances. The first, with the Philadelphia clergyman Charles Wadsworth, is well characterized by Albert Gelpi as "an affair that could not exist beyond the confines of her mind";[14] it was, in other words, an infatuation, carried on by Emily before she became Dickinson, the writer of the poems. The second, an affair conducted by Dickinson when she was fifty with the elderly widower Judge Otis P. Lord, was very real, and as delightful as it was strangely tardy.[15] Millicent Todd Bingham reports that Susan, Emily's sister-in-law, remarked to her mother when her mother called one day, "You will not allow your husband to go there, I hope!...I went in there one day, and in the drawing room I found Emily reclining in the arms of a man."[16]

We find an explanation even for this late lapse in the poems. Dickinson's romance is the result of a minor rebellion against her own principles, against sumptuous destitution and the ego's freedom as a "Nobody." "I was always told that conjecture surpassed Discovery, but it must have been spoken in caricature, for it is not true," Dickinson tells Higginson in a letter written either just before or just after Lord's first visit (L 459). She then concludes the letter with a poem which directly turns on "I'm Nobody!" by praising "The long sigh of the Frog"[17] as an ideal. Earlier and more seriously, in "Renunciation—is a piercing Virtue—," Dickinson lauds "The letting go / A Presence—for an Expectation—." But as the poem continues, a doubt concerning this characteristic recommendation is cast in the form of a further definition:

> Renunciation—is the Choosing
> Against itself—
> Itself to justify
> Unto itself—
> When larger function—
> Make that appear—
> Smaller—that Covered Vision—Here—
>
> (745)

To paraphrase these badly crabbed lines, renunciation must renounce itself at the appropriate time. Dickinson is aware that her "White Exploit" may have a neurotic component; she wishes to assure herself that, when the time is ripe, she can accept an ending to her quest. In the poem, the ripe time is after time, not "Here." But in her last years, this fear that her isolation was an escape may well have aided Lord in his courting.[18]

Yet the quest fiction even influences Dickinson's rebellion against it. Apparently, Lord proposed marriage; perhaps he proposed something less honorable. In any case, she answers him in the language of sumptuous destitution: "Dont you know you are happiest while I withhold and not confer—dont you know that 'No' is the wildest word we consign to Language?" (L 562); and again, with some irony, "I have a strong surmise that moments we have *not* known are tenderest to you" (L 750). Still, when Dickinson informs Judge Lord of "The withdrawal of the Fuel of Rapture" (L 842), we cheer the renunciation. Perhaps it is unfortunate that Dickinson formulated libidinal love and the quest as an either/or. Perhaps she broke her own rule of recognizing the real and the ideal as separate in leading her life according to a bodiless ideal. But with "thoughts—and just two Heart—," with love, that is, "Immortality—can be almost— / Not quite—Content—" (495). Dickinson deserves a less qualified contentment; she deserves the destiny patterned for her by her mind.

The third threat to Dickinson's poetic quest is of a different nature. It is the poetry itself. At times, poetry seems enough. In "I reckon—when I count at all—," Dickinson "reckons" poets, the sun, summer, and "the heaven of God":

> But, looking back—the First so seems
> To Comprehend the Whole—
> The Others look a needless Show—
> So I write—Poets—All—

The Necessary Veil: A Quest Fiction

The "Further Heaven" may be as beautiful as the heaven the poets prepare "For those who worship Them," but "It is too difficult a Grace— / To justify the Dream—" (569). Fine as it is, this is nonetheless a poem of fatigue and impatience, part of that minor complaint of recalcitrance which gives the major affirmation of quest such force. Elsewhere Dickinson will write, "No message is the utmost message, for what we tell is done" (L, p. 913). Poetry is part of the "done" which the imagination must outrace. It is "when I cannot make the Force, / Or mould it into Word" that Dickinson knows she is "From mathematics further off / Than from Eternity" (1668). The mind is bestowed to pattern the life, not to replace the goal. Surely it was the poetic imagination to which a teenaged Dickinson referred when, shortly after she had refused to stand for an orthodox Christ and sometime before she had begun to compose actual poems, she wrote to her friend Jane Humphrey of "a long, big shining fibre which hides the others—and which will fade away into Heaven while you hold it, and from there come back to me" (L 35). Poetry was to be Dickinson's thread to heaven, not the heaven itself.

Yet poetry as the mind's continual thrust toward the ungraspable, as questing rather than completed vision, could replace the goal of a final heaven; the ideal of imaginative desire could persist even within a mediated eternity. True, in poems which describe the difficulties of an arduous quest the goal is desirable simply as an end to questing; and in a poem like "Renunciation—is a piercing Virtue—," Dickinson schools herself to be ready to accept the goal when it presents itself. The goal, so far as its nature may be assumed, is assumed to be an equatorial "Zone" of sublime rest, "Whose Sun constructs perpetual Noon / Whose perfect Seasons wait—" (1056). It is "a safer place" from which we "look down some day, and see the crooked steps we came" (L 263). But when Dickinson contemplated that vision of eternity in itself, she must have been dissatisfied. In life, one continually pushes desire beyond the barrier of the accessible:

> I find my feet have further Goals—
> I smile upon the Aims
> That felt so ample—Yesterday—
> Today's—have vaster claims—...
> (563)

One is constantly outgrowing his prior desires and fashioning new ones which will provide an ample fit. Will not an unchanging eternity go against the belief that "Utmost is relative" (1291), that "Desire's perfect Goal" is by definition "Within its reach, though yet ungrasped" (1430)? Though "Hope never knew Horizon" (L 871), will not this static eternity replace expectation with an inferior contentment? It is with some fear that Dickinson asks, "Unto the Whole—how add?" (1341). She cannot specify an answer, but she can affirm that "Immortality contented / Were Anomaly" (1036). In "Each Life Converges to some Centre—," the poem in which the "Centre" can be reached in life no more than the rainbow can be touched, Dickinson can prophesy that eternity will not provide access to the "Centre" but will "enable the endeavoring / Again" (680). She can see the immortal self as a "limitless Hyperbole," limitless and more dynamic and desirous than ever before. Eternity need not epitomize completion, but endlessness:

> As if the Sea should part
> And show a further Sea—
> And that—a further—and the Three
> But a presumption be—
>
> Of Periods of Seas—
> Unvisited of Shores—
> Themselves the Verge of Seas to be—
> Eternity—is Those—
>
> (695)

Eternity will bear a newer goal surpassing it as it surpasses life, and that new goal will bear yet another surpassing it. On and further on, to the endless end, Dickinson's quester will voyage forever.

3

The poet always frustrates the man of order who demands perfect consistency. Dickinson's mind is no jigsaw; the fictions of regulation and quest will not "fit." They will rub against each other briefly, as in this prose fragment: "Paradise is no journey because it is within—but for that very cause though—it is the most Arduous of Journeys— because as the Servant Conscientiously says at the Door We are always—out—" (L, p. 926). But in the regulation fiction, where heaven is always available, the self's absence is a sure sign of self-abnegation; while in the quest fiction, where heaven is always absent or, if present, thrown further on, this absence is a boast of questing courage. We said earlier that Dickinson always confronts the same world, whether as an all-sufficient God or a never-sufficient votary. But that choice is basic and the dual answers argue for a division of belief, a division in no way regrettable since it creates a prismatic spectrum of visionary colors. Nonetheless, we can go some way in defining the one light which the fictions split. Both fictions value a continual dynamism of the spirit. Dickinson will not attend church because "instead of getting to Heaven, at last— / I'm going, all along" (324). Whether the self is flung from the common to the wild unknown, or actively flings out a wild vision which she then quests toward, she is always inviting and retarding truth:

> Escaping backward to perceive
> The Sea upon our place—
> Escaping forward, to confront
> His glittering Embrace
>
> Retreating up, a Billow's height
> Retreating blinded down
> Our undermining feet to meet
> Instructs to the Divine.
>
> (867)

Dickinson is always retreating forward, escaping from one danger to find herself another. In both fictions, skepticism and fear somehow strengthen faith, for this is a poet who believes that "Faith is *Doubt*" (L 912). "Peril as a Possession / 'Tis Good to bear" (1678), and both fictions value a dynamism fired by dread. Vitalizing peril is the only possession this poet finally will "own."

We cannot see Emily Dickinson safely home. The bridge of faith has no pier. We must leave her as she rushes toward and rushes past that point in existence "Beyond the Dip of Bell," where syllable grows into silence and the language ends.

Notes

Chapter One

1. *The Letters of Emily Dickinson,* ed. Thomas H. Johnson and Theodora Ward, 3 vols. (Cambridge, Mass.: Belknap Press of Harvard University Press, 1965). References to this edition appear in the text in parentheses with the abbreviation "L" followed by the number of the cited letter. Unless otherwise noted, the poems are reprinted in accordance with Johnson's choice of variants in his one-volume edition, *The Poems of Emily Dickinson* (Boston: Little, Brown, 1960). References to this edition appear in the text with the poem's number placed in parentheses. Johnson's earlier, three-volume edition, "including variant readings critically compared with all known manuscripts" (Cambridge, Mass.: Belknap Press of Harvard University Press, 1955), is cited only when a variant argues for or against a particular interpretation. No attempt is made to modernize or regularize Dickinson's spelling or punctuation.
2. This is Dickinson's own metaphor. See my discussion of "This is a Blossom of the Brain" in chapter 3.
3. In fact, when Dickinson, at the urging of her admirer Helen Hunt Jackson, allowed Roberts Brothers to publish "Success—is counted sweetest" in a collection of anonymous poems, *A Masque of Poets,* the poem was generally attributed to Emerson. See L 573d, a letter from Thomas Niles, the publisher of Roberts Brothers, to Dickinson, and Johnson's note following.
4. Raymond Williams, "Dickens and Social Ideas," in *Dickens 1970,* ed. Michael Slater (New York: Stein and Day, 1970), p. 98.

5. Allen Tate, "Emily Dickinson," in *Collected Essays* (Denver, 1932); rpt. in *Emily Dickinson: A Collection of Critical Essays,* ed. Richard B. Sewall (Englewood Cliffs, N.J.: Prentice-Hall, 1963), p. 17.
6. "Emily Dickinson: The Problem of the Biographer," pp. 120-28 in *Occasional Stiles,* no. 5 (Yale University, April, 1968), esp. pp. 125-26.
7. Three of Edward Dickinson's letters to his fiancée are included in Jay Leyda's *Years and Hours of Emily Dickinson,* 2 vols. (New Haven: Yale University Press, 1960), pp. 3-4. Others may be found in the Dickinson collection presented by Gilbert H. Montague to the Harvard College Library.
8. There is some doubt about whether this event actually occurred; it may be Dickinson's fictional dramatization of a general attitude. Either way, it remains as her first definition of herself in opposition to prevalent expectations.
9. *This Was A Poet: A Critical Biography of Emily Dickinson* (New York, 1938; rpt. in softcover, Ann Arbor: University of Michigan Press, 1957), p. 180.
10. In the Apocalypse, for instance, the white horse named "The Word of God" is "clad in a robe dipped in blood." White ("gay") and crimson imagery combine in the paradox of creative destruction throughout Revelation.
11. *Middlemarch,* ed. Gordon S. Haight (Boston: Houghton Mifflin, 1954), p. 144.
12. Dickinson's admiration for George Eliot includes an element of identification. When George Eliot died, Dickinson wrote, "The gift of belief which her greatness denied her, I trust she receives in the childhood of the kingdom of heaven" (L 710). This is not the condescension of a believer toward a skeptic; Dickinson might as well have been writing of her own "denial" and hope. Her particular admiration for Eliot's sense of the failure of hope is indicated in her description of *Daniel Deronda* as "full of sad (high) nourishment" (L 974).
13. A. Dwight Culler, *Imaginative Reason: The Poetry of Matthew Arnold* (New Haven: Yale University Press, 1966), pp. 282-83. For a similar, but broader analysis of the relation of the Victorians to the romantics, see the chapter "The Anti-Romantics," pp. 14-40 in Jerome Hamilton Buckley's *The Victorian Temper: A Study in Literary Culture* (New York: Random, 1951).
14. Noted by F. O. Matthiessen in *American Renaissance: Art and Expression in the Age of Emerson and Whitman* (New York: Oxford University Press, 1941), p. 3. Matthiessen then quotes Emerson on the problem of "double consciousness."
15. Ibid.

Chapter Two

1. Yvor Winters, "Emily Dickinson and the Limits of Judgment," in *Maule's Curse: Seven Studies in the History of American Obscurantism* (Norfolk, Conn.: New Directions, 1938), rpt. in *In Defense of Reason,* 3d ed. (Denver:

Swallow Press, 1947), p. 287; Jay Leyda, "Introduction," in *The Years and Hours of Emily Dickinson,* p. xx; Ruth Miller, *The Poetry of Emily Dickinson* (Middletown, Conn.: Wesleyan University Press, 1968), p. 160.

2. For a most recent example, see Eleanor Wilnor, "The Poetics of Emily Dickinson," *ELH* 38 (March 1971): 126–54. I quote a pertinent passage of this article in my fourth chapter.

3. Thomas Wentworth Higginson, "Letter to a Young Contributor," *Atlantic Monthly* 9 (April 1862), rpt. in *Massachusetts Review* 6 (Spring-Summer 1965): 570–80.

4. T. S. Eliot, "The Metaphysical Poets," in Eliot's *Selected Essays, 1917-1932* (London: Faber and Faber, 1932), p. 273.

5. Ibid., p. 268.

6. I am employing the word "scene" in the usefully expandable way by which Kenneth Burke defines it, "as a blanket term for the concept of background or setting *in general,* a name for any situation in which acts or agents are placed." See Burke's *A Grammar of Motives,* "California" edition (1945; Berkeley: University of California Press, 1969), p. xvi.

7. Among others, Charles Feidelson, Jr., has argued effectively for a collapse of dualism as a prime characteristic of American romanticism. In *Symbolism and American Literature* (1953; Chicago: Phoenix Books, University of Chicago Press, 1959), Feidelson writes, "The philosophy of symbolism . . . is an attempt to find a point of departure outside the premises of dualism—not so much an attempt to solve the old 'problem of knowledge' as an effort to redefine the process of knowing in such a manner that that problem never arises. . . . The new starting point, both philosophic and literary, is designed to recapture the unity of a world artificially divided" (pp. 50–51).

8. Charles Rosen, "Isn't It Romantic?" (review of M. H. Abrams, *Natural Supernaturalism* and William Empson and David Pirie, eds., *Coleridge's Verse: A Selection), New York Review of Books,* 20 no. 10 (14 June 1973): 16.

9. John Lynen, *The Design of the Present: Essays on Time and Form in American Literature* (New Haven: Yale University Press, 1969), p. 45.

10. Lynen, "Three Uses of the Present: The Historian's, the Critic's, and Emily Dickinson's," in *College English* 28 (November 1966): 134.

11. Richard Wilbur, "Sumptuous Destitution," in *Emily Dickinson: Three Views* (Amherst, 1960), rpt. in *Emily Dickinson: A Collection of Critical Essays,* ed. Sewall, p. 130.

12. William Howard, "Emily Dickinson's Poetic Vocabulary," in *PMLA* 72 (March 1957): 237.

13. David T. Porter, *The Art of Emily Dickinson's Early Poetry* (Cambridge, Mass.: Harvard University Press, 1966), p. 135.

14. Other examples of the single, extended analogy are considered in chapter 4.

15. Charles R. Anderson, *Emily Dickinson's Poetry: Stairway of Surprise* (New York: Holt, Rinehart and Winston, 1960), pp. 172–76; Thomas H. Johnson,

Emily Dickinson: An Interpretative Biography (Cambridge, Mass.: Belknap Press of Harvard University Press, 1955; paperback, New York: Atheneum, 1967), pp. 138–40.

16. This hunt may have symbolic import, but it is useful to note Dickinson's attitude toward actual hunting.

> His Bill is clasped—his Eye forsook—
> His Feathers wilted low—
> The Claws that clung, like lifeless Gloves
> Indifferent hanging now—
> The Joy that in his happy Throat
> Was waiting to be poured
> Gored through and through with Death, to be
> Assassin of a Bird
> Resembles to my outraged mind
> The firing in Heaven,
> On Angels—squandering for you
> Their Miracles of Tune—
>
> (1102)

If the hunt in "My Life had stood" is for love or poetic images or whatever, it is difficult to believe that this poet would employ the image of hunting in unironical approval. Even as a symbolic hunt for beauty, Dickinson would condemn it:

> Beauty—be not caused—It Is—
> Chase it, and it ceases—
> Chase it not, and it abides— . . .
>
> (516)

I cite this poem not as proof but only as correlation of the hunt's plainly negative implications in "My Life had stood."

17. The phrase "Eider-Duck" itself reinforces the second stanza's negative image of hunting. The master's comfort is bought at the expense of nature.

18. In "The Zeroes—taught us—Phosphorus—" (689), Dickinson uses the yin-yang formulation to describe death and resurrection: "Paralysis—our Primer —dumb— / Unto Vitality!" Our life-gun has been activated too early. It has tried to achieve immortality in this life, and the ironic result is *anomie*. For further examples of Dickinson's yin-yang, see my final chapter.

19. The dating of nearly all the poems and many of the letters is highly conjectural. Johnson's handwriting-and-stationery analysis is remarkably careful, but he himself asks readers not to ascribe precise accuracy to his dating.

20. Tony Tanner, *City of Words: American Fiction, 1950–1970* (London: Jonathan Cape, 1971), pp. 15 and 18.

21. There are three "Master" letters, full of passionate avowals of love and of the

power of suppressed love. Dickinson's biographers often use them as proof of a secret love affair. The letters were never sent, they say, because the poet was shy. I find more plausible the notion that the letters were written as fictions, for in them, as in the "Master" poems, the master is a deliberately ambiguous figure who may represent a beau, a deity, or a principle of inspiration. Perhaps Richard Sewalls's forthcoming biography will illuminate their intent. In any case, the kind of thoughts (though not the mood) that went into those letters went into "My Life had stood—a Loaded Gun—."

22. Another poem likewise appears at first to support an optimistic reading of "My Life had stood":

> The Spirit lasts—but in what mode—
> Below, the Body speaks,
> But as the Spirit furnishes—
> Apart, it never talks—

But as this poem continues, we note the crucial difference that the speech is not made destructive, directed against nature; here it is musical, a tune of infused being.

> The Music in the Violin
> Does not emerge alone
> But Arm in Arm with Touch, yet Touch
> Alone—is not a Tune—

Finally, the absolute contrast between the two poems becomes clear as the underlying spatial analogy is revealed.

> The Spirit lurks within the Flesh
> Like Tides within the Sea
> That make the Water live, estranged
> What would the Either be? . . .
> (1576)

A positive interpretation suits this poem perfectly because of the "within" formulation of the two terms. It is this kind of merger which the life-gun-master relationships make impossible in "My Life had stood."

23. If we wish to interpret the killing of the master's foes as the writing of satire, then we have to recognize that the poem implicitly condemns a satirical purpose—just as another poem which uses gun imagery condemns it:

> My friend attacks my friend!
> Oh Battle picturesque!
> Then I turn Soldier too,
> And he turns Satirist!

How martial is this place!
Had I a mighty gun
I think I'd shoot the human race
And then to glory run!
(118)

24. A phrase coined by Roy Harvey Pearce in his "Introduction" to Whitman's *Leaves of Grass: Facsimile Edition of the 1860 Text* (Ithaca, N.Y.: Cornell University Press, 1961), p. xxvi.

Chapter Three

1. Eleanor Wilnor, "The Poetics of Emily Dickinson," p. 131.
2. William Howard, "Emily Dickinson's Poetic Vocabulary," p. 237.
3. Geoffrey H. Hartman, "Beyond Formalism," in *Beyond Formalism: Literary Essays, 1958-1970* (New Haven: Yale University Press, 1970), p. 50. For complementary remarks, see Northrop Frye's essay on Blake, "The Road of Excess," pp. 119-32 and especially pp. 127-30 in *Romanticism and Consciousness: Essays in Criticism,* ed. Harold Bloom (New York: Norton, 1970); and Paul deMan, "Intentional Structure of the Romantic Image," pp. 65-77 in the same collection.
4. Angus Fletcher's phrase in *Allegory: The Theory of a Symbolic Mode* (Ithaca: Cornell University Press, 1964), p. 23.
5. David Evett, " 'Paradice's Only Map': The *Topos* of the *Locus Amoenus* and the Structure of Marvell's 'Upon Appleton House,' " *PMLA* 85 (May 1970): 507.
6. Hartman, "The Voice of the Shuttle: Language from the Point of View of Literature," in *Beyond Formalism,* p. 349.
7. See Lynen, *Design of the Present,* pp. 328-32, for a comparison of Whitman's merging of immediate and infinite times with Wordsworth's "smooth, progressively developing flow of perception and meaning."
8. This is Emerson's introductory paragraph to his essay "Circles."
9. Miller, *Poetry of Emily Dickinson,* p. 93.
10. In their study *Goethe: Poet and Thinker* (London: Arnold, 1962) E. M. Wilkinson and L. A. Willoughby describe a similar opposition that runs through Goethe's works in the images of *Wanderung* and *Hütte,* "wandering" and "cabin." Like Dickinson's "sea," Goethe's *Wanderung* "is a symbol for expressing every conceivable manner and mode of his 'wandering,' from the simple impulse to roam in space, through the urge to dalliance and philandering, or the limitless aspiration of individual striving, to every variation of self-fulfilment, including that soaring of the human mind which we call poetic vision." Like Dickinson's "home," Goethe's *Hütte* "represents the other pole of man's being and symbolizes an equally wide range of experience: the comfort of home, the cramping ties of domesticity, the irksomeness, but also the fulfilment, of self-limitation." And, most tellingly, for Dickinson as for Goethe, "The one impulse at once calls forth its cor-

responding opposite, its regulative counterforce" (pp. 35–36). In *Thoreau as Romantic Naturalist: His Shifting Stance toward Nature* (Ithaca, N.Y. and London: Cornell University Press, 1974), James McIntosh cites this same passage and applies it convincingly to Thoreau (p. 180). His claim that this opposition (between the self as adventurer" and as "reflective guardian") is common among the romantics finds its fullest confirmation in Dickinson.

11. Feidelson, *Symbolism and American Literature,* p. 29.
12. Anderson, *Emily Dickinson's Poetry,* p. 29; Johnson, *Interpretive Biography,* p. 110; Porter, *Emily Dickinson's Early Poetry,* pp. 10–11; Miller, p. 45.

Chapter Four

1. "Three Uses of the Present," p. 134.
2. Ernest Benson Lowrie, "A Complete Body of Puritan Divinity: An Exposition of Samuel Willard's Systematic Theology," Ph.D. diss., Yale University, 1971, pp. 71–72.
3. *City of Words,* p. 19.
4. A typical example:

> Papa above!
> Regard a Mouse
> O'erpowered by the Cat!
> Reserve within thy Kingdom
> A "Mansion" for the Rat! . . .
>
> (61)

5. *City of Words,* pp. 27–28.
6. Albert J. Gelpi, *Emily Dickinson: The Mind of the Poet* (Cambridge, Mass.: Harvard University Press, 1965), p. 60.
7. This is equally true of all the major romantics, and we should not praise Dickinson at their expense. In his comparison of metaphysical and romantic poetry, W. K. Wimsatt offered the first modern refutation of the idea that romantic poetry is irrational, a matter of "swelling, swirling notions." See "The Structure of Romantic Nature Imagery," pp. 103–18 in Wimsatt's collection of essays, *The Verbal Icon* (Lexington: University of Kentucky Press, 1967). First printed in 1949, this landmark essay has instigated a retreat from the simplistic equation of romanticism with purely subjective emotion. For added argument, see Walter Jackson Bate, "The English Romantic Compromise," pp. 149–73 in *Romanticism and Consciousness,* ed. Harold Bloom. Bate too dogmatically considers the English romantics a specially sensible bunch but the basic points of his argument may be applied to the great romantic poets of Europe and America.
8. Dolores Dyer Lucas, *Emily Dickinson and Riddle* (DeKalb: Northern Illinois Press, 1969), pp. 9 and 14.
9. Ralph W. Franklin, *The Editing of Emily Dickinson: A Reconsideration* (Madison: University of Wisconsin Press, 1967), p. 120.

10. Porter, *Emily Dickinson's Early Poetry*, p. 143.
11. Charles Olson, "Projective Verse," in *Selected Writings*, ed. Robert Creeley (New York: New Directions, 1966), pp. 15–16.

Chapter Five

1. Erick Auerbach, "Figura," in *Scenes from the Drama of European Literature: Six Essays* (New York: Meridian Books, 1959), p. 53.
2. Ibid., p. 41. This is Auerbach's paraphrase.
3. Frank Kermode, *The Sense of an Ending: Studies in the Theory of Fiction* (New York: Oxford University Press, 1967), p. 35.
4. There is concrete evidence that Dickinson was fully aware of the traditional typology. See her precise use of the words "typic" and "typify" in poems 1115, 1515, and 1068.
5. In *The Complete Poetry of Richard Crashaw*, ed. George Walton Williams (Garden City, N.Y.: Doubleday Anchor Books, 1970), Williams provides a helpful footnote: "Isaac, carrying the wood for the burnt offering of himself (Genesis 22:1–18), anticipates Christ carrying his own cross; manna, given to feed the Israelites in the Wilderness (Exodus 16:1–15), anticipates the body of Christ given to feed mankind; Paschal Lamb, the means of deliverance from captivity in Egypt (Exodus 12), anticipates the Lamb of God, the deliverance from sin" (p. 185).
6. This tension, which we noted earlier in other contexts, is yet another characteristic of Dickinson's romanticism. In his general article on the romantics, Charles Rosen describes the romantics' discovery "of stripping forms of their original significance and of giving them a new sense.... What they looked for was the tension between the new meaning and the inevitable residue of the old" ("Isn't It Romantic?" *New York Review of Books*, 14 June 1973, p. 14).
7. Though David Porter does not recognize that Dickinson's use of typology focuses on end terms, he does recognize the poet's penchant for figural interpretation and he accurately states Dickinson's derivation from the puritan norm: "She interposed a strong secularism in the Puritan habit...and the result was a greater objectivity on her part, an awareness of the ironic possibilities within the language of metaphor, and a movement toward individual skepticism, in direct contrast to the humility and acceptance which characterize Puritan usage" (*Emily Dickinson's Early Poetry*, p. 81).
8. Kenneth Burke, *The Rhetoric of Religion: Studies in Logology*, California ed. (1961; Berkeley: University of California Press, 1970), p. 7.
9. See Burke, *A Grammar of Motives*, pp. 21–23 and 430.
10. *Sense of an Ending*, p. 8.
11. Cited by Auerbach, "Figura," p. 35.
12. Ibid., pp. 12 and 56.
13. Nietzsche, *Ecce Homo*, cited by Eugen Fink in his "The Oasis of Happiness: Toward an Ontology of Play," translated by Ute and Thomas Saine and excerpted in *Game, Play, Literature*, ed. Jacques Ehrmann (1968; Boston:

Beacon Press, 1971), p. 25.
14. William G. Madsen, *From Shadowy Types to Truth: Studies in Milton's Symbolism* (New Haven: Yale University Press, 1968), p. 5.
15. Richard Poirier, *A World Elsewhere: The Place of Style in American Literature* (New York: Oxford University Press, 1966).
16. "I measure every Grief I meet" provides another example:

> The Grieved—are many—I am told—
> There is the various Cause—
> Death—is but one—and comes but once—
> And only nails the eyes—
>
> (561)

Here, characteristically, Dickinson is less interested in the particular situation, "the various Cause" of the agony, than in "the fashions—of the Cross— / And how they're mostly worn—." Her concern is with what happens after and internally.
17. A possible source for this image of silence is located in a letter written to Austin in 1853. Dickinson writes of "A splendid sermon from that Prof Park" and describes the audience's attention in these terms: "The students and chapel people all came, to our church, and it was very full, and still—so still, the buzzing of a fly would have boomed like a cannon" (L 142). Dickinson describes Professor Park as a type of God on Judgment Day and thus, in this poem, when the fly interposes himself between the persona and God, the letter's supposition of a booming fly is actualized to create irony.
18. We find another expression of a disappointingly undramatic death in poem 255:

> To die—takes just a little while—
> They say it doesn't hurt—
> It's only fainter—by degrees—
> And then—it's out of sight—...

Here, too, this debunking is imaged in terms of "fainting" sight.
19. In a passage from another poem which stresses the ghastly paralysis of the dead, flies again are employed in contrast:

> Buzz the dull flies—on the chamber window—
> Brave—shines the sun through the freckled pane—
> Fearless—the cobweb swings from the ceiling—
> Indolent Housewife—in Daisies—lain!
>
> (187)

But conversely, "Death is like the insect" (1716). This compound fly is both death and vitality, two worlds reduced to meaninglessness.

20. Dickinson's lack of admiration for houseflies is documented:

> Those Cattle—smaller than a Bee
> That *herd upon the eye*—
> Whose tillage is the passing Crumb—
> Those Cattle are the Fly—....
>
> (1388, my italics)

They "gallop on the Furniture— / or odiouser offend—," but our main concern here is with their attack on the eye. Because they preclude sight, they are a likely image for the preclusion of spiritual vision. In a letter supposedly written shortly before "I heard a Fly buzz" was composed, Dickinson remarks to Mrs. Bowles, "The Dust like the Mosquito, buzzes round my faith." The old and rightly disputed idea that the fly represents the coming dissolution in the grave may be revived in a less literal way. As I will show, the grave is itself a symbol of Dickinsonian doubt, and the fly, for its very lack of symbolic meaning, equally suggests that doubt—which in Dickinson is tantamount to nihilism.

21. More supportive evidence from a poem whose expression is more direct:

> Fight sternly in a Dying eye
> Two Armies, Love and Certainty
> And Love and the Reverse.
>
> (831)

Love is directed back at the world we know. As for the unknown future, the battle of belief is resolved only in "uncertain certainty."

22. This is most emphatically not a poem about the onset of actual blindness, but much of the remarkable imagery may derive from a serious eye ailment Dickinson suffered. Though her treatment in Boston for the unknown condition occurred in 1864-65—that is, after the date conjectured by Johnson for the poem's composition—it is just possible that Dickinson could draw on problems she was having with her own sight.

23. In a poem which ribs the Transcendentalists, Dickinson observes that "Size circumscribes—it has no room / For petty furniture—." She concludes:

> ...intrinsic size
> Ignores the possibility
> Of Calumnies—or Flies.
>
> (641)

Dickinson wants to keep herself small enough to include calumnies and flies within her circumference.

24. Most speculatively, an "aftermath" to this poem could be posited in another poem where a persona dies only to return as a comforting but puzzled Lazarus:

> If any sink, assure that this, now standing—
> Failed like Themselves—and conscious that it rose—
> Grew by the Fact, and not the Understanding
> How Weakness passed—or Force—arose....
>
> (358)

The point is that we know from our study of the "Hamlet" poems that all burials in Dickinson's poetry may be metaphorical.

25. The attempt of the everyday mind to counteract agony is rendered more directly, but with the same resultant futility, in a similar but less complex poem:

> I felt a Cleaving in my Mind—
> As if my Brain had split—
> I tried to match it—Seam by Seam—
> But could not make them fit.
>
> The thought behind, I strove to join
> Unto the thought before—
> But Sequence ravelled out of Sound
> Like Balls—upon a Floor.
>
> (937)

Here the failure is expressed in terms of consciousness. But a variation of the second stanza, which Johnson presents as a separate poem, makes the problem ontological and epistemological:

> The Dust behind I strove to join
> Unto the Disk before—
> But Sequence ravelled out of Sound
> Like Balls upon a Floor—
>
> (992)

The past of experience, now dust, *does not* lead by an easy hyphen to a surmise of the world beyond experience, the mysterious "Disk." If we could combine both versions of this poem, the internal emphasis of the first with the external, metaphysical emphasis of the second, we would come up with "I felt a Funeral, in my Brain."

26. Dickinson elsewhere complains,

You cannot even die
But nature and mankind must pause
To pay you scrutiny.

To die might be supposed "An undisputed right—," Dickinson writes, but

Attempt it, and the Universe
Upon the opposite
Will concentrate its officers—...
(1692)

The "Universe" presumably includes the reasoning self, the sane and/or cowardly half of the mind.

27. Clark Griffith, *The Long Shadow: Emily Dickinson's Tragic Poetry* (Princeton, N.J.: Princeton University Press, 1964), pp. 249-50.

28. Like many of Dickinson's best poems, "I felt a Funeral, in my Brain" combines conflicting attitudes which are sorted out in lesser poems. " 'Twas like a Maelstrom, with a notch" obviously interprets the mind's free-fall as horrific,

From Dungeon's luxury of Doubt
To Gibbets, and the Dead—...
(414)

But another poem speaks of "Paralysis" as "our Primer—dumb— / Unto Vitality" (689). By that formula, the paralyzed corpse of "I felt a Funeral" is being primed for the only real life and his fall is the antecedent to his rise. In further rebuttal, consider this interpretation of the silence which begins and accompanies the fall:

When Bells stop ringing—Church—begins—
The Positive—of Bells—
When Cogs—stop—that's Circumference—
The Ultimate—of Wheels.
(633)

This note could grow and grow, arguing for positive or negative readings of "I felt a Funeral" by reference to analogous poems. Either kind of reading would be partial and wrong, for the poem's achievement is its attitudinal balancing act. Agony creates possibility, possibility is achieved through agony. And only possibility, no more but no less.

Chapter Six

1. For examples, see Miller, *Poetry of Emily Dickinson,* pp. 52-54; and Johnson, *Interpretive Biography,* pp. 106-13.

2. Johnson very usefully presents all four versions of the poem (with the notes

between Emily and Sue which contemplate the changes) in his three-volume edition of the *Poems* 1: 151-55.

3. Ibid., p. 153.

4. Elsewhere, Dickinson writes,

> Better a grave of Balm
> Toward human nature's home—
> And Robins near—
> Than a stupendous Tomb
> Proclaiming to the Gloom
> How dead we are—
>
> (1674)

5. Poems which contrast natural vitality to the stillness of the tomb abound, and we considered some examples earlier. See also poems 529, 592, and 813.

6. "Lie" is substituted for "sleep" and a few minor changes in punctuation are made which do not change the stanza's meaning.

7. *Poetry*, p. 53.

8. There are no major alterations in the third version.

9. Elsewhere, Dickinson speaks of "Immortality" as "a shapeless friend" and cannot quite decide whether he is intrinsic or an external force or both, given as grace:

> Neither if He visit Other—
> Do He dwell—or Nay—know I
> But Instinct esteem Him
> Immortality—
>
> (679)

As usual, Dickinson tries to negate the inner-outer dichotomy.

10. The poem's sources are many. In an early letter, Dickinson mentions to her brother that she rode in a carriage "last evening with *Sophomore Emmons,* alone" (L 72). Poor Emmons! Discarded for "Death"! A literary source is suggested by Jack Capps in his excellent work, *Emily Dickinson's Reading, 1836-1886* (Cambridge, Mass.: Harvard University Press, 1966), pp. 88-89. Capps points out limited similarities to Browning's "The Last Ride Together" and proves that Dickinson had read the poem. But "Death" as a "supple Suitor / That wins at last—" is largely Dickinson's own invention, inspired perhaps by metaphysical conceits, dependent no more on Browning than on Sophomore Emmons:

> It is a stealthy Wooing
> Conducted first
> By pallid innuendoes

And dim approach
But brave at last with Bugles
And a bisected Coach
It bears away in triumph
To Troth unknown
And Kindred as responsive
As Porcelain.

(1445)

This later poem emphasizes the more implicit beguiling of the persona by Death in "Because I could not stop." Both Poems deny the hope of a heaven of restored human relations.

11. The logic of this correction is fleshed out in another poem:

Day—got tired of Me—
How could I—of Him?...

(425)

Dickinson's personae cannot stop for death or tire of day. Her radical passivity is equaled only by her love of this life.

12. See the following chapter for examples.

13. We find this ironic description of the grave extended in an early poem:

What Inn is this
Where for the night
Peculiar Traveller comes?
Who is the Landlord?
Where the maids?
Behold, what curious rooms!
No ruddy fires on the hearth—
No brimming Tankards flow—
Necromancer! Landlord!
Who are these below?

(115)

Those who wish to ascribe a "romantic death wish" to Dickinson must ignore these poems of the grave. Death in itself, as stoppage rather than passage, is anathema to Dickinson. She is in favor of dynamic life, life on either side of the grave.

14. "Three Uses of the Present," p. 134.

15. Stephen E. Whicher, *Freedom and Fate: An Inner Life of Ralph Waldo Emerson* (1957; New York: A. S. Barnes, 1961).

16. "Our young people are diseased with the theological problems of original sin, origin of evil, predestination and the like..., These are the soul's mumps and measles and whooping coughs..." ("Spiritual Laws").

17. Georges Poulet, "Emily Dickinson," in the appendix, "Time and American

Writers," to the American edition of *Studies in Human Time*, trans. Elliott Coleman (Baltimore: Johns Hopkins University Press, 1956), pp. 346-47, 349.

18. "Three Uses of the Present," p. 132.

19. Poulet, p. 347.

20. In "The Birds begun at Four o'clock—," the same process occurs:

> A Music numerous as space—
> But neighboring as Noon—. . . .

The sudden disappearance of the birds' evanescent melody is more explicit in this earlier version, and may serve as a supportive gloss:

> The Sun engrossed the East—
> The Day controlled the World—
> The Miracle that introduced
> Forgotten, as fulfilled.
>
> (783)

Here, the bird song is a foreshadowing type of the day, and yet we suspect that the introductory "forgotten" miracle is granted superiority over its fulfillment.

21. One of John Lynen's finest insights applies here, his notion of the stylistic equivalent to Dickinson's concern with eternity and the individual moment: Dickinson's typically "successful ending brings us simultaneously to the level of highest generality and the point of keenest immediacy" ("Three Uses of the Present," p. 133). But again, as with Lynen's larger theory, we would want to add the qualifier "sometimes."

22. The mute confederate who has died is Carlo, Dickinson's beloved dog. Carlo's death is mentioned in letter 314.

23. Auerbach, "Figura," p. 59.

24. The idea of heaven as a locale always bothers Dickinson if the spatialization (unlike her own) is naive and dogmatic. In "We pray—to Heaven—," she teases:

> Is Heaven a Place—a Sky—a Tree?
> Location's narrow way is for Ourselves—
> Unto the Dead
> There's no Geography—
>
> But State—Endowal—Focus—
> Where—Omnipresence—Fly?
>
> (489)

Chapter Seven

1. Much of my discussion of other poets in this chapter and the selection of some of my illustratory citations are indebted to a landmark essay on

American romantic poetics by Harold Bloom, "The Central Man: Emerson, Whitman, Wallace Stevens," in *The Ringers in the Tower: Studies in Romantic Tradition* (Chicago: University of Chicago Press, 1971), pp. 217–233.

2. From an 1846 journal entry.
3. From Stevens's poem, "Asides on the Oboe."
4. Several versions of "As I Ebb'd with the Ocean of Life" are extant. I quote from the 1859 original as reproduced in *Leaves of Grass: Facsimile Edition of the 1860 Text* (Ithaca: Cornell University Press, 1961). Strangely, Bloom does not comment on these lines in his article.
5. See Nathalie Sarraute, *The Age of Suspicion: Essays on the Novel,* trans. Maria Jolas (New York: Braziller, 1963).
6. Georges Poulet, *The Metamorphoses of the Circle,* trans. Carley Dawson and Elliott Coleman (Baltimore: Johns Hopkins Press, 1966), p. 95.
7. See Bloom's essay, "The Internalization of Quest-Romance," in *Romanticism and Consciousness,* pp. 3–24.
8. René Dubos, (New Haven: Yale University Press, 1965), p. 14.
9. For an extended comment on Dickinson's handling of the Burkean sublime, see Gelpi, *Emily Dickinson,* p. 125.
10. *Design of the Present,* p. 3.
11. This paraphrase of several passages from Willard's *Compleat Body of Puritan Divintity* appears in Lowrie's unpublished dissertation, "A Complete Body of Puritan Divinity," p. 63.
12. Bloom, "Internalization of Quest-Romance," p. 11.
13. H. J. C. Grierson, *Classical and Romantic* (Cambridge: Cambridge University Press, 1923), abridged as "Classical and Romantic: A Point of View," in *Romanticism: Points of View,* ed. Robert F. Gleckner and Gerald E. Enscoe, rev. ed. (1962; Englewood Cliffs, N.J.: Prentice-Hall, 1970), p. 54.
14. Bloom, "Internalization of Quest-Romance," p. 21.
15. Richard B. Sewall, *The Lyman Letters: New Light on Emily Dickinson and Her Family* (Amherst: University of Massachusetts Press, 1966), p. 77. The quotation is an excerpt from a letter sent by Dickinson to her distant relative, extant only in the form of Lyman's recopied version.
16. Poems 573, 1151, and 1432 similarly encourage risk as a moral value.
17. "Introduction" to *The Meditative Poem: An Anthology of Seventeenth-Century Verse,* ed. Martz (New York: New York University Press, 1963), p. xxxi.
18. From "Self-Reliance." Winters condemns Emerson's influence on later poets in his essay "The Significance of *The Bridge* by Hart Crane, or What are we to think of Professor X?" in *In Defense of Reason,* pp. 575–603.
19. Walter Jackson Bate, "The English Romantic Compromise," in *Romanticism and Consciousness,* p. 155.
20. See Angus Fletcher, *Allegory,* p. 41.
21. For similar treatments of memory *qua* guilt, see poems 1242, 1273, 1406, and 1753.

22. See poem 1247, "To pile like Thunder to its close," for a similar definition of poetry.

Chapter Eight

1. "Classic and Romantic," p. 46
2. *A History of Western Philosophy and Its Connection with Political and Social Circumstances from the Earliest Times to the Present Day* (1945; rpt. New York: Simon and Schuster, 1965), p. 707.
3. *Grammar of Motives,* p. 191.
4. Ibid., p. 187.
5. Denis Donoghue, *Emily Dickinson,* University of Minnesota Pamphlets on American Writers, no. 81 (Minneapolis: University of Minnesota Press, 1969), p. 22.
6. "God" here equates with Kant's things-in-themselves. Nature, when capitalized, gains the same status and the same advantage over the mind:

> We pass, and she abides.
> We conjugate Her Skill
> While She creates and federates
> Without a syllable.
>
> (811)

7. A phrase coined by Geoffrey Hartman for Hopkins in *The Unmediated Vision: An Interpretation of Wordsworth, Hopkins, Rilke, and Valéry,* rev. ed. (New York: Harcourt, Brace and World, 1966).
8. In another poem which denigrates analysis in comparison to intuition, Dickinson concludes with a remark which I hope the reader will not apply to the present occasion:

> "Eye hath not seen" may possibly
> Be current with the Blind
> But let not Revelation
> By theses be detained—
>
> (1241)

9. "I reason, Earth is short—" expresses a similar impatience. It concludes, bitterly,

> I reason, that in Heaven—
> Somehow, it will be even—
> Some new Equation, given—
> But what of that?
>
> (301)

See also poem 1706, "When we have ceased to care."

10. William K. Wimsatt and Cleanth Brooks, *Literary Criticism: A Short History* (New York: Alfred A. Knopf, 1957), p. 391.
11. "Sumptuous Destitution," pp. 131 and 132.
12. *The Changing Nature of Man* (*Metabletica*) (New York: Norton, 1961), excerpted as "The Subject and His Landscape" in *Romanticism and Consciousness*, pp. 64–65.
13. "The Internalization of Quest-Romance," in *Romanticism and Consciousness*, p. 3.
14. Gelpi, *Emily Dickinson*, pp. 24–25.
15. One must take care in interpreting Dickinson's loving language as an avowal of libidinal love. But Dickinson's letters to and about Lord are unmistakable. To Higginson she writes, "Judge Lord was with us a few days since—and told me the Joy we most revere—we profane in taking" (L 477). Those who wish to concoct other loves for Dickinson must take into consideration her avowal to Lord, "I never knelt to other—" (L 750).
16. Millicent Todd Bingham, *Emily Dickinson: A Revelation* (New York: Harper, 1954), p. 59.
17. Reprinted by Johnson as poem 1359.
18. Indeed, in the absence of this fear, Dickinson would not have debated with herself the value of a "Master" (see my second chapter).

Index

197

Index